GRUMPY GIBBY

THE WEST STAND

HIBBIE

www.twitter.com/wowte_hibs

www.facebook.com/weonlywanttheearth

Braidwood Books

Also by Sandy Macnair:

CARSPOTTING: THE REAL ADVENTURES OF IRVINE WELSH

GROWING UP IN GREEN: HIBS SUPPORTING THROUGH THE SEVENTIES

MOONSHINE ON LEITH: HIBERNIAN'S 2015/16 SCOTTISH CUP-WINNING SEASON

THE HIBS GO MARCHING UP: HIBERNIAN'S 2016/17 CHAMPIONSHIP-WINNING SEASON

WE ONLY WANT THE EARTH: HIBERNIAN'S 2017 / 18 RETURN TO THE PREMIERSHIP

GRUMPY GIBBY THE WEST STAND HIBBIE

SANDY MACNAIR

Sandy Macnair

Published by Braidwood Books
4 Nellfield Gardens
Braidwood
Carluke
Lanarkshire
ML8 5GX

ISBN 978-0-9931012-4-3

Printed and bound in the UK by Witley Press Ltd
www.witleypress.co.uk

ACKNOWLEDGEMENTS

Many thanks to Braidwood Books and in particular Graham Ewing, whose idea it was to bring former Hibs fanzine one-man freak-show Grumpy Gibby back from the dead. (Although he is probably now fairly keen to return him there, a.s.a.p.)

Ta also to Roanna at Blackwell's Bookshop, Neil and staff at the Hibernian Clubstore, Steven, Amanda and staff at Football Nation / Six Yard Box, all at Hobs Reprographics, John Urquhart and all beatific bar-persons at The Iona, Four-in-Hand and Robbie's.

Front cover of His Royal Grumpiness has been wonderfully recreated by Megan Donaldson with her own fair hand from an original illustration by David Todd. Bunnets are also duly doffed in the direction of a hastily arranged Mass Hibsteria Editorial Committee allowing the use of their iconic masthead on the back page.

INTRODUCTION

When Braidwood Books offered me the prestigious mission codenamed 'Go Find Gibby', my first instinct was to refuse outright. Surely the former Hibs fanzine columnist and daft old curmudgeon had died years ago, along with (or possibly even in) his favoured haunt, The Volunteer Arms? Or if not, maybe he was seeing out his days at either Carstairs State Hospital or HMP Edinburgh, a.k.a. Hotel Saughton? Alas, no. After rediscovering him purely by accident in The Central one evening and pitching the publishers' proposal his way, he finally agreed to issue one more manifesto. On its completion, my task was then to proof-read and edit it, which was every bit as thankless a task as you might imagine. After removing most of the foul language and correcting his appalling spelling and grammar, I returned the amended manuscript to him for approval, whereupon he instantly changed it all back and threatened to 'boot me up the bahookey' if I dared to alter it in any way again, before publication. So you can't say you haven't been warned...

Sandy Macnair

Summer 2019

PROLOGUE

By Graham Ewing

Alcohol, as we all know, plays bizarre tricks with the human brain at times. Particularly during December, when the normally staid and ever so polite ladies and gentlemen of Edinburgh's workplaces turn into embarrassingly loud-mouthed and obnoxious arseholes at their annual Christmas hooly. Not so for us alumni of Mass Hibsteria, who still meet up after most games to clink our glasses in celebratory joy. Or, to pathetically drown our sorrows, an all-too regular occurrence over the years. Hardened drinkers such as us who frequent the Iona and Robbie's every other Saturday don't do stupid things that are later to be regretted after a few swallies.

Oh no, we don't. Oh yes, we do. (That's enough, Ed).

Setting Hibbie Hippie a challenge of 'Go find Gibby' rates amongst the most stupid of them all. The long-haired sexagenarian (oo-er, missus), as some of you may know, often rises to such challenges with aplomb. Usually at Scorpio Leisure, but that's another story for another day. However, on this occasion, I was confident that even the hirsute, hopeful HH would succumb to certain defeat and my life would remain blissfully peaceful. It had been three long – and very happy – years since the beast of the East (stand, before he was banned for setting the chipmaker on fire) darkened the doorsteps of Hibsteria Towers, now newly re-branded as Braidwood Books. Primarily to confuse the auld goat.

There we were, sitting in Robbie's after a particularly frustrating 2-2 draw against Dundee just before things became formally festive. Cruising in second gear going into the interval 2-0 up, we somehow managed to be fighting for our very lives to avoid defeat after 60 minutes. Despite hitting the double figure mark on pints (chased down with a few drams) HH decided in his Deuchars-drenched wisdom that as the mighty Green Machine were away at Kilmarnock for the start of the festive fixture list, we should meet up for a few pints in Leith instead of miserably sitting in our respective abodes listening to David Francey et al. A fine idea said I, as you do after a thoroughly entertaining night of the company of the Burns Battalion and HH.

***

One o'clock starts are all very well when there's a home game to give livers and bladders some relief from relentless pint-drinking. Not so when Hibs are away to Kilmarnock. A bar full of Grumpy Gibby wannabees were maligning our team's ineptitude to muster up so much as a challenge to an admittedly decent Killie outfit. Lashings of alcohol was the only way to numb the pain we were collectively suffering. Despite HH's cunning plan to have the game abandoned by plotting with the YLT to clip a few electric cables near the Rugby Park floodlights, a 3-0 defeat meant that further sorrow-sorrow-sorrow-sorrow drowning was in order.

And so, we did. As the hours rolled on, so did the puerility of the conversation and standard of the establishment visited. By the time we reached Gladstone's around 8:00, thorough inebriation had firmly taken a grip and we started reminiscing about the good old days of the fanzine and how we could recreate such magical moments.

"Go find Gibby, HH, and he – through the pages of a Braidwood Books bestseller – can single-handedly send our 400,000 fan-base into raptures with his intelligent insight and cutting wit," I stupidly slavered in a moment of temporary insanity.

"But he cannae fuckin' type and I'm fucked if I'm going to write everything down for him, as I did in the past," retorted HH with visceral anger (or was it angst?) in his voice. And, without the slightest hint of irony, I may add. (That, readers, is a very cheap dig on behalf of all former MHHM editors, who have spent infinity nights of desperation trying to decipher and make literate the drunken scribblings of certain contributors.)

"He's probably deid anyway. Haven't seen him since he invoiced me at triple rates for his 2016 League Cup special contribution, claiming that he hadn't been paid for the 2012 and 2013 Cup Final Specials", I responded with as much diplomacy as my drunken state could muster. "In a moment of madness, I stupidly paid him what he asked for. If he does pitch up somewhere unexpectedly, we can exact the perfect revenge on the auld goat by offering him a million then pay him in Zimbabwean Dollars, which works out at about £2.70, give or take a cent or two. Hopefully he'll fuck off to the land of Masvingo, Manicaland and Mugabe, find a boozer that'll serve him with his not-so-hard-earned and we'll never see him again!"

"I like the cut of your jib, Mr Editor", agreed HH in a far more harmonious tone than merely that of a few seconds earlier.

The deal was sealed. Hand clapping all round while HH balanced a football on his nose.

Sadly, HH's searches throughout December proved fruitless. Until derby day...

***

"Oh, what a night,
Late December back in '63,
What a very special time for me,
As I remember, what a night"

said Frankie Valli and the Four Seasons to countless millions of music fans throughout the world in December '75. A wonderful wee ditty that reached number one in the UK charts on 21 February 1976. It would also be rude not to highlight the alcohol-tastic irony that the original draft opening line of Frankie V's hit, written by the great Bob Gaudino, was: "Oh what a night, the 5th December 1933" – written to celebrate the end of the prohibition era!

"Lucky old fucking Frankie," said me, Late December back in eigh-eigh-teen (half past seven, 29th December, to be precise) having witnessed ninety-odd minutes of utter dirge at Easter Road. More (not a lot, mind) of which later.

The day started so well. The Iona Crew arranged to combine Derby Day with our Christmas bevvy session. Well, it would be rude for a group of Hibbie Atheists NOT to mark the event in some way. Yours truly arrived at around 1:30, securing a table and seats for the lads and lassies (despite a few other Ionian regulars making surreptitiously similar plans). The Iona triathlon (7 pints, 7 drams and 7 pishes) began in earnest. I was joined by the usual pre-match crew consisting of HH, wee Lewis (no, not <u>that</u> wee Lewis) Dave C, Brian the statto, team Dusty/Archie, Chrissie, Liz and a supporting cast of other fine Hibernians over the course of the next three and a half alcohol-fuelled hours.

A highlight of the afternoon came in the form a guest appearance from Fraser, one of Biggar's finest, who'd been unable to join us of late. It was indeed "smashing" to see him and enjoy his excellent company. Those of you who have read a copy of Sandy Macnair's wonderful 'Moonshine on Leith' may recall Fraser's immortal line (now used by students of 'No Shit, Sherlock' the world over) after Stokesy's headed equaliser in the 2016 Scottish Cup Final: "This isn't over, lads."

And a fine afternoon it was, with the usual mix of humour and engaging conversation we've enjoyed over the past few seasons. As the afternoon wore on the sheer volume of patrons in Jimmy's fine establishment meant that double rounds became, quite literally, the order of the day for HH and me. Further skills required for reaching the triathlon finishing line were introduced; getting to the bar and back without spilling the recently purchased refreshments. The only slight blemish to a wonderful afternoon was that a pint (purchased from what was supposed to be the last round of the afternoon) ended up being spilt over my previously pristine pants. I consoled myself that it would quickly dry, and thanked the Lord that I didn't put my beige Chinos on. Such an act of folly would have led to a far more embarrassing situation, even if it only brought to the attention of others THAT I WAS WEARING BEIGE FUCKING CHINOS IN A LEITH BOOZER. A final visit to the bar to purchase a double portion of Jimmy's 'Malt of the Month' offering followed before we made the short journey to the Holy Ground and our final ninety minutes before the winter break.

A now-stookieless wee Lewis and I sauntered up the steps to our seats to become two of the quite magnificent 20,200 crowd at ER to witness the night's events. By way of background, wee Lewis is my 10-year-old grand-nephew who, in 2016 was heroically saved by his Uncle Gareth from following in his father's footsteps and becoming a Hun; the rescue operation comprised of buying a half season ticket, an endless supply of juice, crisps and beer mats. Beer mats? Indeed, beer mats; Lewis has developed advanced skills in the ancient art of flipping beer mats onto pint glasses and juice cans. I'm glad to report that the plan worked wonderfully well and the East Stand is now home to him every other Saturday.

Ah, the stookie... well, long story short, Lewie had a spectacular mishap with a rope-swing towards the arse-end of the 2018 summer holidays, requiring a manual manipulation of his arm (yes, I'm cringing at the very thought too). This was followed by a six-week spell of his arm being confined to a stookie. That took us to early October and no sooner had said stookie been removed, he somehow managed to BREAK THE SAME ARM AGAIN IN EXACTLY THE SAME PLACE. The somewhat appositely named green-stick fracture hadn't healed fully, meaning a relatively gentle blow to the arm when playing fitba' at school brought about a recurrence, and a return to Stookieville for a further four weeks. I'm glad to report that at the time of writing there has been no further recurrence.

The last two Derbies had been God-awful, Gorgie-hosted hoofball-fests not for the sore of neck or faint of heart. A 2-1 defeat in May ended our hopes of our first top two finish since 1974/75. I wasn't at the first of the games (arse-end of the 2017/18 season) due to being in Thailand on holiday, and due to the time difference and drinking enough Changi to sink a robust battleship (it was our last hoorah before 14 hours of travel the day after next) I didn't know the final score until waking up on Thursday morning. "Phuket" (to the untrained ear) were the first words I said that day, and nothing to do with the idyllic island I was visiting at the time either.

The aftermath of the game brought Neil Lennon's first (arguably unjustified) outburst and *real* threat of resignation. It only takes a brief glance at Neilly's previous achievements to recognise that he's moulded himself in the 'winner at all costs' mentality. There could be no doubt that he wasn't going to change as Hibs manager. At the after-match presser, he told hacks "We look like we are going to finish fourth, which is unacceptable for me. I will reconsider my position now in the summer." He added, "I've got things to think about myself, my own personal aims and ambitions. But I can't watch that in a derby. It's not good enough. We have a board meeting next week so we'll see. I have been here two years now and we have made great strides, but I've got to think about myself sometimes as well and how I feel about the whole thing. Maybe I am a bit over-emotional at the minute, but fourth isn't good enough."

"Whoah, didn't see that coming!" I thought to myself on the long road back from Asia to Blighty, via the oppressive and inflation-tastic regime of Dubai, where a portion of chips and a milkshake at the airport sets you back TWENTY nabs. There was me thinking that while Lennon's influence had definitely improved the squad's performance levels compared to Sir Alan, greater tests (for both us and him) lay ahead.

The next Gorgie horror Derby-show, the first of the 2018/19 season, was rearranged to All-Saints eve day, or Hallowe'en as you and I more commonly know it. In keeping with the timing of the event, it was an all too familiar thud and blunder horror show, definitely not one for students of the beautiful game. Goalless, classless and clueless sums it up rather well. The clueless part particularly applies to the ref for the night, Andrew Dallas, son of Shug and most likely William too. In sending off Flo Kamberi, he showed blatant disregard for the fact that it was mainly at the request of certain Hearts players and coaching staff. The incident itself was no more or less than had gone on before without recourse to formal punitive measures being taken. We did well to hold on for a draw against our ugliest of ugly opponents in a game which will only be remembered for its ugliness.

Unsurprisingly, the memorable part of the game will be the unsavoury incidents involving fans of both hues. As you know, fellow Hibbies, us fanzine types firmly believe that the pen is mightier than the sword. Apart from, of course, Gibby's 1840s-style quill, which could quite readily take an eye out. The scene was set by a Neanderthal Jambo graffitiing a wall with "HANG NEIL LENNON". Yes folks, in the year 2018, some people still think it's acceptable to advocate the lynching of those whose upbringing doesn't align with their religious ideologies. There can be no other rational reason for this obscene bile. Jesus would have truly wept.

With about ten minutes to go, a Hibbie inexplicably had a go at Hearts goalie Bobby Zlamal when he went to retrieve the ball from behind the goal. Then, in injury time, Neil Lennon was hit by coin thrown by a fan behind the Hibs technical area. Whether Zlamal was actually hit or not (TV evidence isn't conclusive) is completely irrelevant. Similarly, the heated debate amongst fans whether Lennon was hit on the face or chest by the coin (this really happened on Twitter, folks) is low-level whataboutery of the highest order. No-one should be subject to violence doing their job. As Neil Lennon eloquently said after the heat of the moment in his press conference before the follow Saturday game against St Johnstone, "I had a career in England unblemished by this sort of stuff. I had two years at Bolton - again, no abuse, no attacks, no suspensions or anything like that. And as soon as I've come back to Scotland it's started to rear its ugly head again." Rather chillingly – and subsequently prophetically – Lenny once more indicated that he was considering his position with the club in light of what happened during the week.

So, to the New Year Derby, and a chance to put the wrongs of the previous two games right. For once we arrived in plenty of time (5:23 is plenty time for a 5:30 kick-off, OK?) and the atmosphere in the ground was suitably frenzied, in keeping with the occasion. Somewhat surprisingly Rod went against his previous policy of giving Category A away fans (the ugly sisters) only half of the Dunbar end, meaning there was near enough 4,000 Jambos in ER.

The tactical battle was won by Levein. Craigie loves a tussle, keeping skilful football and a decent passing game to the very back of his game plan. Unlike the last Derby in March, we struggled to make meaningful possession count. Despite endless failed attempts, and in the absence of a midfield player in the Allan/McGinn/McGeouch mould, we persisted with punts up to Kamberi that was meat and drink to a Jambo defence known to struggle against decent passing play. The goal? Well, it can be described as a wonder strike or a complete fluke, depending on where your sympathies lie. It was certainly unstoppable, in-form Adam Bogdan's attempt to keep the ball out being futile at best. Referee Kevin Clancy's never done us any favours, and may well have given us a late penalty when Emerson Hyndman appeared to be pulled back late on in the game. But it was not to be. Once again, the negative, putrid Levein machine won the day against a Hibs team who were mediocre at best. The heyday and swagger of last season when we won both ER derbies comfortably seemed a long time ago.

We all trudged off into the moonshine on Leith to drown our sorrows and somehow mentally prepare for the following day's grade A hangover that lay ahead. After our obligatory pint and post mortem of on-the-field events at the Iona, HH and I decided that the only thing for it was to prepare mentally and drink ourselves into oblivion. And where better to perform such an act than a few boozers at the foot of the Walk?

A stop off for a swift one at Robbie's was the first port of call. Surprisingly, the Burns Unit had fizzled out early, meaning HH and I were left to reflect the events of the day with only each other for company. The 'malt of the month' was a palatably pleasant 10-year-old Highland Park. Doubles were ordered along with Guinness and Deuchers chasers.

"Go easy on the water, for fuck sake," I pathetically pleaded with HH, only to discover that we were sitting beneath a big drip.

"Still, better sitting beneath a big drip than being managed by one, especially a Rolf Harris look-a-like," HH suggested in a futile attempt to add some mirth to the misery of the day's event.

"Speaking of big drips, I presume all attempts to uncover the auld radge Gibson have failed?" I queried, half hoping that HH would whip out a copy of the hatches, matches and dispatches section of the Evening News with Gibby's name emblazoned in the obituary section.

"Of a fashion, comrade, but I did see Moany Tony a couple of weeks back who told me that he had been 'spotted' at the Harp and Castle," further explained HH in almost sympathetic tones. "By spotted, the manager took a look at him, diagnosed him with the Gorgie strain of Bubonic Plague that was covering his antediluvian coupon, told him to go home, see a doctor and be cured of his ills before setting foot in the place again."

"That could be tricky," I suggested. "Don't you remember he's now barred from the dole office on account of there being no record of his birth? He blames the Windrush scandal, although the rush of wind he exposed his fellow claimants to in the waiting area couldn't have helped. Well, he's been struck off from his GP Practice for the self-same reason. That was the official line anyway, although I suspect that it's because he's a skint, smelly auld radge with unpaid bar tabs nearing levels of a small African nation's GDP."

After a drunken pregnant-pause, HH added, "Tea-leaf Keith was telling me last week Gibby's trying to put him out of business by doing a clairvoyance show under the stage name 'Gypsy Gibby the Mystic Hibbie'. The branding would benefit from some revision. Anyhoo, at last week's show in the Spey Lounge, he held up a map of South America, a bottle of white rum and a bottle of gin. He claimed that the origins and name of the new owner of Hibs, which will be announced during the upcoming close season, is cryptically contained therein."

"Loadypish!" we said in unison, laughed heartily and chinked our glasses before draining them of their watered-down contents.

We reluctantly agreed that the Central would be our last port of call for the evening, and the year for that matter. Despite the earlier disappointment, everyone's favourite foot-of-the-Walk boozer was stacked out. A significant contributor to the evening's takings was Erse-Faced Eddie, who'd stuck his entire weekly wage on 'Carole's Destrier', a gutsy winner of the 2:25 at Newbury, at a whopping 12/1. This was despite him scrawling 'Carole's *Derriere*' on the betting slip. The manager of the local Ladbrokes took sympathy on the repellently-couponed puller of pints and paid out to avoid scaring the other customers away.

Mysteriously, a table towards the back of the bar was completely unoccupied. HH performed his world-famous Usain Bolt impression (usually reserved for short dashes to catch the last number 1 bus home) to claim it on our behalf. That, of course, left me having to get the final round of the evening in, a common theme for the evening. Drinks were ordered, and I made my way to the table to rest my drunkenly wearisome feet and wallet.

"Fuck sake, no wonder the table's vacant," boaked HH with a face reminiscent of Erse-Faced Eddie as I wandered over with our refreshments.

The stench – one that is normally only associated with Gorgie – hit me, full on the nostrils. What on God's green (and white) earth could be the cause of this death-inducing reek that could – and probably has – removed paint from walls?

"Loadypish, ya long-haired Hippie erse, it's ma table, so fuck off back tae where ye came fi." The unmistakable tones of Gibby were heard for the first time since 2016.

"Great to see you, Gibby!" enthused HH.

"Whit? That's a loadypish and fine ye ken it, ersehole. Last time I clapped eyes on ye, ye were tryin tae defraud me ootae hard-earned wages wi that erse eh an editor fellie. Ye'll no dae that again," yelped Gibby in a defiant tone.

"Fancy becoming a millionaire, Gibby?" enquired HH as he whipped out the previously prepared Braidwood Books contract from the pocket of his drip-drenched denim jacket. Always one to rise to a challenge placed upon him, HH smugly prepared himself to deliver his speech that had been carefully prepared and rehearsed: "Sign the dotted line, submit 70,000 words of your impeccable wisdom and you're on your way (aha-aha) from misery to happiness today. A *million*, Gibby, which is only the start of it. That's enough to see you through your days *and* your family can commission a statue to adorn the East Stand where your legions of followers can idolise you for ever more."

Gibby greedily grabbed the documents from HH's hands. "That soonds awrite. Goat a pen, Hippie?" he enthusiastically enquired.

With equal eagerness I reached for a pen from my jacket pocket and handed it directly to the prince of puerile pish purveyance. The document, without being read, was duly signed.

That, readers, is the tale of how this book came into being. Do enjoy.

FIELD – WHIT FIELD??

Aye, well, if youse were expectin me tae wish youse aw a 'Happy New Year' youse can bloody well think again n nae mistake! Cos it can hardly be a happy yin when ye're jist comin aff the back eh a defeat tae *that* lot, can it?

"But Whittaker hit the post, man!" says this gadgie in the pub there, as I made ma feelings loud n clear, aboot the Hibs – Hertz game.

"Whit in the name eh Pat Stanton hus that goat tae dae wi it?" I yelped. "Fur whit it's worth, I hit the postman this morning tae, cos the cunt still husnae delivered ma Christmas cairds!"

"Maybe that's cos naebody actually sent youse any," says this other smart-erse.

"Well, that's aloadypish furra start," I countered, as aw thae bastirts started sniggerin intae their lager. "I ayewis get yin fae ma auld flame June Whitfield, whae I met many moons ago when she wis filmin 'Carry On Up The Volley' in Leith back in the sixties."

There wis a sorty stunned silence at that, ye ken. Fair stopped them aw laughin anyway.

"Youse mean *the* June Whitfield – *the actress??*" someone finally piped up.

"The very same," said yours truly. "I used tae tread the boards masel, ye ken, back when The Gaiety wis the tap theatre in the whole eh Embra, no jist Leith."

"Aye, I heard youse were treadin the boards awright," says this boy sarcastically, "when ye trod on a rotten plank n crashed through the flair straight ontae the stage below. Wis that no when youse were tryin tae burglarise the safe while workin as a cleaner there?"

"Not true," I snapped. "I wis workin as a stage-door Johnnie n met aw the stars eh the day. The lovely June bein amongst them, when she came tae a special performance eh 'Moonshine on Leith'. That wis when we first goat taegether. Aye, never mind Terry and June, wi a bit mair luck it could well have been Gibby and June!"

There wis another pronounced silence at that point, but mair eh an awkward yin this time around.

"Eh...I take it youse havenae heard the news then, Gibby?"

"Whit news?"

"Well...there's nae easy way tae tell ye this – but June Whitfield jist died."

"Jist dyed whit – her hair?"

"Naw – she's broon breid, ya auld radge!"

Well, ye could have knocked me doon wi a feather. (In fact some cunt did.) But efter that, it wis drinks fae aw n consolin pats on the back n much toastin eh the dear departed, tae cries eh "Sorry fur yer loss, Gibby!"

Aye, I wis in some state eh shock awright – *Aftershock,* mainly. Fur efter aw thae daft mugs hud bein buyin me bevvy aw night even as I wiped away another manly tear, I could find nae words tae describe how I felt. Well, if push comes tae shove, two words, then. Aye – Absolutely Fabulous!

BARBIE DOLL

So I see in the paper there that Eddie Howe hus recawed Emerson tae Bournemouth. Well, I bloody hope he's sendin Lake n Palmer in the opposite direction, cos wi mair injuries in the Hibs dressin-room than ootside The Spey Lounge on a Setirday night, we need aw the help we can git! I've never seen the like. N noo, in addition tae aw thae yins whae were crocked awready, they send Boyle tae the other side eh the world only fur him tae get his knee knackered in a bloody Asian Cup warm-up gemme! Thinks he's entitled tae play fur Australia cos his dad wis born in Sydney – divine as that sounds, youse widnae catch me playin fur the country eh ma auld man's birth. He hud a tragic life though did ma dad, servin wi distinction in the Second World War. Died in Auschwitz, ye ken. He fell ooty a guard-tower efter losin his balance when he wis tryin tae machine-gun a group eh prisoners. He wis never the same efter that. (Mainly cos he wis now deid, as opposed tae alive.) So I could have played fur ze glorious Fatherland, as a result eh ma Aryan birthright. (If I hudnae been pish at fitba, that is.) But ma conscience widnae allow it either.

So if The Boyler n that other pair want tae play fur the land Down Under, they might as well jist bloody stay there n see how much they like drinkin pishy Foster's roond the barbie aw day while Aboriginal warriors are chuckin spears at their heids (one sure way tae lance a Boyle) in the swelterin heat listenin tae Rolf Harris n Kylie Minogue records. Tie me kangaroo doon, sport, they should be so lucky. Lucky, lucky, lucky. Bunch eh bloody traitors! (N as ma dear auld dad used tae say, there's only one Barbie I've goat any time fur, n his first name is Klaus. Seig Heil!)

SPIT ROAST

Meanwhile, the Hibees are aff on their winter holidays – tae Dubai! Christ, in ma day they were lucky if they goat a wet weekend break tae Dunbar. Noo they go tae the Middle East – then it wid have been tae the middle eh East Lothian. Which I suppose is better than gaun tae the Heart eh Midlothian.

Talkin eh which, it's long been an Embra tradition tae gob on the aforementioned thing, which I wis only tae happy tae dae, when I wis up toon the other day. Pits me in mind eh yon Hertz crest, ye ken. So I'd jist howked up a great green globule eh toxic phlegm n let fly, when I wis apprehended by some officious lookin gadgie.

"I jist witnessed whit ye did there," says he, nose wrinkled up in pure disgust. "N I'm cawin the polis right noo!"

"Caw away," I replied defiantly. "Canny prosecute a felly fur uphaudin long-standin historical traditions."

Sure enough, afore long this spotty constable built like an emaciated rake wi a pus on him like a welder's bench is giein me gyp. Polis – I swear they're gettin younger every day! Anyway, I wisnae slow in gettin him telt, that a guid spit wis perfectly acceptable under the circumstances, but he jist shook his heid sorrowfully.

"Aye, spitting on the Heart of Midlothian symbol on the site of the old city jail might have been OK, *but...*"

He paused fur effect, while giein me the evil eye. Of course, wi a sudden blindin flash eh clarity, I then realised ma major mistake. Aye, I'd gatecrashed the Sir Walter Scott Memorial Exhibition at the

National Library fur the free wine n hud jist gobbed a big greener aw ower a mint condition First Edition copy eh the book eh the same name!

“Damaging a priceless historical relic admired by millions is a *very* serious crime,” intoned the polis solemnly, as he snapped on the bracelets.

Afore long, another priceless historical relic admired by millions wis also bein damaged, when the cunt shoved me unceremoniously doon thae notoriously slippy stairs at St. Leonards’ nick. I wis that concussed I couldnae even read the charge sheet – aw the letters kept gettin jumbled up afore ma eyes.

“Allow me,” says the desk sergeant, takin it back aff me. “If you canny spell it then here’s what it says…”

“Anything to say before I pass sentence, Mr Gibson?” yawned the beak up the Sheriff Court the following day.

“Tae bloody right – I’ve goat a sentence eh ma ain tae pass first,” I telt him.

“Which is…?”

“Youse can stick the Scott Monument up yer erse!”

Bastirts!

DRUGS – JIST SAY NAW

Ower at Ibrox, the maist destructive force tae come oot eh Colombia since Pablo Escobar hud been up tae his tricks again. Aye, yon bampot Alfredo Molasses. Durin the Auld Firm gemme he first boots Broony in the baws right at the start, tramples ower Anthony Ralston n then grabs Ryan Christie by the goolies in the second hauf. Yet, when Sellik complained tae the SFA, thae bastirts in blazers says they can dae fuck aw aboot it, cos although the referee saw aw three incidents, he decided tae take nae action at the time. How no?? N there wis me thinkin it jist proved whit maist fans have thought aw along – namely, maist eh thae wankers wi whistles *are* as blind as Stevie Wonder in a war-time black-oot wi a bag ower his heid. As fur Alfie boy – Colombian marchin powder, eh? Should've been gied his Colombian marchin orders instead, via three straight red cairds, but nae chance eh that.

On that subject, I once tried a shot eh that very substance masel. But when I rammed the coke up ma hooter, the tap eh the boatil goat stuck in ma left nostril. Talk aboot makin a right Charlie eh yersel. That's one reason I dinnae haud wi takin drugs, it's a dangerous business. Youse youngsters dinnae ken the hauf eh it. When I tried smokin grass, the whole front lawn went up in flames efter I applied the lighter tae git it gaun n I hud tae caw oot the Fire Brigade. Bastirts took ages tae arrive n aw. I wis that flustered that instead eh phonin 999 I'd been repeatedly cawin up 666 instead. Aye, the number eh the beast. Which brings us neatly back tae Alfredo Molasses. Number 10 in his case. Another big lump eh dope n nae mistake. So stay aff the wacky baccy, kids. Well, that's me aff tae take an 'E'. Aye, McEwan's Export. N ye canny whack *that*.

BANANADRAMA

Glancin at the calendar on the waw, I noticed that the so-cawed 'Twelve Days eh Christmas' wis up at last. Thank Christ fur that. The date when romance is in the air so they'd have us aw believe, the major day eh the year when every singleton is lookin fur a new partner n in the words eh that shitey syrupy song, 'Love is all Around'. Wet Wet Wet – wis there ever a band mair appropriately named? (N I ken that other lot did it first back in the Sixties – The Froggs, if memory serves correct.) Whitaloadyshite. Love is all a round awright, but only if it's on the hoose n maist eh the drinks are comin ma way.

But youse canny help thinkin back fondly at this time n soon I found masel reminiscin aboot ma dear departed. Aye, I ken I dinnae talk aboot her much, but that's cos the memories are jist tae painful. Seems like only yesterday she wis batterin me ower the heid wi that reinforced steel rollin pin. Mumpy Minnie, that's thirty year noo she's been away. Or is it forty...? Mind ye, she was away long afore she wis actually deid – away wi the fuckin fairies. That wumman wis a right bampot. (I might even have gone tae the funeral an aw, if it hudnae clashed wi a Hibs gemme.) We met at a traditional tea-dance in Leith Toon Hall – a YLT dance tae be strictly accurate. It wis a team effort awright tae get her back tae ma hoose efterwards – took a dozen eh ma pals tae lift the fat sow ower the threshold. Later, she telt me she thought I lived in the Red Light area – I hud tae reassure her that wis jist the glare eh the McEwan's Export cans she'd clocked through the curtains. Of course, I mair or less *did* live in the Red Light area – the Banana Flats werenae exactly a million miles away fae the Love Island eh its day, a.k.a. Coburg Street.

Aye, they still talk respectfully aboot her in the pubs at the Fit eh the Walk tae this day.

"Tragic, the way she died, wasn't it?"

"Dae youse really believe it wis an accident?"

"Ye reckon that grumpy auld git did deliberately shove her violently doon the stairs wi overwhelmin force when she wis pished oot her heid on Fowler's Wee Heavy?"

Things like that...

In ma defence (no that I need yin, yer honour), I will jist say that they're cawed the Banana Flats fur a guid reason. Naw, it's nowt tae dae wi the curved shape, it's mair that the stairs – no unlike thae steep yins at St. Leonards' nick – have a reputation fur bein awfy slippery. Hardly ma fault she took a tumble. N efter aw, if I'd really wanted tae dae her in, I'd jist have shoved her doon the rubbish chute. Worked oot fine wi disposal eh ma first missus, anyway.

"Gibby, sometimes I think ye love the Hibs mair than her," I mind ma auld pal Humpty Harry sayin, back in the day.

"Harry, I love the bloody *Hertz* mair than her," I retorted, pittin him straight.

Aye, an auld joke maybe, a bit like masel. Minnie Ha-Ha, eh? Aye, well, she's no laughin noo...

HING LOOSE

By the end eh the first week in January, it wis nae laughin matter on the Hibs front either. It wis confirmed that the Boyle wis burst awright efter that Asian Cup caper, possibly causin him tae miss the rest eh the season, Ambrose wis now sayin he wis aboot tae Efe aff n Lenny wis still far fae happy wi his two main so-cawed strikers, warnin, "Must do better. You know you can do better and I know you can do better." Things can only get better then? Somehow I doot it. He then added, "We want to get some bodies in. Obviously it's an ideal opportunity to do that with the window being open."

Jist whit Dr Knox said tae Burke n Hare in his office up Surgeons' Hall, aboot two hunner year ago. Come tae think eh it, that pair wid have been a great alternative tae McLaren n Camembert up front – they ayewis went aboot their work skilfully n efficiently n their finishin wis usually deadly in the box. (Admittedly though, they did have penalties awarded against them, taewards the end eh their careers.) But Lenny should be thankful that at least in his case someone jist painted 'HANG NEIL LENNON' on a waw doon Russell Road, whereas when 'HANG WILLIAM BURKE' graffiti appeared in the Grassmarket in 1829, the city authorities were only tae happy tae oblige. Typical Embra Cooncil though – they didnae manage tae extend that as far as his striking partner. Jist like the bloody trams situation, couldnae get the job finished. Still, the twa Willies were duly accorded an honour similar tae the yin bestowed upon former Hibs' greats Tommy Younger n Peter Marinello – at least they eventually goat a pub named efter them.

Christ, I think I've wandered aff the subject a bit there. No like me, I ken. Noo, where were we again? Oh aye, the current state eh the

Hibs squad. (Certainly no a firing squad, I'll tell youse that fur fuck aw.) But at least they've goat a promising former Dundee United starlet on loan fae Sporting Lisbon. Aye, I can see the headlines awready, when he scores the winnin goal in the next derby – 'TYNECASTLE ERUPTED IN GREEN, WHITE AND GAULD.' Dream on...

LEVEIN ON A JET-PLANE

Ower at Tynie, Craig Levein wis in soapy wi the Blazers – again – this time fur havin a pop at the blind bastirts in the black. Craigie hud been maddened by Madden's antics the last time the Hertz hud played the huns, where he'd proceeded tae overlook a raft eh misdemeanours committed by – surprise surfuckinprise – Alfredo Molasses. He wis promptly ordered tae the stand fur the jambos' forthcoming cup-tie. Whit ye might caw a *natural order* where he's concerned, Christ, he's been sittin in that bloody stand mair times than he did when he wis the so-cawed Dire Rector eh Fitba! His Nobby Stiles must be killin him. I widnae want tae be sittin next tae that grumpy lookin bastirt fur ninety seconds, let alane ninety minutes, I'll tell ye that. (Nor wid the Hertz owner – last time he kept repeatedly tellin her tae Budge up.) In comparison, I'm a positive ray eh sunshine (on Leith.)

But I've ayewis been mair eh a 'gless hauf-fu' kindy guy. (Especially if it's some other cunt's gless n I'm havin a fly swally oot it.) Honest tae Gawd, I dinnae ken where I've goat this auld sour-puss image fae. Once, I wis entered intae a 'Grumpy-Faced Get' competition fur charity n I only came in *fourth*. Mind ye, I wis up against stiff competition – Levein himself, Steve Clarke n Alex Miller aw finished ahead eh me. Disappointin tae say the least, as Lexo used tae whinge tae the Press, every time the Hibs team on his watch failed tae shine. Which wis the bloody majority eh the time!

Anyway, back tae auld misery-guts in Gorgie. He'd branded bungling Boaby's performance durin Hertz v huns as 'absymal'. Awtaegither noo – Absymal – ah, Absymal – ah, Beelzebub hus a devil pit aside fur me-e-e… He'd also been handed a one-month ban, suspended until the end eh the year. He could jist pit us n himsel ooty his misery n cairry oot his ain suspension. The same kind that pit an end tae William Burke springs tae mind…

SHOOTING AFF TARGET

Aye, suicide – it's a subject that's seldom far fae ma mind. Used tae be even mair so when Butcher n Malpractice were runnin the show, admittedly. That wis when I realised I'd finally hud enough. So I decided tae fling masel under a train on the ootskirts eh toon. Didnae want tae cause a fuss, ken, bein a considerate sorty gadgie. So efter gettin aw prepared – I consulted the timetable again, made ma way tae a nice secluded length eh track, checked ma watch one last time - n then dramatically flung masel ontae the rails. "Goodbye, cruel world!" I cried oot, in the kindy despairin tone that wid have brought tears tae a gless eye. No that there wis anyone there tae hear me, of course. However, that wis when the plan started tae go a bit awry, on account eh bloody Scotrail. Aye – the bloody train wis runnin late! Efter lyin there freezing ma erse aff fur half-an-oor, I gied up n resolved tae try again the next day.

So I goat up nice n early n ate a condemned man's breakfast, afore heidin oot. There wis nae way I wis trailin away across toon again, so I decided tae stay local this time. But efter wanderin aboot fur ages like a heidless chicken gettin mair n mair confused, I hud tae ask some passer-by fur directions.

"Excuse me, pal, but where the fuck is Leith Central Station again?"

This gadgie jist looked at me like I'd goat twa heids.

"Whit?"

I repeated the question as patiently as I could, whit wi him appearin tae be corn beef. But he jist shook his heid slowly, afore giein me the terrible news.

"Leith Central Station shut doon *decades* ago, auld-timer," he says.

"Well, nae cunt telt me!" I yelled in exasperation.

See that bloody Cooncil, ye'd think they'd keep us Leithers informed first afore they start destroyin our local heritage, but aw naw. They'll be knockin doon Leith International Airport next. I blame that Dr Beeching masel, back in the sixties there he made mair cuts than Zorro. N it widnae have happened if Leith hud still been independent, prior tae thae Embra bastirts illegally takin ower in 1920, I'll tell youse that. Aye, the Great Betrayal, I mind it well. Anyway, I wisnae gaun tae be pit aff any longer, so I resolved tae chuck masel aff the bridge ower Leith Walk instead. That'd show em aw n dae the job jist as well. But – n I'm sure ye ken whit's comin next – aye, they'd only gone n goat rid eh that an aw!

I stumped intae The Cenny in a towerin rage (hud tae relocate there when The Volley goat dubbed up - is *nothing* sacred??)

"Whit's up wi ye, Gibby? Yer face is pure trippin ye, jist furra change," says ma pal Moany Tony, fae his usual seat.

So I explained ma problem, efter orderin up a pint n double Grouse. Nae point in toppin yersel on an empty stomach efter aw.

"If I wis gaun tae cash ma chips in, I'd dae it by tablet," he stated. "Overdose job. Nice n peaceful n yid jist drift away wi'oot leavin a bloody great mess behind."

Well that goat me thinkin awright, maybe he hud a point...

The following day I goat up nice n early n ate *another* condemned man's breakfast – but this time it wis the actual brekky that wis gonnae be the means eh ma final exit. Crafty, eh? But I wis soon strugglin. Fur the one thing that radge Tony didnae allow fur is jist how fuckin sickly ye start feelin, afore very long. By mid-mornin I'd eaten twenty-seven bars eh tablet n it wis pure giein me the boak! Went n threw the whole lot up wi'oot meaning tae n that wis another attempt doon the tubes. Even tried tae choke on ma ain vomit like Jimi Hendrix, but aw I goat wis a purple haze in ma brain. Bastirts!

But ye ken me, I'm no the type that gies up easily. Drastic measures wid now have tae be implemented. So the next time in The Cenny I sidled up tae a well-kent local gangster, whae wis rumoured tae be ayewis packin, if ye get ma drift.

"I need a fire-arm," I surreptitiously whispered in his lug.

"A fire-alarm?"

"Naw," I groaned through gritted teeth, havin tae raise ma voice so that the deef daftie could hear whit I wis sayin. So I repeated the same statement.

"Whit fur?" he demanded tae ken.

"Eh...it's fur scarin owls," I said cunningly, thinkin on ma feet. "Aw that hootin is keepin me awake at nights."

"A fire-alarm'll dae that," he says.

I could see I wis gettin naewhere. I'd have tae be mair direct.

"How aboot a Colt?"

"Nae use – owls arenae feart eh hoarses."

"Look, jist forget aboot thae bloody owls furra minute!" I yelped in irritation. "I need a gun!"

"Why didn't ye say so then? Youse fancy a Luger?"

"I dinnae drink the stuff. McEwan's Export only. But aboot the gun..."

He looked around in a furtive fashion.

"Could ye use a Magnum?"

I nodded eagerly. I then watched as his hand reached slowly intae his inside pocket, afore withdrawin it, a pained look on his evil pus. I saw that he wis haudin a wee broon stick.

"Problem?" I sighed.

"Aye – it melted. Tell ye what though – I could dae ye a starting pistol," he offered.

"Well...it's a start I suppose," I said doubtfully.

For by this time I wis gettin right desperate. It wis noo or never. So I telt Moany Tony eh ma latest intentions – causin the cheeky bastirt tae yawn loudly – whilst the other gadgie went aff tae get the necessary fae his hoose. He took bloody ages an aw, by which time I'd skelped back countless pints n nips. Dutch courage, ye ken. However, he finally reappeared n slipped me this package.

"Right, I'm aff tae dae the deed noo," I telt Tony, makin ma way tae the toilet.

"Aye – whitever."

Luckily there wis nae-one else in the lavvy, so I carefully unwrapped the pistol n raised it tae ma heid, lookin intently in the mirror tae make sure ma aim wis true. Unfortunately though, the bevvy hud taken such effect that when I peered closely at the gless, I could see *two* Grumpy Gibsons lookin back at me. Bastirt! I wis seein double! Still, the chances eh gettin it right were fifty-fifty... I closed ma eyes n squeezed the trigger tightly, whereupon the huge BANG gaun aff gied me such a fright I promptly lost aw control eh ma bowels. As the shite ran doon ma legs it dawned on me somewhit forcefully that – against aw the odds – I wis still alive efter aw. Apparently I'd shot the wrong Gibby, i.e. the yin that wisnae actually there in the first place.

Back in the bar, I made a superhuman effort tae pit a brave face on it.

"I thought ye said youse were gaun in there tae shoot yersel?" Tony says in an accusatory sorty tone, while sniffin the air suspiciously.

"Naw, I says I'm gaun in there tae *shit* masel," I clarified, takin a huge slug ooty the whisky gless. Christ kens how it crawled in there unnoticed, but never mind. Whit a loady crap aw roond, quite literally. I'd gone in there tae end it aw n only succeeded in raisin a right auld stink instead. But at least it gied me a renewed will tae live. But only cos committin suicide turned oot tae be such bloody hard work. Take it fae me – it's jist no worth it...

CUP FINAL CATASTROPHES REVISITED

Needless tae say, there's been times since then when I've been mighty tempted tae gie it another go. May 21st, 2016, comes tae mind. Aye, another bloody disaster...

"Are youse gaun tae the cup final then?" says Torn-Faced Tommy, as I sat there in Wilkies, the day afore the big gemme. (I needed a wee break fae The Cenny – whae in fairness hud strongly hinted that they needed a wee break fae me. Especially efter I'd fired a gun in the lavvy n then shat ma breeks.)

"The cup final?!" I yipped. "Wild hoarses widnae drag me there, I can tell youse that!"

"How no?" says he.

"Cos wild hoarses dragged me along Princes Street efter they won it last time," I says. "I fell in front eh the parade when Andy McGeechan's held the cup aloft n goat ma skerf tangled in the hoarses' reins. Then the bastirts stampeded n I ended up wi worse injuries than that daft suffragette lassie whae flung herself in front eh the King's hoarse a few years later. Plus, I hud a shite day at Hampden afore that an aw. Never saw a thing!"

"How come?" says Tommy. "Hibs won, efter aw."

"Aye, but the bloody match wis played at Parkheid!" I yelped. "Nae cunt telt me of course. I wisnae long back fae the Boer War either, where I goat fatally wounded at the siege eh Sarajevo, dinnae forget that."

"Aye, well, youse are startin tae Boer the fuck ooty me, ye silly auld coot," he replied, as he staggered oot the door, drappin something on the flair as he went. Pished, ye ken. Pished aff tae, when he woke up the following morn nae doot, as he'd jist drapped his cup final ticket. Looked like I wis gaun efter aw!

Twenty-four oors later I'm at Hampden, the match hud jist started n I canny see fuck aw fur the smoke. So I complains tae the nearest steward.

"Pit yer pipe oot then, pal," says this daftie in a fluorescent jaikit.

So I bites ma tongue, but did jist that – but I *still* couldnae see!

"Stokesy's on fire!" says this felly next tae me excitedly.

"Naw, *seats* are on fire," I corrected him, as I clocked the huns settin aff flares galore. In ma day ye'd have been wearin them, no pittin a light tae them. So there's nae score as far as I can tell, until suddenly up pops Kenny Miller! Tae be honest, I didnae ken he wis still playin fur Hibs. Must've been in the reserves fur the last eighteen years. Anyway, doesnae matter, cos he scores a cracker in the 27th minute!

"Gaun yersel, King Kenny!" I roars in delight, jumpin up n doon n twirlin ma rattle, accidentally takin this boy's eye oot as I did so. (Later on, when I caught his other eye I thought furra moment I wis standin next tae Dean Shiels.) But I'll tell ye this fur fuck aw, youse Hibbies should be ashamed eh yersels! I wis the only yin cheerin! Bunch eh ungrateful bastirts – nae wonder they never bother tae win nowt, wi a support like that. But that wis how it stood at hauf-time – 1-0 tae the Hibees.

So the second hauf gets under way n the Hibbies are still giein me funny looks fur some reason – like I could gie a fuck. Then aw of a sudden the baw's in the back eh the net again!

"Whae scored there?" I demanded tae ken.

"Halliday?" says the Dean Shiels boy, a bit uncertain-like.

"If I wis on holiday dae youse really think I'd have picked a cowp like Glesgie as a destination??" I yowled. "I'm on permanent vacation anyway – I retired in 1956. But never mind that – *whae scored??*"

"It's a goal fur Rangers ye silly auld goat," says this other lippy loudmooth.

So I looks at the scoreboard fur confirmation. I cannae believe whit I see, so I rubs ma peepers n looks again. But there's nae doot aboot it. There it is –Rangers 2, Hibernian 1. I mean, how the fuck... The boy there scores a goal – n they gie thae bluenose bastirts *two?* Of course, then I tippled. I may be stupit, but I'm no daft. Thae cunts play at Ibrox, but this is at Hampden. Therefore it's an away gemme played in Scotland n Scotland's in Europe n in Europe away goals coont double! The cheatin bastirts! Well, that wis it. I'd hud enough. I starts pushin ma way taewards the exit, takin a big despairin swally ooty ma dark green boatil as I went.

"Whit have ye goat there, faither?" says this whippersnapper eh a weedjie cop.

"I've goat ma gin, super Gordon's gin, I jist don't think ye understand, I'm Una Stubbs's man, I'm a radge auld Hibees fan, I've goat ma super Gordon's gin," I telt him straight.

Well, that wis it, huckled intae the back eh a Black Maria. She didnae look tae happy aboot it, either. On the way tae the nick the polis stopped at a supermarket n got oot n then came back wi his messages, which included a big bag eh frozen vegetables. Silly bastirt slings the lot in wi yours truly n then we cairried on. Well, ye ken me. Never look a gift-hoarse in the mooth – or a bag eh polis shoppin either, come tae that. So ye can imagine his coupon at the other end when he found oot that I'd ripped one eh the bags open n scoffed the lot.

"Whit's the charge, officer?" I said wearily at the desk.

"Breach eh the peas," he replied, his pus trippin him.

So that wis me bound ower fur the night. I wisnae hauf – the cunts tied me tae a bed in ma cell wi a barbed-wire rope.

"Never mind, grandpaw," one eh them shouted through the bars. "Hibs won!"

"Aye, Hibs one, Rangers TWO, I ken fine," I yelped.

Whitaloadypish!

LOST MARBLES

So there wis some relief when I heard that this January shut-doon nonsense hud finally come tae an end n the Hibs were back in business. Aboot bloody time n aw!

"Are youse gaun tae the cup gemme then?" says Torn-Faced Tommy, bringin a distinct air eh deja-vu tae the proceedings.

"Whae's playin?" I demanded tae ken.

"Hibs n Elgin," he says.

"Elgin! I'd only be gaun tae that if I'd well n truly lost ma marbles," I telt him straight.

"So that means youse *are* gaun then," he sighed in response.

"Wild hoarses widnae keep me away!"

No that I haud wi aw thae Hielan League sides bein admitted tae the Scottish Cup, ken. Elgin County, Ross City, Inverness Clachnacuddin Thistle, Peter's Heid n Aiberdeen – we're bein over-run by teuchters! Never mind another roond eh the cup, it's aboot time fur another roond eh the Hielan Clearances instead, that's whit I say.

Anyway, the Hibees goat aff tae a no bad start, as that Camembert stuck away the opener haufway through the first hauf, wi a big cheesy smile on his face. I wis jist aboot tae forgive him fur missin that penalty in the Livi gemme, when biChrist he only goes n misses *another* yin! Wi shootin like that ye widnae want him beside ye in a war situation, I can tell ye that. No very likely, granted – bein Swiss he'd be mair likely tae be standin on the sidelines wi his white flag, pleadin neutrality. At least Hibs were two up through that Darryl Morgan by then, or it could have been a lot worse. Yet it still took another spot-kick tae really make sure – no taken by cheesy wotsit this time thank fuck – n they finally wrapped it up wi a fourth.

"This was a good game to come to," said assistant gaffer Barry Parker efterwards.

"Speak fur yersel," I muttered.

He then went ontae say, "Gettin into the Top Six is still the main target."

"They couldnae even get intae the Tap Twenty wi 'Hibernian (Give Us A Goal)' back in '73!" I yelped. "So how in the name eh buggery are they gonnae crack the Tap Six? Need tae sell a shed-load eh records tae achieve that. N they should never have knocked doon the auld coo-shed anyway. Built that Famous Five Stand in its place ye ken. Whitaloadypish."

Aw eh a sudden I wis aware eh a deathly silence n loadsy people lookin at me wi whit appeared tae be great irritation.

"Excuse me," says that Parker through gritted teeth, "but just exactly which newspaper or media outlet do you represent?"

Aye, nae wonder they caw him Nosey Parker!

"I represent naebody but masel n the guid people eh Leith," I telt him. "No that it's any eh your business. Caw yersel an assistant manager? Ye look mair like a hameless mountaineer whae's been kippin in a ditch fur the last fortnight."

Well, needless tae say, ma feet scarcely touched the ground as I wis unceremoniously huckled oot fae gatecrashin yet another post-match Press Conference. But no afore I'd pauchled a few sannies n a handfu eh sausage rolls, so it wis jist aboot worth it, in the long run. Unlike the gemme itself.

COWDEN CONSPIRACIES

Ower at Central Park, there wis a right stushie efter Cowdenbeath's cup-tie against the huns wis cawed aff at the last minute. Soon the conspiracy theorists were havin a field-day, claimin that the presence eh Rangers' kit-man Jimmy Bell on the pitch hud influenced the referee's decision. Aye, n youse can coont me amongst them! (I ken fine that thae moon landings were faked n that JFK wisnae really shot by Oswald Moseley, jist fur starters.) Cos whit business hud Bell goat, tryin tae ring the changes by gaun on the park in the first place??

"Kit men do," countered Moany Tony, when I raised the subject in the boozer there.

"Kit-Men-Do is the capital eh Nepal," I retorted. "I'm talkin aboot thae huns cheatin as usual. Didnae want tae risk aw thae fancy-dan signings comin a cropper on yon crappy Cowden cairpit!"

But there wis bugger aw wrong wi the pitch as far as anyone else wis concerned, including the Blue Brazil's gaffer n also their chairman, that pipe-smokin radge Donald Findlay. Even mair suspiciously, despite aw this takin place at the last moments afore kick-aff on the Friday, it emerged that the Rangers team were aw still in their hotel

– in Embra! Aye – they'd never hud any intention eh playin the gemme at aw. Fur if they hud, they'd surely have been stayin in one eh the many five-star hotels on the Costa del Cowdenbeath. Stevie G jist fancied a night oot at the karaoke in Tamsons.

Of course, that be-whiskered bampot in the Blue Brazil boardroom is nae stranger tae such a form eh entertainment either. We aw mind how he wis bombed ooty the vice-chairman post at Ibrox, efter bein caught singin sectarian songs on camera. Imagine bein shunned by the huns fur bigotry, that's like bein expelled fae the Ku Klux Klan fur bein a racist. N I'll tell youse this, he's a shite defence lawyer n aw. Never goat me aff on a charge yet! Maybe cos he's never actually represented me, but that's neither here nor there. It's aw one big giant conspiracy when aw is said n done. Frame Gibby at any cost. Aye, they'll be blamin me fur 9/11 next! (Thank fuck I've goat an alibi fur that date at least.)

JUNIOR SHOWTIME

Still, when aw is said n done, at least Hibs were safely through tae the next roond. Nae such luck fur other so-cawed Premier sides against lower league opposition, baith Dundee n Aiberdeen failin tae win at hame against Queen eh the Sooth n Stenhoosemuir, ya hoor. Mair proof that McInnes's mob *should* be in the Hielan League. But the biggest shock eh the day came in Ayr United bein dumped oot by the Juniors eh Auchinleck Turncoat. That Ian McCall's ayewis been one eh the grumpiest gadgies this side eh yours truly at the best eh times n every time the cameras picked him oot in the away dug-oot his face hud fallen even further. Plus he wis gettin through mair chewing-gum in one match than his fellow torn-face Fergie used tae manage ower a whole season at Auld Trafford. Sittin there like a big greetin-faced four-eyed coo munchin turnips fur ninety minutes. Fur Christ sake man, cheer up! It's hardly the end eh the world.

Granted though, ye'll be abused, picked on n reviled throughoot Ayrshire n beyond till yer dyin day – jist mind whit they did tae 'local hero' Ally Macleod when it aw went tits up fur Scotland in Argentina '78. In fact, buggerin aff tae Sooth America faster than Ronnie Biggs might be his best option. N if he'd needed cheerin up efterwards, he could've done worse than listen tae thae marble-moothed muppets on the BBC trying tae pronounce 'Auchinleck' that evening n the following day. Laugh? I almost pit ma fit through the telly. Newsreaders, announcers, sports reporters – bunch eh illiterate dizzylexic bastirts if youse ask me. Canny speak the Kween's Englush! Jist fur starters, it's 'Auch' as in 'loch', not 'ock' tae rhyme wi 'lock'. So, until youse aw learn tae speak proper, away n get tae fock.

OOH-ARR, V.A.R., SAID OOH-ARR V.A.R.

I couldnae help laughin when I read that Neil Lennon hud kindly offered tae help thae bastirts in the black wi pittin their hoose in order, sittin doon fur a meeting wi various big-wigs (plus some wee hairpiece fae Stenhoosemuir) tae discuss the disconnect between the clubs n SFA officialdom. The Stenny boy said optimistically, "This needs to be dealt with as a single piece of joined-up thinking." (Fat chance eh that wi the Blazers, eh?) He then added dramatically, "Tear down barriers!" Well thae G4S clowns tried daein that at Hampden back on May 21st, 2016, tae save the Hibbies the trouble eh daein it themsels. The thought eh Lenny actually 'sitting down' at the table seemed a trifle optimistic tae – he'll mair likely be runnin roond n roond it wi airms outstretched, daein his aeroplane routine. Stenny Boy's next point wis that the issue eh VAR must noo be looked at closely.

"Whit's VAR?" Humpty Harry demanded tae ken, as we sat there in The Cenny.

"Vodka Assisted Refereein," I explained. "Thae cunts canny dae the job tae save themsels when stone cold sober, so if there's any dispute they take a big skelp eh the Smirnoff n then review it on a screen. Works wonders apparently. They goat the idea fae that Mad Vlad in charge eh Russia, whae ensures that his cabinet ministers are tanked up on the stuff afore they make any major decisions. N they've no goat it wrong yet!"

"Apart fae annexing Crimea, startin a cross-border pagger wi Ukraine, helpin tae prop up Assad's dictatorship in Syria n poisonin folk in Salisbury?" he says.

"Precisely!"

Jist then the barmaid comes ower – ken that Girnin Gertie? Aye, her wi the coupon like a well-skelped kipper.

"I'm afraid I'm gonnae have tae ask youse tae leave, Gibby," she says.

"Whit! Whit fur?"

"We've goat guid reason tae suspect youse are responsible fur the charity boatil that wis on the bar gaun missin."

Of course she wis talkin shite fae the aff, cos it wisnae missin at aw. How could it be, when I kent fine it wis safely tucked away at the back eh my kitchen cupboard? N why no, fur Chrissake? I'm one eh the biggest charity cases gaun. When I wis bangin on recently aboot how skint I wis, some cheeky joker suggested gaun tae a food-bank.

"I'm no short eh money fur scran, I'm short eh money fur bevvy!" I yipped in agitation. "So unless they've started openin up whisky banks, I'll be deid eh thirst afore the week's oot!"

But naturally I wisnae gaun tae admit any eh this tae Girnin Gertie.

"I've never been so insulted in ma puff!" I howled. "Charge denied – n if youse continue tae accuse me wi'oot a shred eh evidence, may I jist remind ye that I've goat Donald Findlay on speed dial."

There wis a silence eh the pregnant variety, prior tae that auld witch wi the pus that could curdle milk giein me a big malicious grin.

"Oh, but we've goat the evidence awright," she says, pointin tae this security camera behind the bar linked tae the big screen, which I'd somehow failed tae spot. Bastirt! So the whole pub are watchin as she gleefully rewinds the incriminatin tape n then presses 'Play'. Wi sinkin hert, I wis reluctantly forced tae look n aw.

"There ye go!" she says triumphantly, pointin a gnarly finger in the direction eh yours truly up on yon screen, surreptitiously stretchin ma hand oot fur the boatil. "That's whit ye caw VAR evidence n nae mistake!"

"VAR?" mumbled Humpty Harry intae his Heavy.

"Aye – Very Auld Radge, caught bang tae rights!"

Bastirt again! I knew I wis beat awright, but wis determined tae retain ma sense eh dignity. I goat aff the bar-stool n started walkin slowly taewards the door, wi heid held high. Mainly cos Gertie had jist delivered a sickenin upper-cut tae ma jaw.

"I'll no be back! I'm takin ma custom elsewhere!"

(Which I thought, rather than spoke, due tae ma mooth bein fu eh blood n broken teeth.) Aye, n I've been speechless ever since...

ON THE ROAD AGAIN

"Motherwell?" enquired Moany Tony there, in his usual nosey fashion.

"Hardly. She's been deid fur fifty year."

He sighed deeply.

"I mean, are youse gaun tae see the Hibs at Fir Park?"

"Wild..."

"Yeah, yeah. I ken, I ken. Wild hoarses widnae drag ye there, am I right?"

"Wild Turkey's on special offer at the bar – three quid fur a double, is actually whit I wis aboot tae say, afore bein rudely interrupted," I snapped. "However, if ye dae the honours, I'll say nae mair aboot it."

He sighed again. Christ, the radge could sigh fur Scotland!

"A double then?"

"Aye."

Next thing, he comes back fae the bar n plonks doon a gless in front eh me.

"Whit's that?"

"Jist whit ye asked fur, Gibby, fur Chrissake! A double Wild Turkey!"

"Aye – but I says I wanted a double!"

Ye could almost hear the cogs turnin slowly in whit passes fur his brain.

"Ye mean ye want a *double* double?" he croaked, as the penny finally drapped.

"Aye, that's whit I says!"

He went grumblin aff back tae the bar, still tryin tae dae the arithmetic in his big thick heid.

"A quadruple then?!" he finally yelled, upon workin it oot, luckily jist as the barman hove intae earshot.

"Comin right up, sir," says the latter, pourin four mair measures intae a fresh gless.

So, six Wild Turkeys later, I wis ready fur the aff. Cos in this case, wild hoarses wid have been quite welcome tae drag me tae the gemme, if they so desired. First League gemme efter the break, ken, I felt I hud tae make the effort. Aye, I wisnae gonnae miss this yin. I goat on the blower right away tae enquire aboot the trains.

"Ye'll have tae change at Glesgie," says this bammer at the other end indistinctly, nae doot as a result eh him operatin ooty a call-centre in Mumbai.

"Will I buggery!" I yelped. "I'm jist gaun in the claes I'm standin up in, fur Chrissake."

Nae way wis I packin a suitcase fur a journey tae Motherwell. Rip-aff bastirts wid probably charge extra fur luggage an aw like that cheeky cunt whae runs Brian-Air, n there wid be every chance eh it bein choaried if we goat stopped by highwaymen at Wishaw. Well, I'd jist have tae travel on the cheap efter aw. Looks like it wis hitch-hikin fur me. I dived back tae the hoose, made up a cardboard sign wi ma intended destination written on it n then bussed it tae the ootskirts. Soon I wis standin by the roadside, thumb stuck oot at a jaunty angle. Motherwell, here I come!

Luckily, there are still some guid people in this sorry world – although conspicuous by their absence in the bloody pubs eh Leith – n soon I wis heidin doon the highway at a fair auld rate eh noughts. Some solo motorists get awfy lonely n are ayewis happy tae pick up hitchers fur a bit eh chat – which wis jist as well, cos it took sixteen separate lifts tae get tae the other end! Funnily enough a lot eh them seemed tae be awfy absent-minded bastirts, cos efter tellin me they were heidin aw the way there, they kept suddenly rememberin they were actually only gaun as far as the next junction, as soon as I started giein them ma life-story. But I goat there in the end, which wis the main thing.

I'll tell youse this though – ye widnae think that wis a Premiership groond, naw, no by a long chalk. Whit a cowp! A guid while since I'd been tae Motherwell, but Christ, it hudnae hauf deteriorated. Like yours truly, it wis fawin tae bits. Despite bein near kick-aff time there wis hardly anyone else aboot n I appeared tae be the only yin proudly sportin colours green n white. The place wis deid as a doornail. So I stood outside the main entrance fur ages until some local gadgie came intae view.

"Which is the right entrance fur Hibbies?" I says tae him.

"Eh??"

See, the trouble wi thae yokel types, thae hicks fae the sticks wi straw in their mooths, they're like furriners sometimes, in that ye've goat tae SHOUT at them LOUDLY tae get them tae understand the Kween's Englush.

So I bawled oot the same question intae his lug at maximum volume, causin him tae leap back several feet in alarm.

"I dunno whit ye've been smoking, grandpaw, but I can assure ye that Hibs are certainly no playin here the night. N nor are Motherwell, fur that matter."

"Whit?!"

I fumbled aboot fur ma ticket which naturally hud the match venue printed on it n waved it in front eh his bemused coupon.

"There – whit does that say there, then?"

He scrutinised it closely n then started noddin thoughtfully.

"Uh-huh. I think I can see where ye've gone wrong, auld-timer."

Wi that, he pointed above at the plaque wi the stadium's name on it, while shakin his heid sorrowfully. So I glanced up, rubbed ma eyes furiously n glanced again. Then I looked at the sign I'd made up fur hitchin n a horrible cauld feelin came ower me. Aye, I'd been in such a hurry, I'd somehow pit an 'S' efter the word 'FIR' in 'FIR PARK' – n the bloody sign on the front eh the stadium only went n confirmed it. Aye – I wisnae in Motherwell at aw – I wis outside East Stirlingshire's groond *Firs* Park! Christ on a bike!

"Whit the hell am I gonnae dae noo?" I howled tae nae-one in particular.

"Actually, it's turned oot that this is yer lucky night," says this local boy, once I'd calmed doon a bit, "cos I jist happen tae have a spare ticket fur tonight's gemme right here."

Which, tae cut a long story short, is how I ended up watchin East Stirling draw 0-0 in a friendly against Auchenshoogle Athletic in the pishin rain wi nae roof ower ma heid n only a cauld pie at hauf-time tae keep body n soul taegether, instead eh watchin Hibs gettin gubbed by Motherwell. (Nae wonder they're nicknamed 'The Stealmen', cos they stole aw three points by aw accounts, but at least I wisnae there tae see it.) So it could have been worse, I wis philosophically thinkin, on ma way back tae the station efterwards. A bit prematurely as it turned oot, cos that wis jist afore I wis jumped by the Auchenshoogle Casuals, whae gied me a Chinese burn n then nicked ma bunnet. Whitaloadypish!

POET'S CORNER

"Wee, sleekit, cowrin', tim'rous Gibby / O, what a panic's in thy Hibbie..." says Torn-Faced Tommy there on January 25th, as I walked intae the appropriately named Bam O'Shanter. Aye, persona non gratis fae The Cenny – again. Normally, I'd have punched him in the pus fur gettin lippy, but it wis that time eh year fur celebratin the life n works eh oor national poet efter aw.

"Fair fa' yer honest sonsie case / Great Chieftain wi a pudding face," I answered correctly, in my Address Tae A Haggis-Faced Huddy.

Already I could see the barman – Erse-Faced Eddie – glarin at me suspiciously, clearly thinkin, should auld acquaintance be forgot n never brought tae mind? Well, I bloody hope so, cos if he minded whae I wis, nae doot I'd have been huckled ooty there an aw.

Exactly a year ago, he'd caught me swingin to n fro on the illuminated panel above the door bearin the pub's name, efter a few bevvies. It wis bloody ancient anyway n stretched the whole length eh the bar, so nae surprise really when it suddenly broke apart n fell tae pieces on the pavement. As did yours truly.

"Ye auld vandal! Whit did ye dae that fur, fur fuck's sake!?" he yelled, runnin ootside in a rage.

"Fur the sake eh auld lang sign," I explained, dustin masel doon afore takin tae ma heels.

Anyway, it seemed like he hudnae recognised me, at least no yet. So we goat stuck intae the bevvy, Tommy n I, 'inspirin bold John Barleycorn,' as Rabbie B might well have pit it. Efter a while, I lit up a Capstan's Full Strength n wis jist aboot tae enjoy a nice relaxin smoke, when Tommy gied us a warnin nudge in the cabbage n ribs.

"Uh-oh, see approach proud Edward's power..."

I looked up, tae see Erse-Faced Eddie bearin doon on us.

"Pit that fag oot! Youse canny smoke in here!"

"How no?" I retorted. "Dinnae gimme yer pish."

I blew a big smoke ring right up his hooter, jist tae make ma point.

"It's bloody well illegal, that's how no. Now pit it oot!"

"It may be illegal in the city eh *Embra*," I graciously conceded, "which I shouldnae have tae remind ye doesnae start till south eh the border which used tae run doon the middle eh the flair eh whit used tae be the Boundary Bar which is haufway up – or doon – the Walk. However, everythin north eh that demarcation line is the Independent People's Republic eh Leith, so thae daft nanny-state jambo-type laws dinnae apply here."

But as I wis gettin him telt – in a rather long-winded fashion admittedly – two unfortunate things occurred in quick succession. When I opened ma mooth tae speak, the Capstan fell fae ma lips intae ma lap. I'd jist bought the packet eh fags ooty the garage doon the road n hud slipped n fallen on the forecourt on ma way back ower, as a result eh some clumsy get spillin fuel all ower the groond by the petrol pumps. Therefore ma breeks goat soaked through wi the stuff. Next thing – WHOOOOOOSH! – I've gaun up like a bloody Twelfth eh July bonfire in Belfast!

Eddie n Tommy jumped back in alarm as the flames engulfed me n ma skin started tae melt. It wisnae long afore the Fire Brigade are on the scene n this big galoot in a yelly helmet is hosin me doon wi this giant extinguisher.

"Whit the hell happened here, Grandpaw?"

"Nowt tae worry aboot," I says stoically, as I bubbled away like a bit foosty blister. "It's Burns night efter aw."

"So ye're a fan eh oor national poet then are ye?" yelled Erse-Faced Eddie, lookin even mair pissed aff than usual, possibly cos part eh his pub wis now on fire an aw.

"Tae right I am," I stated proudly. "Noo's the day n noo's the hour."

"Tae right it is. N you're Bard."

Bastirt! But I suppose that's whit they caw poetic justice.

CZECHMATE

Meanwhile, it wis a case eh 'up wi the bunnets eh Bonnie Dundee' in Gorgie. Aye, Hibs might have goat beat, but at least we didnae get turned ower at hame by the League's bottom club. Hertz scored one eh the luckiest goals ye'll *ever* see intae the bargain, as a mis-hit free-kick took a massive deflection aff a defender n somehow looped ower the keeper's heid intae the net. It wis so unexpected the jambos looked even mair scoobied than the Dark Blues. No that it did them much guid in the long run, as the visitors still went ontae win 2-1.

The Hertz fans were aw waitin eagerly tae see their much-vaunted new striker Vanacek, but sadly there wis nae sign eh a Prague Spring in his step. This wis one Czech that wis simply never gaun tae bounce – the only thing he wisnae slow aboot wis wi gettin himself booked.

Of course, one eh the main tasks eh a fitba manager is tae instil a sense eh confidence in his charges, particularly if he's dealin wi a furriner makin his hame debut whae's maybe feelin a wee bit nervous. So efter hookin the hapless huddy on the hauf-oor mark, Craig Levein proceeded tae chuck aw his toys ooty the big maroon pram n telt the assembled Press pack, "I thought he was rubbish." Well, whae fuckin signed him in the first place, eh, it wis youse whae placed the natural order, sayin, "Czech, please," ya soor-faced specky radge! Cannae blame Cathro fur that yin. Should dae wonders fur the boy's self-esteem right enough, let's hope his translator does the decent thing n tells him that 'rubbish' is jist another word fur 'brilliant'. Much like Craigie's recruitment capability...

LISTED MISSING

Another player whae'd been on the sharp end eh the managerial tongue eh late wis Florian Camembert, whae – as befitted his name – goat awfy runny when his gaffer laid intae him again. In fact he threatened tae run away awtaegether, afore bein talked ooty it by his team-mates. Fur by that time it wis Lenny's run that looked tae have come tae an end instead, as a result eh gettin himself suspended, even afore the 'HING NEIL LENNON' graffiti hud appeared ootside Easter Road. Well, that's whit ye get, by appointin a hot-heided radge tae the position in the first place (as maist eh ma former employers hud frequently asserted, in the past.)

So how wid that affect the Hibs' next gemme, the televised encoonter in Paisley? Fur the better as it turned oot, despite the way Lenny hud been gaun on, where ye widnae have thought they'd have been capable eh beatin *Helen* Mirren. Naturally, I wis careful wi the travel arrangements this time, no only efter the East Stirlingshire fiasco, but cos eh long-ago memories eh an island-hoppin fuck-up still fresh in mind. This wis no long efter thae new-fangled telly companies started showin the gemmes live n some erse hud telt me that Hibs were gaun oot live on Skye. The upshot eh that wis yours truly gettin stranded in a polis station in Portree fur a fortnight efter makin the trip, durin which I nearly caught ma death on the swim across tae the Misty Isle (aye, nae bloody bridge back in thae days!)

So this time I wis even prepared tae change in Glesgie if necessary – which I wis telt in nae uncertain terms wid be the case again. So I changed intae a suit wi arries runnin up n doon it as soon as I reached Queen Street, efter carefully slashin ma pus in several places wi a sharp knife, jist tae blend in wi the local populace, ken. Then it wis aff tae Central, tae buy a second-class economy aff-peak day return pensioners' discounted ticket fur the hoarse n cart express tae Paisley. Unfortunately though, the hoarse wis aff seek, so I hud tae push the cart there masel.

Haufway through the first hauf, I wis wonderin why I'd bothered. Fur a start, Hibs were sportin that eye-waterin fluorescent outfit which made them look like a gang eh bloody buildin-site labourers in thae hi-vis jaikits! N ma ain visibility certainly wisnae eh the high variety, as the effect eh that plus the glare fae the low-lyin sun meant I could see fuck aw. Apart fae the Saints' goal of course. Oh aye, I've missed loadsy things throughoot ma long life – ma ain weddin, Hibs' goals in the 2016 Scottish Cup Final (allegedly – I still dinnae really believe they happened), Mumpy Minnie's funeral, the No. 1 bus, the double twenty on the dartboard – but I somehow never bloody well miss the opposition scorin. I suddenly realised whit wis happenin, as God in His infinite wisdom wis punishin me fur missin the Motherwell gemme an aw, n wis noo condemnin me tae watchin a repeat performance in Paisley! Well, that wis that, then. It wis total pish tae, but bein the loyal Hibernian servant that I am, I decided tae gie them a full oor eh ma valuable time, but nae mair.

Naturally as soon as I'd bailed oot fifteen minutes intae the second hauf, I heard the roar gaun up tae signal another goal. That'll be 2-0 tae them I thought resignedly – wrongly as it turned oot, as some young whippersnapper cawed Shaw hud goat yin back. But I didnae find that oot till I goat back tae Glesgie, havin hud tae push that bloody cart aw the way back there tae. I could have goat a train I suppose, but bein Scotrail there nae doot wid have been a delay due tae the wrong kindy snaw or leaves on the line or somethin similar, so I wis quicker walkin. Sittin in The Hoarseshoe a wee while later – efter clockin that they'd mis-spelt 'hoarse' as 'horse' on the sign – I wis delighted tae see that Saints' auld boys Mallan n McGregor hud done the biz fur Hibs, as the final scores came up on the telly. Jist as I wis thinkin it wis maybe ma day efter aw, the large ornamental hoarseshoe above the door somehow detached itsel n fell on ma napper on ma way back oot, knockin me oot cauld. Whit bampot said that hoarseshoes were lucky, eh? By the time I goat ooty the Southern General wi a big bandage wrapped roond ma heid like a turban, I'd missed the last train back tae Embra. So I hirpled roond tae Buchanan Street, tae find I'd missed the last bus n aw. I caught sight eh ma reflection in a shop windae n looked exactly how I felt – Sikh. Then the passin polis clocked ma arrie-bedecked suit n kindly conveyed me tae where they assumed I'd escaped fae in the first place – Barlinnie. Needless tae say when I awoke late the followin mornin, I'd missed bloody breakfast. Aye, wi ma luck, I'll miss ma ain bloody funeral...

YE'LL AYEWIS WALK ALANE

The next night, there wis a double petrol bomb attack on two eh the pubs owned by Hibs' legend Paul Kane, namely The Four-in-Hand n The Tor, which made front-page news. Christ, I ken Lenny must have hud the hump efter bein suspended, but surely that wis jist takin things tae far. In the past he'd been mair on the receivin end eh bomb threats, rather than cairryin them oot himsel. Still, it maybe wisnae that surprisin, seein as he grew up in Northern Ireland throughout the Seventies n Eighties, where hurlin petrol bombs aboot the place wis mair or less compulsory. Indeed, it wis actually enshrined in the school curriculum. A quick glance at Lenny's daily timetable fur Lurgan Primary only serves tae prove the point. 9 a.m. Assembly. 9.15. Arithmetic (how many British sodjers does it take tae change a light-bulb?) 10.00. English (n why ye should hate their guts). 10.45. Geography (how best tae funnel airms shipments fae the USA n Libya). 11.30. Kneecappin fur Beginners. 12.15. Lunch. 1 p.m. (If ye know yer) History. 1.45. P.E. (Pyrotechnic Explosions, i.e. Advanced Bomb-Makin). 2.30. Chemistry (mair eh the same). 3.15. Art (paintin big daft sectarian gable-end murals). 4.00. End eh school day n time tae throw stanes n rocks at the Army, whilst mobbing n riotin on yer way hame.)

The polis did a thorough investigation, even checkin oot Tamson's, which also forms part eh Kano's property portfolio. Clockin the state eh the place, they instantly assumed that it hud been bombed an aw, but that turned oot no tae be the case. Aye, havin Garry O'Connor drinkin in yer pub can produce a very similar effect. However in his case it's the Jagerbombs rather than the petrol yins that are usually the cause eh the damage.

Of course, I wisnae exactly in the clear masel. Ever since I discharged that firearm in The Cenny when under severe mental strain, the bizzies hud been on ma case. It wis nae different this time, as they chapped ma door first thing Monday mornin, askin me tae accoont fur ma movements between 3.30 n 4 a.m. Luckily I hud a cast-iron alibi – aye, I wis still in Barlinnie, prior tae paddin the hoof back fae Glesgie! So once they'd checked the relevant CCTV I thought I wis in the clear. But ye ken me, if I didnae have bad luck, I widnae have any bloody luck at aw. I might have goat aff wi the bombin, but the cunts drapped me in it fur illegally walkin along the motorway instead! Fined £200, the bastirts! Pish!

MANAGERIAL MISUNDERSTANDINGS

Two days afore the end eh the month, Hibs finally released a statement regardin their manager n assistant, confirmin that they were now their ex-manager n ex-assistant. Pretty much everyone kent that awready, but as wi classic Hibernian statements eh the past, it made nae sense whitsoever. They hudnae been sacked apparently n the suspension hud now been lifted. They hudnae been found guilty eh any wrongdoing either. Chairman Rod Pear-Tree said nice things aboot Lenny whae reciprocated by sayin nice things aboot him. So why the hell were they leavin? Apart fae possibly petrol-bombin pubs, arguin wi n slaggin aff referees, daein aeroplane impersonations in front eh thoosands eh irate huns, cawin Camembert a lazy bastirt, pickin fights wi Craig Levein n Jim Duffy n threatenin tae jack it in efter one disappointin derby result, Neil hud been the very model eh restraint. Aye, ma erse!

So whae wis gaun tae replace him? Well, as much as I hate tae toot ma ain trumpet, ye're lookin at a guy here wi plenty eh experience n a personal knowledge eh aw things Hibs gaun back ower a century. Efter aw, if the fans can now get seats on the Board, why should they no be able tae sit in the manager's chair tae? So I bunged ma CV in the post pronto n sat aboot the hoose fur days waitin fur the phone tae ring. But I heard bugger aw! Ye'd have thought ooty courtesy that Pear-Tree might have acknowledged it at least, cos I put that in a wee note wi ma credentials, tellin him no tae caw when 'River City' wis on n no tae reverse the bloody charges either, as I heard he hud the habit eh daein.

"That bloody phone still husnae rung!" I telt Humpty Harry, finally stormin intae Wilkies efter four days eh gaun stir crazy trapped in the hoose wi nowt tae eat except foosty Wagonwheel biscuits n Werther's Originals.

"Hardly surprising, since it wis cut aff fur non-payment eh bills back in 1971," he retorted.

Christ, right enough – I ayewis meant tae pay up, but that became tae complicated when decimalisation came in.

"Why don't ye send him an email?" he then suggested.

Or at least that wis whit he *claimed* he'd said, when the shite hit the fan later on. See the bloody racket in that boozer, I could hardly hear him, but I thought I'd goat the gist eh it anyway. Aye, I hud the feelin that might jist be the way forward. Goat tae use every means at yer disposal, ken. N truth be telt, I'd ayewis thought I'd dae a great job in the Hibs' hoat-seat.

"Ye reckon that'll dae the trick?" I asked cautiously.

"Well, it's bound tae make him sit up n take notice," reasoned Harry. "Shows that ye're a man eh the modern world an aw that."

"Aye, it wid certainly dae that awright!"

So I hurried aff, tae pit the plan intae action. Once that stage wis done n dusted, aw I hud tae dae wis await a reply fae Easter Road. I wis pretty sure this time I wid hear somethin at least. N sure enough, the following efternin back in Wilkies, I did!

"Mr Gibson?" said the voice suddenly in ma lug.

I looked up, but instead eh the green n white bedecked emissary fae Hibernian Fitba Club I'd been expectin, this glaikit-lookin polis is standin there instead.

"Aye?"

"You do not have to say anything you may later rely on in court, but I have to advise you that you are now under caution..."

"Aw naw!" I yelled in a towerin rage. "Have youse bastirts goat it in fur me or whit?! So whit's the charge this time?"

"Pimping," he says succinctly, lookin at his notebook, like he could actually read.

"But how..."

"Do you deny that, yesterday afternoon, you engaged the services of a known prostitute, one Senga McGlumphar, c/o an address in Cables Wynd House and induced her to make herself available in person to one Mr Roderick Pear-Tree, heid bummer and chief bottle-washer of Hibernian Football Club, to engage in perverted sexual practices in return for favours to be of benefit to yourself?"

"It wis his bloody idea in the first place!" I yelped in some excitement, pointin an accusin finger at that bampot Humpty Harry, sittin there like butter widnae melt in his mooth. "He pit me up tae it!"

A growl eh disapproval fae the other drinkers arose at that, wi dark mutterings eh "Gibby the grass" n such like. Meanwhile, Harry's lookin at me like I've goat twa heids.

"Whit the fuck are youse talkin aboot?" he finally spluttered.

"Dinnae gie me yer Lilian Gish! Ye telt me clear as day tae send that Pear-Tree a female!"

He continued tae gaze at me open-moothed fur a few seconds.

"Naw, ya corn-beef auld coot, I says tae send him an *email*!!"

I clutched at the nearest table fur support. Surely I hudnae picked him up wrong? N even if I'd heard right, there's nae way I'd have risked sendin Pear-Tree Ecstasy through the post. Could get yersel in trouble wi the polis fur daein that. But then I heard the familiar jingle-jangle eh the Polis Scotland bracelets n remembered I wis in trouble wi the polis awready.

“Come on Gibby, let’s go,” he says, clampin on the cuffs. “Your carriage awaits outside.”

The Leith police dismisseth us? Aye, that’ll be the bloody day!

LOAN MOAN

So even afore the cell-door wis slammin firmly shut on yours truly, so wis yon transfer windae. McLaren hud apparently taken ma advice regardin stayin put Down Under n with Efe effing aff fur guid tae, we clearly needed some boadies comin the other way. Some fans arenae that keen on players pitchin up on a temporary basis fae other clubs, but I personally have never decried the system n ayewis been optimistic that we might unexpectedly unearth the next Eduardo Hurtado. As Moany Tony said admiringly eh ma attitude, “wi hope, in yer hert, n ye’ll never mock a loan,” which jist aboot sums it up. So apparently we had a Gael blowin in fae Motherwell, McNulty hopin tae make his Mark efter heading fae Reading n Darnell Johnson bein sequestered fae Leicester. As long as they dinnae send him north in the club helicopter, we should soon be flyin high wi that trio. Could be the best threesome I’ve experienced since I last goat taegether wi Senga McGlumphar n her pal fae Scorpio Leisure. (That wis a loan deal n aw – they took a fuckin loan eh me awright, the following mornin ma wallet wis as empty as ma bawbags.)

MAIR PISH

So the next question tae trouble us aw wis – wool bleat the Sheep? N the answer wis – no Hibs anyway. In fact it wis them that were left lookin awfy sheepish efter throwin away an early lead, tae go in the break trailin 2-1. It goat worse straight efter the restart tae, when they conceded a penalty.

"Loadypish, Lennon!" I yelled in the direction eh the dug-oot.

"It's May," says this interferin get, stood standin there sittin next tae me.

"Is it fuck, it's February," I pointed oot.

I smiled modestly tae masel, as the Hibs fans proceeded tae gie me a huge cheer fur statin the bleedin obvious – or possibly they were reactin tae the Sheep shearing the spot-kick aff target instead. Gemme on? Ma erse it wis.

I then decided tae vote wi ma feet – but it wis that bloody cauld I couldnae even feel them. I carefully poured some Bovril ower them tae aid the defrostin process, but unfortunately some eh it splashed on the expensive tan loafers belongin tae that eejit whae didnae ken whit month eh the year it wis. He let oot a yelp eh pain n annoyance.

"Whit's your beef?" I demanded tae ken.

Bloody nerve! Gie someone a wee heat fur free n that's aw the thanks ye get. Anyway, by the time ma plates eh meat hud thawed oot enough fur me tae actually move, Hibs hud jist made a third substitution.

"It's Gauld," says the daftie in the Bovril-stained shoes.

"I ken it's bloody cauld," I retorted, "aye, ye'd hardly get temperatures like this in the merry month eh May, wid ye? Anyway, I'm aff hame now."

Which sadly turned oot tae be a statement akin tae Lewis Stevenson's next crap pass taewards McNulty, aye, it wis somewhit wide eh the mark.

I stopped aff in the lavvy n it wis that bloody Baltic, ma stream eh pish only went n froze solid against the urinal. Christ Almighty! Try as I might I couldnae free masel n afore I kent it the final whistle hud blawn n every other cunt in the stadium hud bloody left! So I bravely tried tae look on the bright side, namely, that at this rate at least I'd get intae the Raith Rovers gemme the followin week fur free. Of course by that time ma tadger wid probably have dropped aff n I'd be deid fae frostbite, so it wisnae much eh a consolation. But finally, efter at least an oor, ma piteous cries fur help must have penetrated the inner sanctum eh the Boardroom n the Chief Executive hersel appeared on the scene wi a blowtorch tae set me free. Whit an embarrassment, I can tell ye. I resolved tae keep it a closely-guarded secret, but somehow word leaked oot (as did the residual pish fae ma thawed-oot tackle.) I wis made aware eh that the next night in The Cenny, when someone casually remarked, "Another first fur youse at Easter Road yesterday, Gibby, so I heard!"

"Aye, lastin the whole ninety minutes – n mair," I says suspiciously, expectin some bloody folly-up smart-erse comment.

"Naw, I'm talkin aboot youse gettin a blow-job aff Leeann Dempster in the lavvy under the West Stand."

Aye, life sucks sometimes...

NAE HOPE DOPE CANNY COPE IN POPE-FREE SOAP

...Especially if youse happen tae be a player or supporter eh St. Mirren, facin up tae the bluenosed hordes at Fort Ibrox. Durin the fixture takin place at the same time as ma tadger trouble, referee Andrew Dallas awarded the hame team *four* spot-kicks. Christ, the last time the huns were given that many penalties it wis courtesy eh Her Majesty's Revenue & Customs (HMRC that is, no tae be confused wi HMFC – an equally sinister organisation.) Perhaps the maist surprisin thing wis that one eh them might even have been justified. But certainly no the other three.

Proof positive that wherever Dallas features, a ghastly farcical unrealistic soap opera promptly unfolds. In the American version, Bobby Ewing came back fae the deid by appearin in the shower, here St. Mirren failed tae come back fae the deid by appearin in front eh a shower eh bastirts. The Yanks hud Victoria Principal, the huns have goat nae fuckin principles. Personally though, I wis ayewis mair eh a 'Dynasty' man, as that hud John Collins in it. He might have lost the dressin-room at Easter Road, but at least he never lost the plot like Dallas at Ibrox.

EL TEL HARD SELL

A mere four days later, the main action switched ower tae the other side eh dear auld Glesgie toon, as Hibs pitched up at Parkheid.

Needless tae say, efter ma recent experiences in the Wild West, I wis gaun naewhere near this yin. Predictably, the only thing the Hibees picked up were three injuries, as opposed tae three points. Sellik finally sealed it through Burke – naw, no the bodysnatcher partner eh Hare whae I earlier pointed oot wid have been a guid signin fur Hibs – unfortunately, this wis the goalsnatcher version, Oliver that is, whae made it 2-0 jist efter the oor mark. Nae mair than we expected really n Motherwell's win in Paisley saw them jump ower Hibs intae seventh place, pushin us back doon tae eighth. Only a point above Livi in ninth spot n aw, I tell ye, relegation's gettin nearer by the minute! So if we're gonnae go on slidin doon, it's surely aboot time tae appoint a manager whae kens how tae dae things properly in that department. Aye, let's send fur Terry Butcher, pronto! D'ye hear me, Pear-Tree?? Mark ma words, if ye continue tae deny ma guid self the chance eh a shot at it, El Tel's yer man! Mind where ye read it first!

No that there's anything wrong wi bein relegated, of course. In fact, I'd prefer it. Nae bigoted weedjie hordes invadin the Capital City, gemmes aw kickin aff at the proper time eh three o'clock on a Setirday efternin n plenty room in the pubs roond aboot the Holy Groond afore n efterwards. Whit's no tae like, fur Chrissake? Maist fans were awfy pissed aff at the conclusion tae seasons 2014/15 n 2015/16, as indeed I wis masel. But the difference wis that the daft majority were hacked aff Hibs hudnae been promoted back tae the Premier, whereas I wis scunnered that we hudnae dropped even further doon – tae Division One. Cos when we were in the Championship we still hud tae endure visits fae the bloody huns. Aye, if Pear-Tree hudnae been so keen tae give El Tel n Miss-Pass their jotters, I have every confidence they'd have goat the job done. Maybe even goat us as far doon as Division Two – even better! Derbies against Edinburgh City, regular trips tae oor happy Hibbie huntin ground eh Hampden (tae play Queen's Park) n a chance tae look up a few auld pals when visitin Peterheid. (Behind bars, rather than in the bars, ye ken.) Aye, we missed a trick there. Then Stubbsy n Lenny came along n ruined it aw. Guid riddance tae baith, I say!

FUCK YER 1902

There wis still nae sign eh a gaffer gadgie in the manager's chair, when Raith came rovin ower the Forth Bridge tae face the Hibees on February 9th. As for the visitors, at the helm there is a former Swinecastle shinyheid, allegedly spotted at Easter Road recently on a spyin mission. They've goat McGlynn, snooper John McGlynn, I just don't think you understand. He's Val McDermid's man, he husnae goat a tan, they've goat snooper John McGlynn.

Fur some reason, I hud an awfy job gettin intae the stadium in the first place. Every time I tried tae go through the turnstile it jist made that irritatin noise like a rhinoceros fartin in the bath n refused tae open. So I finally grabbed a haud eh one eh thae dafties in the yelly jaikits n explained ma predicament. He then hud a go, wi nae luck either.

"Er...I take it ye've actually paid fur the day?" he says.

"Whit!? That's a bloody season ticket there!" I yelped. "I'm no payin twice ower. Whae dae ye think I am – Aristotle Onassis?"

"That's aw very well, but this is a *Cup* gemme," says Yelly-Belly. "Yer season ticket's only valid fur League gemmes."

"Is that right? Well, correct me if I'm wrong, but last time I looked, Raith were in *League* One n Hibs were in the Premier *League*. Ye concede that much?"

"Aye, I suppose so," he says guardedly.

"Well that makes it a bloody League gemme then, doesn't it? So dinnae gie me yer pish, tryin tae treat me like one eh thae Walk-Up Willies."

"No it doesnae," says Yelly Fever. "I repeat – this is a *Cup* gemme. So it's *not* valid."

"But I've goat the Cup top-up anyway," I says, tryin another tack.

"The Cup top-up wis cancelled, the season efter they won it," he replied, sighin deeply.

"Whit – in 1903?"

"Naw, when they won it *last* time!" he yelled, gettin a trifle excitable, unless I wis much mistaken.

"Aye, that wis in 1902," I pointed oot. "N I wis telt by Michael Whelehan himsel that the top-up wid last until they actally won it again – if ever – n so far that husnae happened. So it's still valid."

But now he wis squintin closely at ma ticket again. Soon his pus wis turnin purple n steam wis startin tae pour ooty his lugs.

"Never mind fur a moment the fact that youse havenae paid fur the Cup gemme!" he yelled, in a right auld tizzy. "That bloody ticket's no even valid fur League gemmes at aw! It's ooty date!"

I grabbed it back aff him in a towerin rage eh ma ain n jabbed ma finger at the number on it pertainin tae the year.

"See? Whit does that say there – 19!"

"Aye, bloody *19*19!" he roared. "It's *a hundred* years ooty date, ye auld fraud! This ticket wis issued jist efter the First World War!"

"Aye, tae think I fought the war fur the likes eh you," I said, shakin ma heid sadly, but secretly fearin that the gemme wis jist aboot up. "But surely ye'd let an auld sodjer in fur free, son, a man whae gied his life fur Queen n country n disabled intae the bargain."

"But ye're no disabled!"

I swiftly pulled oot ma trusty auld Webley service revolver n shot masel through baith kneecaps.

"I am noo."

So by the time I'd goat carted intae the West Stand wi the help eh a team eh stretcher-bearers, the Hibs were awready one up. Only *one*, mind – against a team fae *two* divisions below. Hardly guid enough really. I wis on the verge eh askin fur ma money back, afore rememberin that I hudnae actually paid. Then I clocked whae the referee wis – that bloody Bobby Madden, who gied the Currant Buns four penalties against St. Mirren!

"Madden – ye're a midden!" I yelled. "Away back tae the Lodge, ye Orange bastirt! Aye, n how aboot a penalty whilst ye're at it?"

"Nae sooner said than done, sir," says this polis, materialisin suddenly at my shuder n thrustin a piece eh paper intae ma paw.

"Whit's this?"

"A Fixed Penalty notice. Ye've jist contravened the 'Offensive Behaviour at the Fitba Act' n are hereby forthwith hitherto fined £60."

"I thought that had been repealed?" I yelped.

"It hus, but we're happy tae make an exception in your case," he says.

So there I wis, gettin huckled oot even afore that wash-hand basin in the black hud blown his Partick Thistle fur hauf-time. Then ma pins gave way n I sank tae the ground in mortal agony.

"Whit's wrong wi ye now?" says the polis suspiciously.

"Ma auld knees are shot tae pieces," I groaned piteously.

"Aye – that'll be an age thing," he replied sagely.

"Mair eh a bullet thing," I retorted, bus he wisnae listenin.

"Nae dancing in the streets eh Raith fur you, eh, grandpaw!" he sings oot cheerfully, giein me a nane tae gentle shove in the direction eh the meat-wagon, courtesy eh a boot up the bahookey.

Still, I wis delighted tae later find oot that Hibs hud gaun ontae win 3-1. I tell youse, this could be the season that the hoodoo is finally broken, efter 117 long years. I vowed back in 1902 that one eh thae days I'd see Hibs lift the Scottish Cup again, n – God willin- I will! That's one thing I simply couldnae miss...

EVERY PICTURE TELLS A STORY

...Of course, it wid help if the cup draws were conducted on a metaphorical level playin field, as opposed tae one wi a dirty big metaphorical slope on it, like Easter Road in its heyday. Aye, the odds eh a favourable outcome are against ye fae the start, especially wi an ex-hun n ex-Celt daein the business wi the baws. Numbers 1 through tae 8 were allocated tae each team n the fact that it wis a bloody fix fae the start became obvious when the hame teams were promptly drawn oot on aw the odd digits – 1, 3, 5 n 7. No that bein at hame did Hibs much guid either, as the hardest yin eh the lot then followed – Sellik. They might jist as well have goat that radge Rod Stewart tae make the draw again, at least there's never a dull moment wi him.

BOTTOMS UP

Shockorooni – we've finally goat a new manager! Some gadgie cawed Frank Sidebottom apparently. Naw, me neither. A bit eh a surprise, as the Leith rumour-mill hud been indicatin fur the last week or so that it wis gonnae be someone else naebody hud heard eh afore, Mike Applesauce. However, one look at his scowlin coupon n Mr Universe physique soon hud aw thae cry-babies in the dressin-room runnin fur the hills. If they were feart eh Neil Lennon, Christ kens whit their reaction wid have been tae him turnin on the hairdryer n chuckin teacups aboot the place. But is Sidebottom oor cup eh tea? Or have we goat a bum deal? Well, time will tell, but he widnae have been ma first choice. As ye ken, I wis hopin tae get the job masel, but failin that – n much as I hate tae repeat masel – a return eh Terry Butcher wid have been jist dandy. Or perhaps Colin Caldercruix. Or maybe Jocky Scott...

JOIN THE BOOZE CREWS

I see in the paper that yon writer felly Irving Walsh (author eh bestsellin birdwatchers' manual 'Cranespotting') wis havin a pop at rugger buggers, claimin that their pished-up pish-poor behaviour is generally worse than that eh fitba fans. Says that the polis tend tae turn a blind eye tae it, cos the Hooray Henrys are 'posh'. Pish! I mean here's me, mair posh than Peterborough or Spice, so how come I keep gettin huckled when on the hooch, on ma way tae n frae Easter Road? This ban on drinkin at the fitba is aloadyshite anyway, jist cos a bunch eh weedjies spurred on by religious hatred decided tae have a pagger on the Hampden turf nearly forty year ago efter overdaein it on the Buckfast. But, as I've pointed oot afore, the laws eh the land dinnae apply in the People's Independent Republic eh Leith, or at least no the yins that I dinnae agree wi. That's why I've made it ma personal mission tae reintroduce drinkin on the terracing, fae the Coo-Shed tae the Dunbar End n back again.

At the start eh the season I tried tae smuggle a Grouse intae the Famous Five Stand – unfortunately the bastirt flew away afore I goat tae the turnstiles n a boy at a tap flair windae in Albion Place shot it wi an airgun. So the next time I opted fur the dark green boatil, but the steward clocked the bulge under ma jaikit.

"Whit have ye goat there?"

"Gordon's Gin," I reluctantly admitted.

"Ye'll have tae hand it ower then," he says.

"I cannae dae that. It's no mine tae hand ower anyway."

"Oh aye?" he says disbelievingly. "Whae's is it then?"

"I've jist telt ye – it's Gordon's."

"Be that as it may, ye cannae take it intae the ground."

Aye, I wis dealin wi a right awkward bastirt here. Luckily it wis still early doors n there wisnae many folk aboot.

"Look, I'll gie youse a wee nip."

Somethin aboot his general demeanour eh quiverin wretchedness, shakin hands n broken-veined purple coupon alerted me tae the fact that a wee jag widnae go amiss, fur medical reasons. He glanced around nervously, but the coast wis clear.

"OK then, but make it quick."

So I quickly reached doon n pinched his scrotum tightly between ma thumb n forefinger n then lunged through the turnstiles. I could still hear his screams as I bounded like a geriatric gazelle across the concourse n up the stairs.

Then of course there's beer. Fur years I've been smugglin in at least a gallon a time tae Easter Road – n I've never been caught yet. Mainly cos it's awready inside me, admittedly. But often that's no enough, so ye've goat tae be creative – I find ma 1970s-era flared troosers are the business there. I once walked six cans eh Belhaven intae Ibrox, wi three strapped tae each leg. Thought I wis hame n dry until an Orange bar steward inside saw me tryin tae surreptitiously detach one.

"Hey Grandpaw! Whit have ye goat there?"

"Simply the Best," I telt him.

Better than aw the rest, that's yours truly, when it comes tae standin up fur ma rights. N yours tae! So I urge youse aw tae join the campaign tae bring back the bevvy tae Easter Road n sign ma petition pronto. 'Perseverance is oor motto / At the fitba let's get blotto / So join the cause eh this auld heider / n follow Gibby – Scottish Leader!'

NOVEL IDEAS

Mention eh that Irving Walsh there eyewis pits me in a bad mood (aye, an even worse yin than usual) due tae the bastirt rippin me aff years ago. Or as they caw it in literary circles, bein 'plagiarised'. Which I used tae think meant catchin The Plague. Anyway, this wis back in the early '90s, when I wis writin aloadypish fur Hibs fanzines, but at the same time I wis secretly pennin whit I fondly imagined could be a best-sellin novel. The experts aye advise ye tae write aboot whit ye ken, so I naturally set maist eh it in Leith. It wis a dark tale aboot a bunch eh junkies whae get intae trouble fur gobbin at a ticket-collector on Scotrail. I even hud a catchy title fur it tae – 'Trainspitting'. Aye, n ye ken whit happened *next,* efter I let that slip oot in The Cenny one night! (He also choaried the title eh the prequel I wrote later, aboot the same gadgies burglarisin jewellery shops n cairryin the gear aff in holdall bags. Aye, 'Swagboys'...)

I should have learned ma lesson though, cos aboot ten years afore that I wis uptoon, drinkin in The Oxford Bar, on account eh bein Scotland Yard fae maist pubs in Leith at the time. Got talkin tae this big skinny galoot whae said he came fae Cardenden in Fife originally, n also mentioned that he wis quite keen on the auld writin gemme. Needless tae say, I hud nae idea that I wis Uptown Top Rankin, so tae speak, as I went ontae tell him aboot a series eh murder mystery novels I wis workin on, featuring a crime-solvin mathematician cawed Inspector Rhombus. Aye, n ye ken whit bloody well happened in that case n aw!

Still, it aw paled intae insignificance against the occasion when I met this blonde bint in a café up the Soothside. I'd been thinkin that contributin tae Hibs Monthly / Mass Hibsteria wis excellent trainin fur breakin intae the kids' market (as I wis essentially writin fur badly-behaved bairns whae sniffed glue n spray-painted 'YLT YA BASS' on bus shelters, anyway.) I'd been jottin doon a few ideas when Blondie sneaked a glance at ma notepad afore startin up a conversation. She seemed awfy interested n wis particularly taken wi the name eh a fictional boy wizard I'd jist come up wi.

"Aye, it's no much tae be gaun on wi really," I said modestly. "I mean, a boy wizard cawed Larry Cotter – that's never gaun tae take aff, is it?"

So years later when she became famous, I pilled her up at a signin session in Blackwell's Bookshop, efter gettin pished in The Royal Oak ower the road aw day. Cos truth be telt, it wis that thieving cow that wis now giein me the royal boak. No that I goat very far – she promptly shoved me oot the door n proceeded tae boot ma erse doon the Sooth Bridge. Aye, she's a feisty yin awright. Of course, an Evening News photographer wis on hand tae take a bloody incriminatin photie n I wis pure mortified when it appeared on the front page the following day. That wis quite bad enough, but it wis the bloody caption underneath that really stuck the knife in – 'J.K. ROWLING JAKEY ROLLING'...

YE DINNAE NEED A WEATHERMAN TAE KEN WHICH WAY THE WIND BLAWS

Hamilton were due at Easter Road in the middle eh the month, a team (n place) I've goat mair reason tae hate than maist other Hibbies. There wis that relegation play-aff nightmare double-heider back in 2014 of course n I've still never recovered financially fae the away leg. Ended up no seein the gemme at aw, jist aboot died eh frostbite intae the bargain n goat attacked by a moose. "But surely ye're no feart eh a wee cheese-eatin cowrin tim'rous beastie like that, Gibby," said aw thae radges in The Cenny smugly, when I finally arrived back a week later. N the answer is, naw, I'm *no* feart eh *them* – but this wis the other kindy moose I'm talkin aboot here. Aye, I'd ended up in the wrong Hamilton by mistake – the yin in Ontario, Canada – n this muckle great big-horned bastirt suddenly appeared ooty a snowstorm n butted me up the bahookey afore I even saw it. So in a fit eh temper I stuck the heid on it in retaliation, efter which arrest by the Mounties fur animal cruelty wi deportation tae folly wis purely Academical. No that it wis that straightforward, mind. At the airport they couldnae understand ma accent regardin ma destination, nae matter how many times I repeated 'EMBRA' at the tap eh ma voice. Twenty-four oors later I got aff the flight n failed tae recognise ma surroundings, which I initially pit doon tae the results eh chronic jet-lag. But I soon realised it wis mair the result eh thae incompetent cloth-eared Canadian bastirts sendin me tae Canberra, Australia instead. Which wis a bloody roondaboot way eh gettin hame n an even mair roondaboot way eh explainin why I hate Hamilton.

There wis an ex-Hibbie cawed Brian in the opposition dug-oot fur this yin, a man whae looked like he'd been addin curry tae his Rice thrice daily ever since hingin his boots up at Easter Road. These days he cannae even *see* his boots, much less tie his laces. But he hud a fat chance eh presidin ower a victory efter Camembert opened the scorin, although the stadium announcer seemed tae think it wis Morgan or Forgan or Corgan or whitever he caws himself. Then McNutcase stuck away a penalty n the Hibees were hame n dry even afore hauf-time. Played awfy well fur long spells n they could've scored mair than two. New gaffer Sidebottom telt the media he'd hud that many things tae dae since takin on the gig that 'my head is spinning now.' Aye, well, ma heid wis spinnin n aw, no unlike that foul-moothed lassie in 'The Exorcist', when I clocked the photie eh him in the Hibs programme. Maybe a trick eh the light, maybe a trick eh the teeth, but still a deid ringer fur that simperin smirkin shirt-liftin TV weatherwatcher Sean Batty. Whit a double-act in the dug-oots, eh – Batty n Fatty. Still, brighter spells forecast in the East fur the time bein, no tae mention sunshine on Leith.

LET DOON – BY BLUE N MAROON

But of course grey skies are seldom far away n there wis an overcast aspect tae the League no long efter, thanks tae thae bigots in blue n muppets in maroon failin tae dae us a turn. Bloody typical is it no, aboot the only time ye're actually rootin fur that pair tae beat St. Johnstone n Motherwell, thereby enabling Hibs tae jump up the table, but they baith go n blaw it. No surrender ma erse! 'No tempo, no quality, no intensity, no urgency,' instead, in the words eh reporter Scott McDermott, aboot the nae score bore at Ibrox, which sounds tae me like the cry wis four surrenders. He also branded it arguably the worst display since Gerrard took ower n the Scouse git himself appeared tae agree, sayin they could forget aw aboot winnin titles n closin gaps.

Then the jambos went tae Fir Park a day later n conceded a last-minute howler, the direct result eh which wis the Wellies leapin past Hibs intae seventh spot efter garnerin aw three points. I bet thae great Gorgie galoots went n lost it on purpose, jist tae spite us. I'd a guid mind tae write another letter tae the SFA on the subject, but fur some reason every time I make the effort, the envelopes jist keep bouncin back tae me fae the Royal Mail unopened. Moany Tony reckons it's maybe somethin tae dae wi the fact that I ayewis address them in bright green ink tae 'BAMPOTS IN BLAZERS', c/o HAMPDEN MIDDEN, GLESGIE', mark 'SUBJECT – CHEATIN HERTZ BASTIRTS' in the tap left-hand corner, never pit stamps on them n seal the backs wi ma ain bodily fluids...but whae can tell fur sure?

Actually, readin Levein's comments in The Evening News a day later, it seemed like he wis hopin Hertz wid faw ooty the Premiership awtaegether. He wis quoted as sayin, "We won the Championship when Robbie Nielson was in charge and I took a great deal of pride in that, but that goes down as Robbie's Championship-winning team. I would like to have that opportunity for myself and be recognised as the person who won that trophy. I think that is possible here, I really do."

Well, it's possible awright, but ye'll have tae drop doon a division tae make it so! Talk aboot a lack eh ambition. Which personal pinnacle eh achievement's on his bucket list next – the Tennents' Sixes? Winnin 'The Pink Bus Shelter eh The Year' Award? He also added, "I want to be continually reaching Europe." Well, that's whit the Eurostar's fur, Craig – dinnae hurry back. Paris first, then a one-way ticket tae Dignitas in Switzerland. I've been dyin tae go there masel...

THE GREEN GREEN GAS EH HAME

At the same time as Levein's lot were faffin aboot at Fir Park, Sellik fans were gettin a trifle Killie cranky. At Rugby Park they proceeded tae smash up the seats, hurl coins n other missiles ontae the park, invade the pitch n jostle Kilmarnock players. N this wis at a gemme they *won*! Imagine the reaction if they'd lost. Kris Boyd – whae'd been hit by a coin which turned oot tae be a historical relic dug up fae the Fields eh Athenry – later said he wis gettin tired eh bein cawed 'a fat Orange bastard.' Well, if the cap fits...

Fur some reason, the Green Brigade n their ilk's bad behaviour is sometimes overlooked, in comparison tae that eh ther city rivals – n naw, I'm no talkin aboot the rampaging hooligan hordes fae Firhill.

Mind back in the day when yon Sellik bampot fired a tear-gas canister fae the Dunbar End intae the auld East Stand at Easter Road durin a League gemme? When all the Hibbies there piled ontae the pitch in a panic, the medics wanted tae treat me right away, efter clockin ma distressed demeanour.

"You've clearly been badly gassed, Gibby! The tears are streaming down your face!"

"That's goat fuck aw tae dae wi any weedjie gas," I telt him. "Jist greetin ma eyes oot at Hibs' performance as usual – total pish!"

It widnae have been the first time I'd been gassed efter aw – as maist eh the publicans in Leith could testify. But on a mair serious note, ma auld man wis quite badly gassed durin the Second World War. He inadvertently inhaled a blowback eh the auld Zyklon B, when tryin tae pump it intae yon fake shower cubicles at Auschwitz. Wis only daein his job, ken.

Anyway, it wis total pish fur the Sellik radge at Easter Road that day, when the polis captured him later. Cheeky bastirt appealed against his original sentence eh eighteen months n life certainly wisnae a gas fur him when the Appeals Court judge ruled it tae lenient n promptly doubled it! Aye, it's no often ye'll get yours truly agreein wi the cops n the courts, but on this occasion they goat it spot on. Of course I felt a bit differently, when I wis up before the same beak a fortnight efter that. I'd been charged wi stealin a double-decker bus whilst pished ooty ma heid on Double Diamond, n youse can probably guess whit the gadgie in the wig did, regardin ma original sentence? Aye, only went n fuckin *quadrupled* it! The justice system, eh – whitaloadypish!

TUNNEL VISION

Sellik were on ma mind again, as the week progressed, wi the announcement that tickets fur the forthcomin cup gemme against them wid be gaun on sale shortly. So how tae get ma mitts on yin wis uppermaist in ma thoughts, as payin fur it wis clearly ooty the question. Then I hud a sudden flash eh inspiration, efter watchin that film aboot the Hatton Gairden safe-deposit box robbery, where a gang eh auld codgers almost pilled aff the heist eh the century. Aye, I wis gonnae have tae break intae the Hibs ticket-office n help masel. At first I planned tae maybe get in through that transfer windae, but as it hud shut at the end eh January, they'd have probably hud it well-secured by this time. So I wis forced tae think ootside the box, which wis hardly a stretch fur yours truly, as I'm ooty ma box maist eh the time anyway. It finally came tae me when I ruminated on a possible combination between the Hatton Gairden job n famous Second World War prisoner escapes – aye, I wid simply dig a tunnel fae the Eastern Cemetery under Albion Place n come up through the flairboards across the road. A piece eh pish in other words, as indeed Steve McQueen said tae Angus Lennie, jist afore The Great Escape.

So efter a couple eh days' intense preparation n plannin, buyin aw the equipment n calculatin aw the necessary measurements wi pinpoint accuracy, I assembled ma crack team eh burglars taegether in Tamsons at closin time. (They were referred tae as such cos maist eh them *were* on crack unfortunately, but on a big job like this I obviously needed back-up.) So tae make it worth their while, I gied them the inducement eh cairryin aff aw the briefs they could lay their hands on, which could then be sold on at a small fortune, tae enterprising weedjie ticket-touts, as a last resort. Aw I wanted ooty it wis a seat in the West Stand fur masel. One advantage eh collaboratin wi a bunch eh criminal druggies wis the opportunity tae hoover up a massive amount eh speed they'd provided, jist afore we goat started, tae hopefully aid us in daein the job as quickly as possible. So we climbed ower the cemetery waw, selected a likely spot n then went tae toon wi the high-tech drillin equipment.

Several oors later, efter whit seemed like an eternity eh diggin n drillin n swallyin big handfuls eh earth n earthworms, sweat pishin ooty us wi the effort, I reckoned we'd be jist aboot on target. The auld amphetamine sulphate hud done the trick n we'd torn through the terra firma at a fair auld lick, in fact progress hud been a lot better than I'd expected. I consulted ma intricately drawn map one mair time by torchlight, did a few arithmetical calculations in ma heid regardin distances n depths n so on n then gied the signal tae start heidin upwards.

I watched anxiously as the giant drill burrowed up taewards the surface, but we didnae have far tae go noo. Sure enough, an ominous sorty sound indicated that we were through the layers eh earth n were aboot tae break through somethin solid.

"Nearly there, boys!" I shouted in encouragement. "One mair push should dae it!"

The boy wieldin the drill cranked it up tae max, n the next minute there wis an almighty 'BOOOOOM' as we broke through at last, tae be suddenly flooded wi light. I hudnae expected that, as I'd imagined the office wid be shrouded in darkness in the middle eh the night. Nor did I expect anyone tae be on the premises either of course, so it wis wi some considerable shock that I heard whit wis a worryingly familiar tone eh female voice.

"Gibby – is that really you?? Whit the fuck are ye playin at noo, ya auld radge?!" shrieked this screechin harpie in amazement, as ma heid popped up through the hole in the flair.

I blinked in equal amazement, at the sight eh ma neebor Senga McGlumphar's work colleague n best pal, Fifi Phanni-Phlapz herself.

"Whit the fuck are ye daein here?" I demanded, in a state eh total confusion.

"I bloody well work here – mair tae the point, whit the fuck are youse daein comin up through ma flairboards?!"

Then it struck me somewhit forcefully – we must've somehow overshot the target, cos we werenae in the Hibs ticket office efter aw – we were in the basement eh Scorpio Leisure on Albion Road!

Afore long, the rest eh the team hud followed me in clamberin oot n were lookin nane tae happy. Nor, it hus tae be said, wis the naked gadgie pinned firmly tae the bed under the formidable form eh Fifi. Aye, like him I wis in a sticky situation awright. Despite ma state eh shock I wis gonnae have tae pill masel taegether n dae some awfy quick thinkin.

"I hope ye've goat a guid explanation fur this, Gibby," says the leader eh the crack burglars grimly. "Because once ye've made a promise tae us, ye'll either fulfil it or suffer the consequences."

"Look, I promised youse free briefs if ye gied me a hand taenight, isn't that right?" says I, choosin ma words carefully.

"Aye, ye did that," he replied suspiciously.

"There ye go then," I says, flingin Fifi's client's discarded underpants in his direction, wi aw the force I could muster. "Have this pair tae be gaun on wi, fur now."

I then quickly slid back doon through the hole in the flair n took tae ma heels along the tunnel as fast as ma legs wid cairry me. Luckily, the speed wis still coorsin through ma system n I goat back tae the cemetery in record time. I then fled doon tae The Marksman on Duke Street fur openin time at six.

"Well, that wis a fuckin waste eh time n nae mistake," observed Humpty Harry, efter I'd breathlessly recounted the sorry events eh the night tae him.

"Anyone can make a mistake," I protested. "N at least it proves whit a loyal Hibs fan I am – I'd dae *anythin* tae see that gemme."

"Jist turn the telly on, then – it's live on the box, ya silly auld cunt. *That's* whit I mean by it bein a waste eh time."

For once, I wis lost fur words. See if only someone hud mentioned that fact earlier...

QUESTION TIME

The followin day, I wis relieved when the opportunity tae get ooty Leith fur a wee break presented itsel. The crack burglars hud turned oot tae be crap burglars an aw, but they probably widnae be shy in crackin ma heid open n kickin the crap ooty me tae, if they caught up wi me any time soon. Hopefully though, they'd still be stuck in the tunnel under the Eastern Cemetery, especially since I thoughtfully blew up the entrance wi a dirty big stick eh dynamite on ma way oot.

Anyway, I'd ayewis fancied bein on the telly, but imagined that if it did ever come tae pass it'd be on one eh thae daft reality 'I'm an X-Factor Big Fat Gypsy Celebrity in the Jungle wi Ant n Fuckin Dec, Get Me Ooty Here' type programmes. So when the invite came through tae appear on that 'Fastermind' wi John Humphrys, I could hardly believe ma luck. Granted, I'd been applyin regularly since the days when auld Magnus Magnesium wis still hostin the proceedings, but noo ma time hud come at last!

...See when ye're actually sittin there in that big black chair though n the lights go doon – talk aboot stage fright! (Talk aboot stage shite n aw, it wis runnin doon ma legs afore he'd even goat started.) Wis it any wonder therefore, that I made a total erse eh ma specialist subject?

"Who was the manager when Hibs last won the Scottish Cup?" demanded that Humphrys, glowerin at me like I'd jist shagged his wife n shat in his shoes. (He hud nae worries on that score, it wis ma ain footwear that wis noo bearin the brunt there.)

"That's an easy yin tae start wi!" I yipped confidently, as relief flooded me. "Dan McMichael."

"I'm sorry, but it was Alan Stubbs."

"Whit?? But..."

"Next – who scored the winning goal in the 1972 Scottish League Cup Final?"

"Well I ken that yin anyway – it wis Hibs."

"Mmm, it was actually the player's name I was looking for there – Jimmy O'Rourke. Moving on – which legendary manager was at the Easter Road helm immediately after the Second World War and died in 1948?"

"Paul McCartney?"

"Close. But I'm afraid I can't give you that – it was *Willie* McCartney. Who then was the manager who replaced Alan Stubbs?"

"John Lennon."

"You certainly know your Beatles, Gibby, but unfortunately 'Neil' was the Christian name there. OK, which Hibs player had his leg broken by Graeme Souness, in the latter's debut game as player / manager of Rangers?"

"Oh Christ, I dinnae ken... Eh...George Harrison...?"

"Yes, I can see your train of thought, but George *McCluskey* was in fact the answer. What was the name of the campaign launched by Hibs supporters to counter-act Wallace 'Fat Tory Bastard' Mercer's hostile takeover bid?"

"Hertz aff Hibs!"

"*Hands off* Hibs, I'm afraid. Where was Eduardo Hurtado from?"

"The Planet Zorg?"

"An understandable answer, perhaps, but it was the country we were after there – Ecuador. Who is Hibs' top scorer of all time?"

"George Best! Even scored at hauf-time once, at least accordin tae the title eh one eh his books. Scored wi mair burdz than I've hud hoat dinners!"

"Alas, I was looking for scorers of the 'goal' variety there. Gordon Smith is the answer to that one. What was the nickname of the swashbuckling Hibs side of the early 1970s?"

"Turnbull's Torpedos?"

"Again, very close, but I can't give you it. Turnbull's *Tornadoes,* I'm afraid. Last question – what is the technical term whereby one player conveys the ball to a team-mate by the use of his foot?"

"Oh fuck, I dinnae ken. Pass."

"...is the correct answer! Gibby, you have now scored one out of ten in your specialist subject, which is, if I may be absolutely frank, aloadypish. You may however do better in the general knowledge round to follow."

Well now I wis shitin masel even mair! I wis that nervous I didnae even notice whit the other contestants were asked or whit they scored, but naturally I wis first back in the spotlight efter Round One, due tae ma utterly shite performance so far. But bizarrely, a peculiar calm sensation descended upon me as I made the long, lonely walk back tae the chair. I began tae feel strangely optimistic...

"Which musician released the best-selling album 'White Ladder'?" barked Humphrys, glarin at me like I'd jist shagged his shoes n shat on his wife.

"David Gray," I replied confidently, luckily rememberin tae omit the 'Sir' at the start.

"Correct. Who wrote the best-selling series of books about a

Yorkshire vet, later made into the TV series 'All Creatures Great and Small'?"

"James Herriot. Or Jim, as I caw him," I added flippantly, as memories eh oor 1970s goalie floated through ma mind.

"Correct. In children's literature, which Enid Blyton group of characters comprised Julian, Dick, George, Anne and Timmy the dog?"

"The Famous Five."

"Correct. Which film featured brothers Jeff and Beau Bridges, and also starred Michelle Pfeiffer?"

Never mind Jeff n Beau, I thought, whit aboot Gerry n Joe?

"The Fabulous Baker Boys."

"Correct. What do you get if you combine the name of Top Cat's smallest sidekick and the largest country in South America?"

"Benny Brazil."

"Correct. Complete the name of this small Leicestershire town. Melton..."

Christ, I should win a Tony Award if I get this yin right.

"Mowbray."

"Correct. What comes before 'Buzzard' in the name of a small Bedfordshire town?"

I'm away wi the goalie again!

"Leighton."

"Correct. How would two minutes past seven in the evening be represented on a twenty-four hour clock?"

"1902."

"Correct. What is the surname of the respected late American actor who starred in 'Paris, Texas' and had the forenames Harry Dean...?"

My God!

"Stanton."

"Correct. What is the appropriate scientific designation for a honey-producing insect, if at a great altitude?"

"A high bee?"

"Correct! Gibby, you have just scored ten out of ten in your General Knowledge, so many congratulations. That was without doubt one of the greatest rounds we have ever witnessed on this famous quiz-show. Unfortunately though, your First Round showing was, as I previously intimated, a complete n utter loadypish. So thank you and goodnight. Cheerio, cheerio, cheerio...

Aye, stormed the second hauf, but fucked it up in the first, it wis like Hibs n Falkirk at Hampden in 2013 aw ower again. So I still came fourth ooty four, relegation standard it hus tae be said. But I'm no gaun doon wi'oot a fight. I'll be back! 'Leith's Goat Talent', here I come!

FALLING BY THE WAYSIDE, ON THE WAY TAE TAYSIDE

'Leith's Goat Talent' wid have tae wait though, as Dundee beckoned next, a place wi nae discernible talent at aw. Christ, there's mair attractive burdz boakin up their Bacardi in the Bigg Market doon Newcastle on a Friday night, than there are tae be found in the mythical 'city eh jute, jam, jambo heartbreak (1986) n journalism'. N I should ken, cos I once went oot on the pull there wi Moany Tony, efter a Hibs gemme at Tannadice many moons ago. I bagged aff wi this burd whae I actually thought wis Lorraine Kelly, but the next morning when I rolled ower in bed, I found tae ma horror that I appeared tae have somehow woken up wi Ned Kelly instead. I think it wis the three-day stubble, nae teeth n steel helmet that did it. In fairness, she wisnae exactly that chuffed either – cheeky cow said she wis that pished the night afore she thought I looked like Mel Gibson, so therefore wis less than impressed tae wake up wi Grumpy Gibson. As fur Tony, well the least said the better. Goat aff wi this thing whae he reckoned wis a ringer fur yon Irish singer Sinead O'Connor n therefore wisnae amused tae later discover on soberin up that he'd only gone n pulled Jim Duffy.

But this wis a different baw gemme noo. N it wis at Dens, no Tannadice, although if I hud gone tae the wrong groond again, even I could have spotted the right location, jist ower the road. Now at this juncture ye're probably sayin tae yersel, Christ, Gibby, get a grip, we've read aboot youse mixin up Fir n Firs Park n gaun tae the wrong Hamilton, so dae yer bloody hamework this time, afore settin oot. The last thing that we, the readership, want tae hear is how ye went tae Dundee in Florida, USA, by mistake, OK? Well I can assure ye aw that there wis absolutely nae chance eh that happenin this time at aw – mainly cos I wound up in Dundee, Sooth Africa, instead. Quaint wee toon in Natal province, aboot haufway between the borders eh Lesotho n Swaziland. Check it oot, next time ye're in the vicinity.

Meanwhile, in Dundee, *Scotland* (a crap, cauld n dreich country on the periphery eh Europe), a titanic struggle wis takin place in front eh the TV cameras. Swiss bliss wis the name eh the gemme, as Camembert, exhibitin the balance n poise eh William Tell, the precision n timin eh a cuckoo-clock, the shape n strength eh a giant Toblerone bar on legs n the self-belief n serendipity eh Sepp Blatter wi his hand in the cookie jar, stuck away a peach eh an opener. The hame team goat yin back, but it wisnae long afore the Hibees regained the lead, courtesy eh a McNutjob double n whit can only be described as a Mallan streak. His rocket screamed intae the back eh the net n although Dundee did get another consolation goal, the only really sticky moment came wi the appearance eh Kenny Miller as sub. For the *hame* team, mind ye, much tae ma surprise – Christ, I thought he wis still playin fur the Hibs! Scored fur us in the 2016 Scottish Cup Final where we lost tae the huns, unless I'm much mistaken. I wish that Chief Executive wumman wid keep me bloody informed aboot the movement eh players, as I'm seek eh gettin shocks tae ma system like that. Next thing ye ken, they'll be gettin rid eh McGinn n McGeouch! Aye, so they will, ower ma deid body! Anyway, Miller hud the baw in the net twice, but the referee rightly disallowed them on account eh him bein a treacherous turncoat, whae turned his back (n coat) on the Hibees. That'll learn *him*.

Aye, it wis jist as well that coverage extended as far as the alternative Dundee, where I watched the action on the screen in a pub fu eh big fierce-lookin bare-chested gadgies whae were wearin gress skirts n cairryin long spears.

"Zulus?" asked this other white guy nervously, whae hud jist come in.

"On the contrary, we won – n won well," I telt him. "...and the boys in blue, goat fucked 4-2, by the famous Embra Hibees!"

SMOKE JOKE

When I goat back fae the Dark Continent (a direct flight this time, thank Christ, fae Pretoria straight tae Leith International Airport), I wis met by the scowlin visage eh Steve Clarke, aw torn-faced in the tabloids. Reason wis his bein on the receiving end eh abuse fae Rangers fans apparently, although it beats me how gettin described as slim could be construed as an insult. "I'm certainly not a lean yin!" he wis quick tae protest tae the Press, where even yours truly wid have been happy tae take that as a compliment.

Hibs were also on the receivin end eh some criticism fur agreein a sponsorship deal tie-up wi an e-cigarette firm, nae doot fae thae do-gooder nanny state types whae keep insistin that smokin is bad fur ye. (Vapin is another matter of course, but that wis jist gied a bad name by that London taxi-driver pervert John Worbuoys, the so-cawed 'Black Cab Vapist.') Now, while I'm no sure aboot this lot makin fags wi an Ecstasy ingredient, the fact that smokin is actually *guid* fur ye can be validated by a quick glance at ma medical history. Let's face it, I've smoked like a fish n drank like a chimney ever since I wis knee-high tae a Zurich Grasshopper n in the 'fit as a fiddle' stakes I'm positively Stradivarius standard! My doaktir says I'm in no bad shape fur ma age (admittedly I wis a wee bitty economical wi the truth regardin ma birth-date, so he actually thinks I'm thirty years aulder.) He telt me I hud the lungs eh a ninety year-auld, which I took tae be guid news, as that meant each yin wis only forty-five. N it wis even better than that really, cos unbeknownst tae him, I wis born wi an extra lung, a one-aff freak eh nature which husnae occurred since. Spreads the workload, ken, in dealin wi the nicotine. In fact, I've been toyin wi the idea eh gettin a fourth yin installed.

Similar situ wi the bevvy – if yer liver packs in it's nae big deal, jist sign up fur a replacement. I should ken, I've been doon that road a few times. The first transplant didnae go tae well initially, but then I found oot they'd only gone n gied me George Best's! So that hud tae be replaced an aw. Then I goat Jim Baxter's, but luckily I managed tae swap that wi Oliver Reed – whae wis kind enough tae gie me his whilst he wis still alive. (He wisnae fur much longer efter that, it hus tae be said.) So ma general advice wid be – dinnae go fur a celebrity liver, ye're better aff wi a plain civilian job.

But like drinkin, it's surely aboot time that smokin wis reintroduced tae the fitba an aw. Adds tae the atmosphere n if ye dae enough eh it, it can even obscure the view eh the pitch, which wid be a godsend mair often than not. Fur God's sake, it cannae dae ye any harm, never mind whit aw thae namby-pamby health n safety Nazis tell ye. I can honestly say that I've smoked in *every* fitba groond north n south eh the border n it's never been a problem yet. Granted, there wis that one time – n *one* only, mind – when I wis at Bradford City in 1985 n accidentally dropped a lit...

(THE REST OF THIS PIECE HAS BEEN SUMMARILY REDACTED, ON THE STRICT INSTRUCTION OF MR G. GIBSON'S LAWYERS.)

GOGGLEBOX

Sittin in the hoose there, watchin aw thae envelopes comin pilin through the letter-box at a rate eh noughts – I started tae feel a bit like the Beast fae the East hud struck again. Aye, I wis gettin snawed under! Ever since ma appearance on 'Fastermind', thae telly bastirts hud been tryin tae entice me back wi a series eh ever mair outlandish offers. So, as naebody yet hus hud the decency tae pay ma phone-bill n get me reconnected n I dinnae dae email (especially no efter that mix-up wi Senga n Pear-Tree), bombardin me wi letters is the only way they can get tae me.

Latest is fae that Clarkson, wantin me on 'Whae Wants Tae Be A Millionaire?' N the simple answer tae that is – no me. Whit bloody use is a million quid tae anyone these days, eh – if it wis '*billionaire*' then aye, *maybe* I'd have considered it. Plus, I doot very much I'd get through that wi'oot lampin that thick-heided smug owergrown public schoolboy upsides doon, even afore he'd offered me fifty-fifty.

'Tipping Pint' sounded interestin – how many glesses eh Export can ye knock back within a given time – until I realised I wis missin the *Point* there, so tae speak.

'Loose Wimmin' then raised their ugly heids – as if I didnae ken enough eh them anyway, thank youse very much, fae Senga tae Fifi Phanni-Phlapz n ontae Girnin Gertie, Lorraine / Ned Kelly n Christ kens how many others eh a similar stamp.

I wis aw fur that 'New Lives in the Wild' admittedly, but Ben Fogle – a man whae's climbed Mount Everest, faced doon hostile tribes in the Amazonian rain forest n survived winter in the Arctic Circle –

refused on safety groonds tae visit the Banana Flats.

I agreed tae 'University Challenge' in principle, but only if I wis allowed tae challenge thae ken-it-aw Oxbridge smart-erses tae a square-go. No surprisingly, they widnae agree tae that.

The maist alarmin offer probably came fae 'Long Lost Family' – cos if there's one thing I need like a hole in the heid is any other members eh ma aforementioned long lost family suddenly poppin ooty the widwork efter aw this time, tryin tae get their thievin mitts on ma cash in the attic. Hopefully they're aw deid, but youse can never be sure. That Davina McCall wis awfy persuasive though. Claimed tae be hoat on the trail eh ma second cousin twice removed, Stumpy Gibby, him wi the wooden leg. I shuddered at the thought eh whae else she might uncover – his brother whae wis ayewis daein 'cash fur crash' bogus car accident scams – Bumpy Gibby, or even ma uncle best-kent fur takin a shite in public, Dumpy Gibby. Then there wis his sister, the eternal spinster Frumpy Gibby, the list goes on n on. N as fur ma alleged cash in the attic – that comes mainly in the form eh coin-filled charity boatils choaried ooty pubs, hospitals n churches. So thanks, Davina – but at the same time, no fuckin thanks!

Naw, the only yin that *really* appealed tae me, apart fae cowardy custard Fogle's show, wis 'Naked Attraction' – no that they offered it tae me, I hud tae apply fur that aff ma ain bat. But guess whit – the cheeky bastirts knocked me back, efter I sent them a photo eh masel in the scud, apart fi my Hibs bunnet, worn at a jaunty angle. Have youse seen some eh the mingers that get on that programme? I've never been so insulted in ma puff.

Well that jist leaves 'Sportscene' I suppose. Practically tailor-made fur yours truly as a special guest, espousing words eh wit n wisdom.

"Can I jist say, Michael – or can I caw ye Mikey Baby? – that youse are the lowest eh the low, a *double* turncoat. Went fae Hertz tae Hibs n even though the Hibbies were guid enough tae forgive yer past n gie ye yer ain song, ye rewarded us aw by then gaun *back* tae Hertz. Judas bastirt! N as fur *you,* Thommo – or can I caw ye Tommo? – aw ye dae is sit there wi yer daft blue jumper n daft dyed barnet n talk aloadypish. Well, I'd better hand ye back tae Jonathan, whae will now introduce tonight's Premiership highlights. So there now follows twenty-eight minutes eh the huns versus Hamilton, twenty-eight mair minutes eh St. Mirren versus Sellik n four minutes eh the remainin fixtures aw lumped taegether. Nae favouritism on this programme, by the way! No surrender, it's a grand auld team tae play fur..."

Unfortunately though, that wis aw only in ma ain heid, as they didnae want me either. Still, as the producers eh 'Naked Attraction' were kind enough tae point oot, at least I've goat a great face fur radio...

A POKE EH CHIPS NOW

"Gaun tae Perth?" enquired Moany Tony, as we sat there in The Spey Lounge, contemplatin the meanin eh life. (Conclusion – there's nane. It's aw aloadypish n then ye die.)

I wis gettin a bit seek eh ma sidekick's monotonous n repetitive mode eh questionin, along the same lines. I swear tae Christ, if he asked me if I was gaun tae San Francisco tae wear some flooirs in ma hair, he'd dae it in the same lifeless monotone.

"Am I fuck. I'm no long back fae Australia, remember?" I snapped, as memories eh thae moose-shaggers unceremoniously packin me aff tae Canberra came floodin back. For once, I'd have preferred tae end up nearer tae Christophe Berra.

"No *that* Perth," he groaned, lapsin intae his traditional 'sighin fur Scotland' routine. "I mean the Scottish version, Gateway tae The Hielans, n aw that."

"They should knock that gateway doon n build a proper bloody waw instead," I pointed oot. "Keep thae plaid skirt-wearing heuchter-teuchters in their place n stop them fae invading the Lowlands, comin doon here tae steal oor sheep n shag oor jobs. As well as vice-versa. Send fur Donald Trump, that's whit I say! Aye, I ken he's no actually pit his waw up yet, cos he's still waitin on the bricks n cement. Jist wait till he gets gaun though! Keep the Mexicans in Mexico!"

Moany let oot a sigh that wis so long, deep n hertfelt it practically rattled the windaes in The Cenny up the road.

"When ye're finally done talkin pish," he went on, "I wis aboot tae point oot that Hibs are playin there in a League gemme."

"Whit in the name eh God are they playin a League gemme in Mexico fur?"

"No in fuckin Mexico! In *Perth*, ya radge! St. Johnstone!"

Oh aye, auld St. Johnstone himsel, the Patron Saint eh Shitey Hame Supports.

"No can do. I'm busy on Setirday," I lied, hedging ma bets fur the time bein.

"It's Wednesday."

"They play in *Sheffield,* no Perth," I snorted. "So whae's talkin pish noo, eh?"

But as it turned oot, there wis mair than a touch eh Sheffield steel aboot the team in green, as match-day rolled aroond. They weathered a storm fur the first oor or so n I wis delighted when they went in a goal tae the guid at the break. The second hauf wis tightly fought tae, wi the hame team gettin back on level terms, then there wis a sendin-aff, penalty award n finally a spectacular winner fur the visitors right at the death!

Jist then there wis a loud chap at ma door – luckily he rang the bell or I widnae have kent he wis there – n I opened up tae admit that loud chap Moany Tony, whae'd come tae take me fur a victory pint. Aye, I'd opted fur yon wireless instead, rather than risk gettin lost in the Ootback (in Australia *or* The Trossachs, it comes tae the same thing.) It wis still on in the backgroond, as Tony sighed his way ower tae the sofa, wincin as I punched him playfully on the shuder. (I must have owerdone it a bit in ma high spirits, cos it wis later found oot tae be fractured.)

"Guid auld Hibs!" I sang oot, "n tae have Liam Henderson's brother in the team noo, alongside Scotty Broon back where he started oot aw thae years ago, can only be barry news. N at least Scott Bain's finally joined the ranks tae!"

Moany shot me a painful look (hus he even goat any other kind?) n held his hand up imperiously fur silence, his lugs strainin taewards the sound eh the post-match pundits pontificating pish as per usual.

"Uh-huh. So ye listened tae the radio commentary then, did ye?" he finally frowned.

"Sure did! How – whit's wrong wi that?"

"Nowt – except the fact that's been the *Hertz – Sellik* commentary ye've been listenin tae, no the Hibs gemme, ya silly auld goat!"

I gaped at him wi mooth wide open, like a shellshocked goldfish.

"Whit?! But...but...the boy on the radio says the team managed by Neil Lennon won 2-1!"

"Aye – that's Sellik!"

Then I remembered – right enough, he'd scarpered aff tae Soapdodge City n we'd noo goat Sidebottom at the helm.

"But...there wis a late winner..."

"Aye – so there wis at McDiarmid Park."

"There wis a man sent aff!"

"Aye – so there wis at McDiarmid Park."

"There wis a penalty!"

"Aye – so there wis at McDiarmid Park."

"There wis only one goal in the first hauf – but two in the second!"

"Aye – so there wis at McDiarmid Park."

"Has anyone ever telt ye that ye sound like a stuck fuckin record?"

"Aye – so there wis at McDiarmid Park."

(Which turned oot tae be true – 'When The Saints Go Marching In' goat jammed on repeat on the McDiarmid Park hi-fi.)

"Ye realise whit this means, don't ye?"

"Whit?"

"It wis one n the same gemme!"

So we returned tae The Spey, feelin that the world had shifted slightly on its axis noo that they were directly cloning fitba gemmes n passin them aff as genuine, tae the gullible fans. The thought weighed heavily on us, as we sat there contemplatin the meanin eh life in gloomy silence yet again. Ye could have heard a pin drop. In fact, ye could have heard a pandrop – that bastirt wis rustlin a bag eh them aboot in his poakit, but failed tae offer us one.

"Aye, I wish I'd been at the Kilmarnock – Motherwell gemme instead," he sighed eventually, breakin the solemn reverie.

"How come – whit happened there?"

"It goat fogged aff haufway through."

I swallyed ma hauf n hauf n came tae a sudden decision.

"Well I'm gonnae fog aff haufway through an aw."

"Please yersel."

"I will."

Moanin auld misery-guts that he is! I exited ontae Leith Walk n looked up intae an apocalyptic sky, as bolts eh lightnin bounced aff the pavement aw around me. A junkie croaked his last in a shop doorway, as a lone coyote howled mournfully somewhere on a lonely mountain-top, deep within the rural backwaters eh the People's Independent Republic eh Leith. Then, a quartet eh pished-up radges wearin skull masks whae were sharin a single bag eh French fries between them, came staggerin ower the road, singin tunelessly in cracked, guttural voices. I shuddered inwardly at the sight - the four hoarse men eh a poke eh chips.

Aye, it might have been the end eh February, but it truly felt mair like the end eh the world...

JOE, JOE, SUPER JOE

...Super Tortolano. Aye, it wis really him! I saw this big beefy-lookin thuggish gadgie in a bomber jaykit, makin his way doon Sunnyside there, taewards the Hibs Supporters Club n ma hert skipped a beat. Or at least it wid have, if I hud a hert in the first place, which is highly debatable, accordin tae thae self-appointed medical experts in the hostelries eh Leith. But whitever it wis, the cauld hand eh fear wis briefly clutchin at ma shuder. Ma first thought wis that it might have been a hitman fur the crap burglars whae wished tae dae me herm, so it wis wi some relief I finally recognised one eh Hibs' maist, er, 'iconic' players eh the eighties n nineties.

Fur the bold Joseph wis a guest eh the St. Paddy's HSC, efter Neil Lennon fur some inexplicable reason hud tae caw aff, bein the original first choice. But that didnae seem tae faze the former flyin fu-back, whae wis happy tae share some eh his mair revoltin experiences in ye olde Hibernian dressin-room. I dinnae think I've heard the word 'shite' used quite so much fur a guid while, outside one eh ma ain conversations. N we're talkin *literal* shite here, particularly in the tale where one unidentified former Hibee lobbed a fresh jobby intae the communal bath which wis fu eh his team-mates at the time. Joe wis understandably panic-stricken that some eh it might have splashed up n compromised the cut eh his latest meticulously managed hairstyle.

He almost failed tae get the Hibs' gig at aw, efter neglectin tae return a phone-call his wife hud taken earlier, fae someone she said wis cawin himsel 'Blakey'. Thinkin eh that character fae the spectacularly dreadful TV sitcom 'On The Buses', he suspected a wind-up n ignored this, until an impatient second call came through fae the same person. Only it wis fae *Blackley*, aye, 'The Sloop', whae hud evolved fae Hibs player tae Hibs manager n now wanted tae sign him up.

N the rest is, as they say, history. I wis dyin tae address the elephant in the room durin the Q n A, n demand tae ken whit the fuck possessed him tae snap Gordon Strachan's leg near the start eh a Testimonial gemme eh aw things, but fur once I managed tae keep ma trap shut. Cos he looked like he wis still quite capable eh snappin *ma* leg, if he'd taken the hump.

Aye, it wisnae aw plain sailin, as on occasion he hud tae double-up as Budgie's room-mate on away-trips. Poor Joe couldnae get any kip due tae the mad goalie blastin oot tapes eh some sports psychologist's motivational speeches at tap volume, afore blindfoldin himsel n insistin that his roomie flung oranges n other items eh fruit at him repeatedly, tae test his reflexes.

No surprisingly, political correctness wis somewhit conspicuous in its absence durin Joe's meanderings doon memory lane. One struggles tae recaw many occasions thae days when references tae 'fanny', 'Chinkies' n a John Inman-style impression eh a stereotypical mincin sitcom homosexual can garner such applause. However, the 'chinky' remark wis in the context eh 'curry', so ye couldnae tar Joe wi the racist brush fur that yin. N the 'high quality fanny' alluded tae wis nowt but a stirrin compliment tae the lovely ladies eh the Icelandic nation, where he'd plied his trade efter leavin Hibs.

Aye, that fair goat me reminiscin tae. I went tae Iceland masel once, but promptly goat huckled oot fur attemptin tae shoplift a box eh fish.

"The Cod War's no ower yet!" I yelled defiantly, as the store detective booted ma saggy auld erse firmly doon the Kirkgate. So, unlike Joe, I sadly never goat tae bag aff wi any eh the burdz there. I wis lost in thae melancholic thoughts fur ages, when the unwelcome sound eh the bar shutters comin crashin doon suddenly jolted me back tae the present.

"Time tae go, auld-timer! Ye're the last yin left," observed the barmaid, in a kindly tone.

Auld-timer, eh, the cheeky cow! Didnae look a day under ninety hersel! I hirpled reluctantly ooty the deserted Supporters Club n started pechin back up the lane taewards Easter Road like a breathless bulldog. Aye, I might have been on the 'Sunnyside' so tae speak, but I felt mair like the Walker Brothers back in 1966, whae hit the nail squarely on the heid wi the observation that 'The Sun Ain't Gonna Shine Any More'...

TOILET HUMOUR?

So, Cup quarter-final day wis almost upon us, n yours truly wis still ticket-less, efter that crap burglar Scorpio Leisure Fifi Phanni-Phlapz fiasco. But when aw is said n done, it's jist no the same watchin it on the telly, is it? I wis still ruminatin on the problem, when I wis suddenly jolted by an idea eh such overwhelmin brilliance that I felt obliged tae gie masel a pat on the back right away. Cos efter aw, I still hud a perfectly guid tunnel dug under Albion Place, didn't I? OK, admittedly it wis mair eh a perfectly pish tunnel tae be honest, but that could easily be rectified. It wid be a simple job tae folly that along tae the point where it unhappily veered aff course tae the right n extend it fae there straight under the Famous Five Stand concourse. I wid have tae take extra special care wi the measurements this time though, as the sight eh ma napper poppin oot on the centre-spot at kick-aff time wid probably cause Rod Pear-Tree tae have kittens in the Directors' Box.

Of course, when I crept back intae the Eastern Cemetery the night afore, I only then remembered that some panic-stricken ersehole no a million miles away hud dynamited the entrance n I hud a hell eh a job digging a new route in, beneath the sod. But once I goat through that, it really wis a piece eh pish. When I arrived at the bend in the tunnel, I boldly forged straight ahead wi the auld drill, allowin fur the distance between the road above, tae a point behind the Clubstore, which I'd paced oot earlier. Aye, I'd thought eh everythin this time! At last I wis done n started tae burrow taewards the surface like a crazed giant Hibbie mole wi irreversible brain damage. Then, aw eh a sudden – whit aloadyshite! Quite literally. Aye, I'd only emerged in the sewer runnin underneath the Gents' lavvy, but apart fae bein coated fae heid tae toe in the broon stuff, it wis still a positive result. The important thing hud been achieved – I wis in!

However, many *many* oors later, wi kick-aff time nigh, I wis rapidly approachin the end eh ma tether. Sittin in the stand behind the goal on ma lonesome, I wis bored ooty ma skull, starvin, gaspin w thirst n freezin ma Mark McGraws aff intae the bargain. Plus, I ken that the 'live on the telly' factor ayewis significantly reduces the size eh the crowd, but even I couldnae believe how poor it wis. In fact, it wis East Stirling v Auchenshoogle aw ower again, there wis naebody there! No only were there nae fans, there were nae stewards or polis either – which wis a bonus I suppose, but I could have done wi some bloody catering staff. Nae luck there, though, the hoat cuisine remained ooty bounds.

I began tae wonder if maybe it wis one eh thae weird gemmes played behind closed doors, as a result eh some draconian punishment bestowed by the Blazers on account eh the fans' bad behaviour or somethin. Aye, that must be it. But then the flaw in ma internal debate wi masel wis revealed rather forcefully, by the fact that there were nae bloody teams tae be seen either!

Finally, the straw that broke the camel's back. Obviously the bloody gemme hud been cancelled n as usual nae-one thinks tae tell Gibby. Aw naw! Laid doon his life in two World Wars n one World Cup fur his Queen n country, n this is how he gets treated? Makes ye seek. I stormed back intae the Gents in a towerin rage, dived back doon the pan like Ewan McGregor in the first 'Trainspottin' film n stumped aff back along my subterranean sidewalk taewards the cemetery.

I wis however delayed on the way, by a roof collapse in the section beyond the Hibs shop n afore the cemetery boundary. It turned oot that Christian Nade hud been drivin a ten-ton truck along Albion Place n the excessive weight (his, no the truck's) hud caused the cave-in. So that wis ma free route intae the ground fucked, as I hud tae dig ma way oot there, afore the curious gaze eh nosey parker passers-by. By the time I goat back ontae St. Clair Street, I wis puzzled tae see thae Hibs fans heidin the other way, taewards the stadium.

"The gemme's cancelled," I telt them aw.

"Oh no it isn't!" retorted this young whippersnapper, as if he wis at the bloody panto.

See youse young folk the day – nae respect fur yer elders n betters! I'm a patient man as ye aw ken, but I cannae abide been contradicted by ignoramuses.

"Well, if it husnae been cawed aff, perhaps ye can explain how I've been sittin in that stadium fur bloody oors n oors, way past three o'clock, n there's nowt happenin?" I yipped, the sarcasm drippin fae ma tongue.

"The simple explanation wid probably be that the gemme wis never scheduled tae kick aff at 3 p.m. in the first place, it's a 5.15 job, ya daft auld codger."

I felt faint aw eh a sudden.

"Whit...ye mean that..."

Wi a triumphal air, he shoved his match-ticket under ma neb, which confirmed the kick-aff time tae ma jaundiced eye. When in the name eh aw that is sacred n holy, hus a fitba match ever kicked aff at that time, I ask ye?? I didnae even have the presence eh mind tae grab hud eh it n dae a mad runner taewards the turnstiles. I glared at the eejits, whae were grinning at ma distress like a bunch eh glaikit

Cheshire cats.

"It's no right!" I spluttered. "Fitba gemmes ayewis kick aff at three in the efternin n have done fur as long as I can remember. Somethin smells very bad here..."

"Aye – you," they chorused in unison.

Well, I could hardly refute that, could I, given ma breakthrough point intae the stadium n subsequent be-foulin eh ma entire personage. I stamped aff doon Easter Road, thinkin at least I could watch it on a pub telly, as I dinnae get aw thae fancy channels on the black 'n' white job in the hoose. But of course, reality then kicked in n I found oot I couldnae even dae that – naebody wid serve me, jist cos I wis covered in shite! The 2-0 scoreline in Sellik's favour then went ontae show that it hud truly been a crap day aw roond, n nae mistake.

THE FINAL COUNTDOWN

"Consonant please, Rachel!"

"Thank you, Gibby – H."

Aye, H fur Hibees, a guid start, eh? Have youse guessed where I am yet?

"Another consonant please, Rachel!"

"D."

"Thank you, Rachel!"

Aye, I wis on that 'Countdoon' on Channel 4! Hud tae keep repeatin the lassie's name, ken, as I entered under the impression that Carol Vorderman wis still daein it n hud tae remind masel it wisnae her. Disappointin tae say the least, as Alex Miller used tae frequently remark, cos wi'oot doot ma ultimate fantasy wumman wis the eminently cowpable Carol. Mind ye, this wee blonde piece wis quite easy on the eye tae...

"You seem to be lost in thought there, Gibby – is everything alright?"

"Er...oh aye, Carol, sure is, doll. Er, I mean Rachel. Christ, aye."

"That's good. Would you like to select another letter then?"

"I jist have – I!"

"Oh, sorry. I thought you meant the Scottish word for 'yes' there."

"Well, that's only goat three letters, hasn't it? No gonnae get much eh a score fae that, am I?"

Nice enough lassie, ken, but no exactly over-burdened wi a surfeit eh the auld Saughton Mains up tap. Unlike Carol...

"Foul please, Rachel!"

"Er...you mean 'vowel'?"

"Look, I ken whit I mean awright! One eh thae letters that's no a cormorant!"

"You mean 'consonant'?"

"Naw, I want a vowel."

"O."

"Well, there's nae need tae act so surprised."

"No – I mean the letter 'O'."

"Oh..."

"Your next letter, Gibby?"

"Christ, geeza break, hen! Youse goat a train tae catch or somethin? I'll take another condiment."

"P?"

"Thanks fur askin, but I hud a slash on ma way in."

"No, that's your next consonant."

"Aw right, gotcha. Well gie me another eh them then, Carol!"

"My name's Rachel. Y."

"Why? Cos yer parents christened ye that, I suppose."

"No, I mean that's your next letter – Y."

"Ye mean as in 'YLT'?"

"Sorry?"

"Never mind. Hit me wi another foul."

"A."

"Aye, that's the YLT awright – the A-Team. OK, Car...Rachel, another cons... eh...conso...consolation, please."

"S."

"Uh-huh. N one mair eh the same, ta."

"L."

So that wis it up on the board – H D I O P Y S A L.

But, afore I even hud time tae gather ma thoughts taegether, that Richard Shitely is throwin it open tae ma opponent! One – I'm no entirely sure that it's Shitely in the chair efter aw, n Two – I forgot I even hud someone up against me. I wis concentratin that hard on no cawin Rachel Carol I'd been imaginin it wis jist me flyin solo. So as I picked the bloody letters, surely I should get a shot first.

"Look, Dick..."

"Who are you calling a Dick?" says the Almost-Certainly-Not-Shitely felly irritably. "The name's *Nick.*"

He wis glarin at me like that Humphrys hud done on 'Fastermind'. Dae thae jumped-up Groucho Club-patronisin luvvie telly presenter types really think that they can intimidate Gibby? Wi his big frowny face, doon-turned mooth n saggy jowls, I goat the distinct impression his entire coupon wis sufferin fae a severe case eh Hewer's Droop.

"How come she gets tae start?" I demanded, jerkin ma thumb in the direction eh ma adversary, some wumman whae looked like a retired school headmistress ooty 'The Prime eh Miss Deacon Brodie'."

"It's ladies first," says Dick-Nick, gettin chivalrous aw eh a sudden.

I glanced ower again, tae see her starin intently at the board n scribblin on her notepad at the same time.

"Standby!" says Dick-Nick self-importantly, like he's a fuckin train guard or somethin, as that irritatin music n tickin clock start daein ma heid in.

When that hud run its course, the Brodie-type bint is lookin awfy pleased wi hersel, fur some reason. But whitever she hud up her sleeve, I wis ready fur her...

"Eight letters – HOLIDAYS," she says, smugly, as a slow murmur eh appreciation ripples roond the studio.

Dick-Nick looks like he's aboot tae come in his pants.

"*Terrific* start," he says fawningly. "Eight letters indeed, that is going to be very hard – if not *impossible* – to beat, I would imagine. Very, very impressive..."

"LOADYPISH!" I barked oot suddenly, cuttin him aff in his prime.

There wis a stunned silence fur a moment.

"Mr...*Gibson*, is it?" Dick-Nick finally enunciated, through gritted teeth. "There is absolutely no call at all for such a display of unsportsmanlike rudeness! To insult your opponent with such a flagrant, gratuitous comment..."

"Haud yer wheesht, ya specky fanny-baws, I'm no insultin her at aw! That's ma word eh *nine* letters fur youse, right there. Aye, nane eh yer eight-letter ersin aboot fur me. Check it oot – LOADYPISH."

Hewer looked like he wis aboot tae turn intae a spewer. His face wis pure trippin him, renderin him speechless fur a few seconds. He gawped at the board in desperation, as if hopin fur some sort eh divine intervention. But then a brief pang eh anxiety jack-knifed through ma body, as I realised he wis now lookin ower at Dictionary Corner.

"Susie?"

Wi hert in mooth, aw ma hopes were now pinned on the divine dame Dent. I wisnae sure which way it wid go, as I saw her reachin oot fur one eh the two hefty volumes on the desk in front eh her. 'The Standard Oxford English Dictionary', naturally, n then tae ma eternal relief, I saw she wis stretchin oot fur the specially abridged updated 'Standard Oxford English Dictionary – Leith Version' instead! Efter she'd flipped through the pages tae 'L', there wis nae doot aboot the ootcome whitsoever.

"Yes, Gibby, very well played indeed. Here it is – 'Loadypish' – *A Scottish colloquial expression, translating as 'a large amount of urine', usually employed as a derogatory response towards something said, which has not met the approval of the recipient, due to its suspect content."*

Susie, baby – I couldnae have pit it better masel! Rachel n the Holidays wumman were lookin at me wi a new-found respect, but I could see that Dick-Nick wis still far fae happy.

"I don't know if I can allow that," he harrumphed. "It might be in some obscure version of a *Scottish* dictionary, but such *Scottish* slang terminology is not generally recognised as constituting proper English."

Jist listen tae this radge! Tryin tae bend the rules tae suit himsel! N then insultin the Scottish Nation intae the bargain. Aye, he'd finally pushed his luck tae far, wi yours truly. Wi a lightnin move, I grabbed the other dictionary aff Susie's table, then bounded ower n clattered the cheeky bastirt ower the heid wi it, employin aw the force I could muster. Somewhit tae ma surprise, he instantly slumped tae the flair, apparently unconscious.

Well, the whole studio instantly erupted intae pure pandemonium. The audience were cheerin or booin, I couldnae tell which, Susie looked as if she wis aboot tae pass oot hersel n ma opponent wis screamin hysterically n tearin her hair oot. Only Rachel remained cool as a cucumber, lookin at me wi something akin tae love in her eyes. Well, that's how I interpreted it anyway.

"It's the name eh the gemme, doll," I stated, pointin at the inert form eh Dick-Nick.

She continued to gaze at me expectantly.

"Cunt Doon," I explained, afore tippin ma hat tae her gallantly n ridin aff intae the sunset.

IF ONE GREEN BOTTLE SHOULD ACCIDENTALLY FALL

Well, I see the West of Scotland weedjie mob are at the moan again. They're no happy cos the Hibs CCTV at the cup-tie allegedly failed tae record the bottle-throwin incident in its entirety, whereupon a glass missile wis – again allegedly - flung at Scott Sinclair. Emblazoned on the side eh the said projectile wis the ominous word 'BUCKFAST'. Mmm, that kindy narrys doon the likely origins eh the perpetrators, does it no? When hus any self-respectin Hibbie jakey been in possession eh the mad monks' mingin mock methylated spirits, eh, tell me that! Anyway, it wisnae surprisin that footage wis hard tae come by, as once it hud disappeared intae the depths eh that ridiculous thatch that Sinclair seems tae think is a 'hairstyle', there wis nae chance eh retrievin it. Gone fur guid, jist like somethin chucked intae one eh thae black holes in space. The polis spent oors lookin fur it, aided by a team eh highly-trained sniffer dugs, but found fuck aw. A trifle hypocritical eh that shower makin a fuss, efter aw the bother n damage they caused at Rugby Park the other week there! N it's been gettin worse ever since. Still in a wee cream puff aboot Brendan bailin oot, Bhoys?

Actually, when I saw the banner hoisted aloft by Sellik fans at Tiny Castle the week afore, I initially assumed their sulky sentiments were aimed at Neil Lennon. Swapped 'immortality' fur 'mediocrity' – efter aw, he went fae the first tae wear the green / first tae have floodlights / first tae have sponsors' name on jerseys / first tae play in Europe team tae a bunch eh impostors formed thirteen years later, whae copied oor colours, then poached maist eh oor tap players! Still makes ma blood bile, thinkin aboot it.

But back tae the present, n once it became clear the Green-aboot-the-gills Brigade were referring tae Rodgers, no Lennon, ye hud tae laugh at the bitchy aside beneath the main banner. 'NEVER A CELT' it stated, aboot a guy whae'd ayewis spoken emotionally eh supportin the team since boyhood. Admittedly he did so when hundreds eh miles away fae Glesgie, but that's never been an impediment tae the thoosands eh other glory-huntin long-distance sycophants whae 'folly' the Bhoys, the Tim Malloys... But noo he'd hud the cheek tae jump ship fur a better job wi a real challenge n maybe even some proper financial backin (which he never goat at Parkheid), he widnae even be welcome back as a fan.

Then, on tap eh aw the totally ower-the-tap media hysteria aboot bottle-throwin, flares gaun aff, sectarian singin, aw the usual shite, oot comes a report fae somewhere, suddenly announcin that certain Scottish fitba groonds were 'fundamentally unsafe' intae the bargain. Apparently us fans were in mortal danger every time we stepped ower the threshold. N sometimes even afore it – a big Christian Nade shaped hole in Albion Place bein a case in point. Speakin fae ma ain experiences, I can definitely concur wi the report's concerns, regardin Health n Safety at Easter Road. In fact, I'm gonnae send that Chief Executive wumman a letter shortly, aboot the chronic subsidence beneath the Gents' shitehoose at the Famous Five Stand end...

LETTER TAE LEEANN

Dear Ms Dumpster (or may I caw ye Leeann?),

When are ye gonna dae something aboot the stadium lavvies, eh? I'm up tae ma knees in shite hauf the time. Also, how come there's nae chips any mair in the Famous Five Stand? Ye might no ken this, but chips are actually made fae tatties n ye'd dae well tae mind whit happened back in Ireland in 1846 when they ran ooty spuds. Aye - mass starvation! Sellik fans are still greetin their eyes oot aboot it, tae this very day! So ye'd better think long n hard aboot the awfy consequences that nae chips can bring aboot. Plus, is it no aboot time that alcohol n smokin were reintroduced tae the ground? N chips, mind

- dinnae forget aboot thae bloody chips! On a final note, is there any truth in the rumour concernin Neil Lennon's alleged homophobic insults?

Hopin this letter finds ye well,

I remain your humble n obedient servant,

'Grumpy' Gibson

DIRECTIVE FAE DEMPSTER

Dear Mr Gibson,

No, you may *not* call me Leeann. Also, my surname is *Dempster* – a 'dumpster' is an American street receptacle for throwing rubbish into. Such as your letter, for example.

As to your complaint regarding the Easter Road toilets, from my own personal and extremely unwilling experience, you seem to spend an inordinate amount of time causing trouble in them. In fact, the club blowtorch has never been the same since. Furthermore, a recent police investigation strongly points to you being the principal cause of the recent subsidence problem.

I am very well aware of the source of chips, but thank you very much for the invaluable history lesson all the same. As a health (and safety) conscious club, we see no reason to encourage the consumption of chips, alcohol *or* cigarettes on our premises.

In response to your last query – Neil who?? (But mind your own bloody business anyway.)

Hoping this letter finds you well – on your way to either the Royal Edinburgh Hospital or Saughton Prison, where you clearly belong,

Yours in sport,

Ms L. *Dempster*.

TURNING ON A TANNER

As I wis walkin doon the Albion Road, I met a total stranger. N he said tae me, "Are ye gaun tae see, the famous Glasgow Rangers?" So aff I went tae Ibrox Park, tae see...naw, hing on a minute, naw I didnae! It wis a hame gemme, fur fuck's sake! So naturally I telt him tae mind his ain bloody business (much like that Dumpster wumman hud done tae me), but he must have been a bit psychic – cos I actually wis! N there wis nae way I wis makin any mistakes aboot the kick-aff times again – I say 'again', cos I'd awready gone along tae the stadium at 7.45 this mornin. Broke aff fae a breakfast sesh in The Marksman tae, so I wisnae best pleased tae discover that it wisnae takin place till twelve oors later. I swear tae God, I'm gonnae have tae write another letter tae Leeann Dump-Truck aboot thae bloody kick-aff times – it's never the same twa gemmes in a row!

Anyway, as per usual, I wis soon wonderin why I'd bothered, as the first hauf unfolded. Fae a Hibs point eh view it wis quite simply a loady single fish! Nae shots on target. Nae shots *aff* target. That great galoot McGregor in the Total Strangers' goal hud that little tae dae, he actually nipped roond the corner fur a spot eh slap n tickle wi Senga n Fifi – n naebody noticed! It wis jist as well I'd only invested in a hauf-season ticket, so at least I hud tae leave at hauf-time. (I wis forced tae relinquish ma 'expiry date 1919' job, under threat eh bein executed at dawn by Rod Pear-Tree's crack firing squad. Aye, n ye can bet yer bottom dollar thae bloody shots wid have been on target!)

By the time I left, Hibs were trailin tae a Daniel Candelabra goal, but believe me, it could have been a lot mair than that. So I wis expectin a proper tankin n couldnae even face watchin the second hauf on the telly. I strode intae The Cenny n demanded they changed the channel ower tae 'Coronation Street' instead, tae howls eh protest fae the usual armchair 'supporters'. That mob havenae been near the Holy Groond since the days eh Turnbull's Toreadors, the Famous Four or even the Secret Seven! Bunch eh part-timers, so they are. But of course, one eh the problems eh the People's Independent Republic eh Leith is that it's akin tae livin in Ooter Space, the time it takes fur the TV signals tae reach us. Cos ye could have knocked me doon wi a feather when I looked up at the screen, tae see that Elsie Tanner wis apparently aboot tae get married again. Still, Hibs wid be experiencin an ever bigger pumpin than the yin auld Elsie wis aboot tae get, I thought. So ye could have knocked me doon wi *another* feather, when Hibbies started tricklin in an oor or so later, lookin no that doon in the mooth efter aw.

"Cam Berry pit the baw in the net late on!" one eh them says.

Whae the hell's he, when he's at hame, I wondered. Neil Berry's younger brother? Or maybe Chuck's...

"Whit wis the score?" I demanded tae ken.

"Hibs 1, Rangers 1," I wis telt.

"Hibs won – n *Rangers* won??" I repeated back tae this eejit. "They canny *baith* have won, fur Chrissake! It's no even possible!"

See the pish that some folk talk thae days, it's no real. So I stumped aff hame, none the wiser. Still, hope it aw works oot awright fur Elsie this time...

AW WE ARE SAYING IS GIE WAR A CHANCE

People often ask me, "Gibby, whit is it that made ye the fine upstandin figure eh a man that ye are taeday?"

N I reply in aw modesty, "Apart fae the Lord God himsel, it wid have tae be the Army, n ma impeccable military backgroond."

I may no have mentioned it much afore, but I've been involved in maist eh the major conflicts eh the last century, fae the time I first signed on as a fresh-faced boogie-woogie bugle-boy in Company B. Noo that might only have been in the Boy Scouts, but it stood me in guid stead, when I unexpectedly found masel caught up in the Spanish Civil War. Efter aw, I'd only volunteered tae fight against Franco's Office Bar at Tollcross, no actually that cunt Franco himsel. N then I realised quite quickly that the pagger in question wis somewhit misleadingly named, cos it wis far fae fuckin civil, I can assure ye eh that, in fact bastirts fae *baith* sides were tryin tae shoot me!

Then I wis at the forefront eh some eh the major battles in World War Two. Maybe it wis tae assuage the guilt caused by ma auld man turnin oot fur the opposition so tae speak, but I wis never backward in comin forward. Rorke's Drift, Gettysburg, Gallipoli, The Little Big Horn, The Charge eh the Shite Brigade – ye name it, n there's a fair chance that Gibby wis there.

Later on, I took part in the Korean conflict – I didnae fancy the North v South tussle, so I actually took part in the slightly lesser-known war between East n West Korea. Every bit as dangerous, mind. Not least cos I kept gettin caught in the crossfire between the bloody Yanks n Chinkies competin in the other yin!

Then I became a hired gun n took part in the Middle East's famous Three Day War of 1967. Aye, I ken it's mair commonly known as 'The Six Day War' but I jist went fur a long weekend.

"It wis ideal preparation fur the Falkland conflict," I telt ma rapt listeners in The Cenny, maist eh whae were noo wrapped up in their ain thoughts, havin ceased tae actually listen tae yours truly ages ago, the ill-mannered bastirts. But I pressed on regardless. "It wis early one Setirday efternin that day in 1982, when we unexpectedly came across the enemy," I reminisced. "First we heard the strange accents speakin in a tongue that we didnae understand n knew they were close by. Speed n surprise were noo eh the essence cos eh their fearsome reputation, especially if backed intae a corner. So I gave the order tae lead the charge, whereupon..."

But jist at that moment, I wis rudely interrupted.

"Gibson – I've never heard such a load of absolute poppycock in my life! Poppycock, I tell you, man!"

I whirled roond tae be met by the ramrod-backed figure of Lieutenant-Colonel Sir Roderick Farquarharson-Ponsonby-Smythe, an alleged war hero (military fantasist, mair like) whae hung aboot the boozers eh Leith in full battle-dress, n whae wis generally referred tae as Roddy the Squaddie, or, mair succinctly, Rod the Fraud.

"You're a born bloody liar, Gibson! I was there with Colonel 'H' Jones at Goose Green I'll have you know, and I can absolutely state *categorically* for the benefit of your dipsomaniac acolytes here that you were nowhere near the place. You've never faced down the Argentinian Army in your bloody life, man! So what have you got to say for yourself, eh?"

He wis jabbin his forefinger irately at me, aboot three inches fae ma hooter.

"Whae said anything aboot fightin the Argies?!" I yelped. "I wisnae talkin aboot *that* Falklands conflict, I'm talkin aboot the *Falkland* in Fife conflict. The YLT were on their way tae the Hibs gemme at St. Johnstone by bus n hud jist stopped fur chips in said place, when we clocked the Mental Methil heidin fur Bayview. N when *that* aw kicked aff, it wis a damn sight mair bloody than that half-ersed skirmish aff the coast eh Sooth America, I'll tell ye that."

Well, that pit his gas at a peep, n nae mistake. See the number eh times I've hud tae pull rank ower thae impostors, whae've never done their bit fur Queen n Freddie Mercury, er, I mean country!

"Now, did I ever tell ye aboot ma involvement in The Wars eh the Roses?" I continued enthusiastically, gettin back intae ma verbal stride.

Roddy the Squaddie jist stood there helplessly, wi an expression on his coupon like Simon Weston lookin fur the fire-extinguisher.

“It wis a dark n stormy night in Restalrig,” I went on, “N I’d jist been challenged tae a square-go in The Bunch eh Roses...”

I glanced sideways tae check the reaction eh ma admirin audience – only tae find that the bastirts were no longer there, they’d aw crept away when I’d turned roond tae confront that ersehole squaddie! Never mind the Bunch eh Roses, bunch eh bloody traitors mair like! Aye, I noo kent how Davy Crockett must’ve felt at The Alamo. Gallant auld Gibby – the last man standing, again...

HIBERNIAN (GIE US A POLE)

Another weekend, another hoo-hah aboot hauf-wits runnin ontae the field eh play. Jist when oor soothern neebors (the English, no those residin at the wrong end eh Leith Walk) were congratulatin themsels on no bein part eh the *Scottish* fitba problem, one bampot in Birmingham went n effortlessly upstaged aw the rest, at a local derby. This time a player wis actually *attacked*, somethin which hudnae happened north eh the border (despite whit the hun cry-babies claimed efter 21/5/16.) Still, it almost certainly didnae have the desired effect where the Brummie wis concerned, as the Aston Villa boy he lamped then went ontae score the winnin goal.

Of course, the huns theirsels were party tae one eh the maist spectacular pitch invasions eh aw time in the same city, back in 1979. The provocative sight eh an Irish tricolour flutterin in the Villa

Park breeze caused thoosands eh huns tae invade the park at the other end n then storm up the pitch en masse. It didnae end there though, as they proceeded tae systematically dismantle the toon centre brick by brick fur several days efterwards. N the gemme in question wis a 'friendly'! Ideal military preparation fur another major riot at Hampden the followin year, which put the final mockers on the terracing cairry-oot tradition an aw. Still, at least it gied the weedjie polis cavalry an opportunity tae show aff their superior equestrian skills, by randomly tramplin ower flared-troosered miscreants in baith blue n green.

So ye've goat tae sigh at the ineffectiveness eh the daftie whae goat ontae the sidelines at Easter Road tae confront Tavernier durin the gemme against the huns. Cos efter petulantly bootin the baw away fae the Cream Buns' captain, he seemed at a loss as tae whit tae dae next. If ye're gonnae go tae the trouble eh vaultin the advertisin hoardings n preparin tae face the consequences later, fur Chrissake make it worth yer while n at least bop the Bluenose one – make a decent fist eh it, in other words! I dinnae ken whit hooliganism is comin tae thae days, I really dinnae.

They should send thae homegrown half-baked hoodlums on a trainin course tae the stadia eh Sooth America or Eastern Europe, where they still ken how tae hoolie like it's 1979. (I wid recommend the Polish derby between Krakovia n Wisla, where the mass burnin eh rivals' skerves on the terracing is aw part n parcel eh the pre-match entertainment, as well as general violence n mayhem baith inside n ootside the ground.) Then once they've learned their lessons properly there, they could maybe dae a better job when returnin tae these shores. Silly-billys eh Scotland – dae yer duty!

REMIT TAE ROD

Dear Mr Pear-Tree (or may I caw ye Rod?),

I've recently hud cause tae write tae yer underling, Ms Leeann Damp-Squib, but as I got nowt but lip by way eh a reply, I thought it wis time tae deal directly wi yersel. Whit concerns me is Damp-Squib's latest verbal fireworks, threatenin tae close part eh the East Stand in the future, if there's any mair incursions by attention-seekin dafties runnin ontae the park. Well, excuse me fur pointin oot the bleedin obvious, but that wid suggest that the problems are occurring on the pitch itsel, as opposed tae in the Stand. Are ye wi me so far? Waggle yer 'tache once fur 'aye', twice fur 'naw'. Guid, noo we're gettin somewhere! So the obvious solution is tae close the pitch instead, is it no? Efter aw, even I have been known tae enjoy masel at Easter Road Stadium. Ye can place a bet, ye can beef yer strength up wi a Bovril, ye can meet yer mates, ye can play 'coont the seagulls', ye can even enjoy the weather if ye're a sado-masochist, but there's one thing that aw tae often spoils the whole experience fur the discernin punter. Aye, that ninety minutes eh shite takin place on the park! Take that ooty the equation awtaegether n I reckon ye're on a winner.

May I also take this opportunity tae apologise fur that wee misunderstanding re ma manager's job application n Senga McGlumphar, request the immediate reinstatement eh my full season-ticket n fur Chrissake man, dae something aboot thae bloody chips - or lack thereof.

Yours truly,

'Grumpy' Gibson

CHAIN-MAIL FAE THE CHAIRMAN

Dear Mr Gibson,

No, you may not call me Rod. Also, you've got some bloody nerve, getting my surname wrong again. However, as this is the 47th letter penned in bright green ink you've seen fit to send me this year already, I thought that I, in turn, should address you directly. I will happily agree to close any part of the stadium, or indeed all of it, as a means of preventing you setting foot in the place ever again.

Regarding your previous season-ticket; as that has been used fraudulently at Easter Road since 1919, I have calculated that – taking into account a six-year deduction for the duration of World War Two – you are therefore due us a reimbursement for 94 seasons-worth of free attendance. Please find the enclosed bill, which for convenience sake I have rounded up to £33,840 (plus 72 pence for postage.) If this is not paid in full by the end of the current campaign, there will be another season ticket promptly despatched to you – for permanent viewing from HMP Saughton.

Yours insincerely,

Mr. R. Petrie

P.S. You'll have plenty time to stuff your face with chips in there.

P.P.S. Tell Senga that Rod says 'Hi! Let's do it again sometime soon. Luv ye, baby. X.'

GIEIN GENEROUSLY

Sittin on ma tod in The Cenny n hopin fur a bit eh peace n quiet, I wis findin it hard tae get a proper grip on ma pint gless. Reason bein that the auld arthritis in ma hand wis playin up somethin terrible, as a result eh writin aw thae angry letters fur oors on end. Cos I hudnae stopped at Pear-Tree n Dumpster, aw naw, far fae it! The issue regardin a lack eh chips is way tae important fur that. So I also sent them tae the First Meenister, the Second Meenister, Smith, Johnstone, Reilly, Turnbull, Ormond, then another tae the Queen n a final yin tae the Pope, in the interests eh balance. Aye, I wis therefore daein ma bit tae make the world a better place anyway, but there's ayewis some interferin gets whae keep expectin ye tae dae even mair. I shuddered as aw thae do-gooder types came through the door, rattlin their charity collection tins shamelessly in ma direction.

"Charity begins at hame," I telt them firmly, which wisnae jist a glib expression in ma case.

Efter aw, ma ain hame wis burstin at the seams wi choaried charity boatils n tins, which I'd accumulated ower many years.

"But today of all days, Gibby, you've got to make an effort!"

Christ Almighty, I could see that peace n quiet were well n truly oot the windae fur noo.

"You've got to get into the spirit of things, Gibby," persisted this radical feminist Save-the-Whale-Ban-the-Bomb type bint. "Think about the starving children in Africa!"

"I'm tae busy thinkin aboot the starvin bairns at Easter Road wi nae fuckin chips," I muttered under ma breath, but I kent she wisnae gonnae let it lie, until I made some magnanimous gesture.

Jist then, I clocked that mock military muppet Roddy the Squaddie glarin at me fae across the bar. A cauld rage started tae simmer in my soul. Bastirt tryin tae make a monkey ooty me wi his Falklands fantasies, showin me up in front eh ma loyal fan-base! I'll show *him*, I suddenly decided, gettin tae ma feet in a sprightly fashion.

"Ye want me tae get intae the appropriate spirit, tae mark this auspicious charitable occasion, dae ye?" I said tae the Ban the Whale wumman. "OK, watch this then."

I strode across the flair wi a jaunty military two-step n stuck the heid on the bridge eh Rod the Fraud's prominent hooter wi such force that a great geyser eh blood instantly shot up in the dusty air.

"Happy Red Nose Day!" I yelled, as he fell aff his stool n then proceeded tae writhe aboot like a burnin deckhand on the General Belgrano.

There wis a brief stunned silence, afore maist eh the regulars dissolved intae gales eh cruel laughter, dissipatin the tension right away. Even Girnin Gertie had a malevolent grin splittin her mockit coupon fae tap tae bottom.

"Show's over, folks," I announced modestly, takin a bow. "Ye cannae say I've no done ma bit fur Comic Relief noo...

As I lapped up the applause, I wis distracted by the sound emanatin fae the splattered so-cawed squaddie, whae wis now greetin his eyes oot. I couldnae resist one final dig afore I left, so I re-routed masel via the jukebox, stuck on 'Don't Cry For Me Argentina' n then exited stage left.

WELL DONE

Comic Relief wis also on the agenda as Hibs got doon tae business against Motherwell the followin day – well within the first minute tae. They were dickin aboot defensively which led tae Lewis Stevenson skitin the baw aff Marciano's post, n relief wis the principal emotion when that stayed oot. Happily however, that wis aboot Motherwell's lot as a threat in the first hauf. McNutsack stuck away another penalty n Knight eh the Hibernian Realm, Sir David Gray, didnae even need his White Ladder tae get his heid tae a folly-up net-buster. Aw afore the hauf-time whistle tae! I wis almost enjoyin masel, although of course the lack eh chips wis weighin heavily on ma mind throughoot.

Still, mair eh the same efter the break n although Camembert hud me cheesed aff by failin tae convert an easy yin, they never looked like throwin it away. Barryl Organ went close tae n wee Omeonga danced a conga roond the Stealies aw efternin. Best thing tae come oot eh Belgium since Hercule Poirot n Tin-Tin! Tap Six here we come! Aw haud on, we're awready there...

Aye, a guid weekend fur the green, wi every team between us n Sellik at the tap droppin points – aw three in the jambos' case, as Rice's men curried nae favours taewards the maroon balloons. That streak eh misery Levein telt the Evening News that, 'the game had 0-0 written all over it,' n nae-one hud the hert tae tell him it actually hud '1-0 tae Hamilton' written aw ower it. Hopefully, he hudnae yet processed the info that the Hibees were a mere two points behind his lot in the table, wi a far superior goal-difference. Time fur the natural order in the league tae be restored, boys! Bring on the Hertz!

PAYBACK TIME

When I awoke the mornin efter Well hud been well done, the sun wis shinin warmly through the windae n the little birdies were singin prettily in the treetops. I felt so calm n at peace wi the world, I instantly began tae fear there wis somethin wrong. But it wisnae jist the shortage eh chips at Easter Road...I sensed that someone somewhere hud bigger fish tae fry. Suddenly I shot bolt upright as wi an awful clarity I remembered – I wis the loady fish in question n Pear-Tree wid be the yin daein the fryin, unless I came up wi nearly £34,000 fairly pronto! Where on earth wis I gonnae get ma hands on a sum like that?

Fifteen minutes later I wis in the bookies, frantically scannin the day's form. It wis only when a woman screamed in disgust I realised I'd clean forgotten tae get dressed, n wis standin in front eh The Racing Post stark naked. So efter a quick return hame tae don the clobber, I wis back tae consider ma options. Ye could get 10/1 on Soon-2B-Dogfood runnin in the 2.30 at Haydock, but last time I backed that particular three-legged donkey in the same race he didnae finish till 5.15 at Aintree. Must have taken a wrong turn at the first bend. But that wis nae use anyway, as I'd need a stake eh nearly four grand tae make it worth ma while. I looked at that day's special offers. 100/1 on Craig Levein crackin a smile afore the day wis oot didnae strike me as bein that generous, considerin the extreme unlikelihood eh such a thing occurin at aw, never mind afore midnight. I wis beginning tae doot the wisdom eh tryin tae raise the loot via the dubious philanthropy eh Mr William Hill...

Ower the road in The Cenny, I cautiously approached the well-kent gangster, whae'd provided the startin-pistol fur one eh ma least successful suicide attempts. Ye'll notice that I wis careful no tae reveal his name in that sorry tale, fur it wis made crystal clear through the underworld grapevine that tae pit it intae print wid be equivalent tae signin yer ain death-warrant. He *never* wanted it made public. Fuck knows why, cos it's actually 'John Smith', one eh the maist common names around! Hardly gonnae draw attention tae yersel wi a borin run-eh-the-mill handle like that. Tae his criminal cronies he wis simply 'Slasher' Smith, but even that wis a bit eh a misnomer, designed tae pit the frighteners on people. Cos he wisnae referred tae as such due tae his dexterity wi a blade, but cos he hud an awfy weak bladder n wis ayewis gaun fur a slash.

"Awright, Slasher?" I blurted oot, rather inappropriately.

Still, at least I hudnae used his *real* name. His eyes narrowed – although they were quite narry enough tae start wi. They were that close taegether he wis often mistaken fur a Cyclops. But the last gadgie tae caw him *that* hud his ain eyes plucked oot by way eh a punishment.

“Whit dae ye want? Still pittin the fear eh God intae oor feathered friends?”

I wis briefly scoobied by this statement, afore rememberin oor last interminable conversation aboot owls. Silly cunt hud owls on the brain, no tae mention bats in the belfry!

“Naw, nowt like that. Thing is, I need a loan.”

“A lone whit? Wolf? Ranger?”

Here we go again, I thought.

Wi a superhuman effort, I managed no tae lose ma rag wi the hulkin great eejit.

“Naw, neither eh them required, Slasher. It’s mair eh a wee cash-flow problem I’ve goat. I heard ye were, no tae pit tae fine a point on it n nae offence intended, somethin eh a loan-shark.”

“Whae telt ye that?”

“Er...now that I come tae think eh it, it wis mair the sight eh yon giant fin protrudin fae yer back that gave the gemme away,” I clarified. “That, n yer habit eh ye bitin folks’ legs aff.”

“Mmm, I see. How much are ye lookin fur?”

I swallyed nervously n crossed ma fingers tightly behind ma back.

"A five-figure sum?"

"How aboot £100 n 72 pence?"

I wis aboot tae reject this ooty hand, but remembered that the seventy-two pence wid actually help, bein part eh parsimonious Pear-Tree's added expenses.

"Well..."

"There's interest of course," said Slasher suddenly, giein me that evil seemingly one-eyed stare again.

I shuddered inwardly.

"Aye, I imagine there wid be. It's a fascinatin service ye provide efter aw," I went on, tryin tae soft-soap the radge.

"I dinnae mean *that* kind eh interest, ya auld goat!" he roared. "I mean that fur every quid I lend ye, I'll be wantin *two* in return. *Capiche?*"

"Whit a loady capiche!" I snapped in reply, as the glarin flaw in the moneylendin racket abruptly became aw tae clear. "Loan-shark ma erse! Ye're mair like one eh thae Pathetic Sharks that used tae be in that VIZ comic. Away n pish on yer boots, ya weak-bladdered wank-piece!"

So that wis *him* telt, but I wis still nae nearer tae solvin the problem.

Wanderin doon Leith Walk a short while later, I wis deep in thought, realisin that I now maist likely hud a price on ma heid. Shouldnae have spoken tae Slasher like that I suppose. But then I *awready* hud a price on ma heid effectively, through that penny-pinchin prick Pear-Tree! Whit wis a gadgie tae dae?

Aw eh a sudden, a couple eh guys wearin stocking-masks came harin doon the pavement, wi the sound eh sirens n heavy clump eh Leith Police tackety boots no far behind. Fur unbeknownst tae yours truly, the bank on Great Junction Street hud jist been robbed. I couldnae help noticin that the bandits were bein severely impeded by the apparently heavy bags they hud slung ower their shuders. As a result, Leith's finest were gainin fast. Mutterin curses, they reluctantly discarded their loads, instantly pickin up the pace as they raced past me. The polis steamed on by, oblivious tae this, as they were that intent on the pursuit. *"Nee-naw, nee-naw,"* went the panda car back-up, also tearin on by, headin up the Walk. I stood there frozen tae the spot fur a moment, as the cops n robbers disappeared ower the horizon. Then, *very* slowly n *very* surreptitiously, I edged ever closer tae the bags.

Back hame, I dragged them baith intae the livin-room w a considerable effort n then collapsed exhausted on the flair. Nae wonder the masked marauders hud tae drop them, they weighed a ton! But efter gettin ma breath back, I started tae empty oot the contents, n a 'ton' didnae even come close, in terms eh either weight or monetary value! When I finally finished coontin, I discovered there hud been £17,000 in banknotes n coins in each, which gied me a grand total eh...eh...eh...aye, exactly thirty-four grand!

Naturally, I didnae want tae leave a sum like that unattended, so I decided tae stay put, even when Moany Tony dropped by, tryin tae cajole me along tae The Cenny.

"No the day," I said firmly. "But ye're welcome tae have a wee snifter here. In fact, mair than a wee yin!"

Aw ma previous antagonism taewards the moanin auld get

evaporated n I became consumed wi the blithe spirit eh generosity.

"Here – take this," I offered, bungin him a hundred sobs straight aff the tap.

"Go doon tae the offy n get loaded up – we're gonnae party like it's 1902!"

When I awoke some oors later wi a thumpin heid, Moany wis comatose in the armchair opposite, also lookin deid tae the world. The whole flair wis littered wi empty boatils n cans, Christ, we'd pushed the boat oot n nae mistake! I couldnae even mind crashin oot. Still, I wis rollin in the loot n there wis enough tae pay Pear-Tree aff in full, which I fully intended tae dae – unless I changed ma mind, of course. I goat tae ma feet wi some difficulty, as another jolt eh blindin pain zapped through ma napper. I winced n glanced again at ma drinkin buddy, whae tae ma surprise appeared tae be awake efter aw. But he wis still slumped there, starin vacantly intae space. I hud an awfy feelin he wis aboot tae start sighin at any moment.

"Awright, Tones? Looks like ye've lost a fiver n found a farthing!"

Sure enough, a terrible hert-wrenchin gasp eh woe issued forth fae his shakin frame. He coughed nervously.

"Gibby – er, jist tae let ye ken, I actually went back oot fur a wee while, efter youse fell asleep."

"Where tae – The Cenny?"

"Eh...no quite...ye see, when I went tae buy the cairry-oot, I noticed in the bookies that they hud an awfy temptin price on a scoreless draw in the Dundee – Sellik gemme. So I thought there wid be nae herm in havin a wee flutter, like."

"Uh-huh?" I said, only hauf-listenin.

I wis lookin around the room, wi a vague uneasy feelin that somethin wis missin... He gied that irritatin nervous cough again.

"Aye, cos I started thinkin how about *a hundred n fifty grand* or thereaboots wid be even better, than whit ye awready hud. So, I...er...came back here tae borrow...only *borrow*, mind..."

A ghastly otherworldly sense eh foreboding n ootright terror suddenly jack-knifed through me. I felt faint n ma legs turned tae jelly. However, I still managed tae leap across the room n grab him by the throat.

"THE MONEY! THE FUCKIN MONEY! WHAT THE FUCK HAVE YE DONE? TELL ME THE MONEY'S SAFE, FUR FUCK'S SAKE!"

"It's...it's...safe as hooses," croaked Moany hoarsely, probably as a result eh bein slowly strangled. "Safe as William Hill's hooses anyway..."

I fell back on the cairpit, physically n emotionally drained.

"As I wis sayin," he went on, "the draw looked like a guid deal. Eh...did youse hear the result?"

"How could I hear the result – I've been fast asleep!" I pointed oot.

"Right. Well, the guid news is this – it wis a nae-score draw efter ninety minutes."

A wild hope surged unbidden intae ma rapidly beatin hert.

"OK. So that means..."

"It wis even 0-0 efter five minutes eh time added on," he gasped, starin at me imploringly.

A wave eh happiness n relief flooded through me.

"So it finished 0-0?"

That cough again.

"Er...no exactly. Cos Sellik scored a winner in the 96th minute."

I felt as if I wis bein slowly sucked intae the remorseless embrace eh a black hole in the infinite darkness eh ooter space.

"Uh-huh. So how much did ye actually bet?"

"The whole lot."

"The whole..."

"Aye, 34 grand on the draw."

There wis a silence, one jist tae deep n painful fur words.

"But," said Moany eventually, while clearin his throat carefully, "there wis *some* guid news..."

"Oh aye?"

"Aye – I found this change that someone hud dropped, in the gutter outside the shop."

He opened his palm n afore I'd even coonted it, I kent *exactly* how much wid be there. Aw seventy-two poxy pence eh it. Jesus Christ Awmighty...looked like Pear-Tree wis gonnae be waitin a wee while longer efter aw.

SKYFALL

Fae one horror-show tae another – on tap eh the ghastly debacle eh havin n then losin £34,000 in a matter eh oors, a former Hibee n a current yin (McGinn n McNuthouse) played their part in Scotland's catastrophic capitulation in Kazakhstan, wi the visitors gaun doon 3-0. However, ma viewin eh the maist terrible thing I'd seen on telly since I last caught a bit eh 'Loose Wimmin' by mistake, wis brought tae an abrupt end.

But even afore that, ma concentration wis rudely interrupted by the bloody phone ringin. Aye, I'd finally bitten the bullet n hud it reconnected, jist in case any mair lucrative TV deals were floated ma way. Cos let's face it, I needed the dough mair than ever noo.

"Mr Gibson?" says this smarmy-soundin English get on the other end.

"Maybe ayes, maybe naw," I replied cautiously. "Depends whae's askin. If ye're the polis, Europol, Interpol, Inter Milan, the Inland Revenue or a legal representative eh Rod Pear-Tree or Slasher Smith, the answer is a definite, resoundin, unequivocal 'naw'."

A nervous chuckle came doon the line.

"No, I represent none of the aforementioned, Mr Gibson. I am a producer of Channel 5's 'Nightmare Neighbour Next Door' and was telephoning to enquire whether or not you would be interested in taking part in our new series?"

"Tae bloody right I wid!" I yelped, once the initial surprise hud worn aff. "I'm yer man fur that! Cos I've plenty tae get aff ma chest regardin the neebs, startin wi her next door. Ayewis spreadin malicious rumours aboot me daein away wi ma previous wives, the bammy auld bat! Wee humfy-backit hoor-bag, so she is. N the other night I wis disturbed by rattlin at ma letter-box. So I went tae the door tae find that Junky Johnston fae upstairs n he wis bloody rattlin awright! Run ooty gear n gaun through that Cauld Chicken, wi withdrawal symptoms, ye ken. N that Senga McGlumphar, ayewis bringin men back, mornin, noon n night. I ken it's her job, but whae says she's got tae keep takin her work hame wi her? A never-endin procession eh punters, traipsin up n doon the stairs at aw times, n leavin used condoms on ma doormat. Then I've goat tae go tae the bother eh rinsin them oot, afore usin them again. Waste not, want not, ye ken. It's no right though. N see him in Flat 4 wi thae exotic pets! Should be in a fuckin zoo, no a hoose. Aye, the animals as well! That pink elephant goat loose again last week n somehow found its way intae ma bedroom – frightened the shite ooty me when I woke up efter a four-day drinkin sesh! Oh aye, I've goat plenty eh dirt tae dish on thae bastirts, I can tell ye!"

There wis an extremely long silence at the other end, in fact it wis that bloody lengthy I began tae wonder if the marble-moothed midden hud fawin asleep. Well it turned oot that he hudnae done that, but his voice did sound awfy faint when he finally responded, in an irritatin hesitant sorty manner.

"Ah yes, quite. I see...uh-huh. Yes, that's all very interesting, Mr Gibson – but I am afraid that perhaps I did not make myself entirely clear. Because, yes, we *do* want you to participate, but, er, what I mean to say is...uh..."

I wis beginnin tae lose patience wi this stutterin radge.

"Well, spit it oot, man, fur Chrissake!" I yelled. "I havenae goat aw day, ye ken."

There wis another ominous silence, afore he spoke again.

"Well, you see, Mr Gibson, the situation is like this. The programme has *already* been contacted by a large number of residents of Cables Wynd House concerning your own behaviour, so..."

I began tae experience a sinkin feelin, aw the way doon tae the tips eh ma taes.

"Aye, so...?"

"So, Mr Gibson, we want your input, because – according to your fellow citizens at least – it's *you* who is the Nightmare Neighbour Next Door!"

The receiver fell fae ma nerveless hand n hit the deck. If the radge wis still speakin, I certainly couldnae hear him. A white-hot rage swept through me like a firestorm. The bastirts, the cheeky *bastirts...*

Then, afore I hud time tae pick it up n tell him tae go fuck himsel, there wis the sound eh some cunt rattlin ma letter-box again! I ripped the door open wi such force it almost came aff its hinges, ready tae 'smack' Junky Johnston intae the middle eh next week while kickin his needle-punctured erse fae the Banana Flats tae the Bar Brig n back again...but it wisnae him.

"Mr Gibson?" said this officious-lookin gadgie in a suit.

"Maybe ayes, maybe naw," I snapped. "Depends whae's askin. If ye're the polis..."

"Save it, grandpa," says this other cheeky bastirt wi him, flashin some sort eh official caird in ma coupon. "We're from Sky TV. Which, I can see from here, you are now watching. Oooh, cracking goal from Kazakhstan there. Anyway, although you are viewing our admittedly ridiculously over-priced product, our records show that you have certainly not accessed it through legitimate means."

Holy piss-flaps, the bastirts were tryin tae pit the bite on me! Efter aw that hud happened recently...

"Look, I've nae money, right! Moany Tony poured 34 grand eh mine doon the tubes on a daft bet, although tae be honest it wisnae strictly speakin actually mine, it wis the proceeds eh a bank robbery, but ye cannae say they didnae deserve it, bunch eh robbin bandits theirsels, I mean look at that cunt Fred Goodwin, nae wonder they took his knighthood aff him, but anyway this wis jist efter I'd tried tae tap up Slasher Smith, ken him wi the dodgy bladder, but I telt that owl-obsessed ersehole tae go n fuck himsel tae, which is jist whit I'm aboot tae tell youse pair eh comedians an aw, comin roond here intimidatin God-fearin folk in the sanctuary eh their ain hames! So whit have ye goat tae say tae *that,* eh?"

"Can't pay – we'll take it away," they replied in unison, afore rudely pushin past yours truly, unplugging ma telly n cartin it aff intae the sunset.

So how the fuck am I gonnae see the next gemme noo? Oh, show me the way tae San Marino / I'll maybe watch it doon The Torino...

TIRADE TAE TOM

Dear Sir Tam (or may I caw ye Tommy?),

Yer famous advertisin jingle used tae boast that - n I quote - 'Ye can't get better than a Kwik-Fit fitter.' Is that right? Well, accordin tae ma doaktir, I'm rapidly heidin fur a *quick fit* eh ma ain, unless someone does somethin aboot that stadium catering. Cos ye can't get batter in a deep-fat fryer, I'll tell ye that. N I'm also gonnae tell ye a wee personal story set tae music, tae illustrate ma point. When I wis five ma daddy took me doon tae Easter Road / Tae a place which looked jist like a bombsite bunker / I know now that it wis in fact that boozer cawed The Clan / He left me in the rain whilst he goat drunker / Pints n nips n bags eh chips I go Hibee Hibernian / Hibee Hibernian… See the operative phrase there, Farmer? Aye - *bags eh chips*. I'm no even that fussed aboot the bag either, the standard stadium box'll dae jist fine. One eh thae wee plastic forks n aw. Get it sorted, man, fur Chrissake, it's no rocket science! I've awready written tae Pear-Tree n Damp-Squib aboot this important matter n goat naewhere. Dinnae make me come doon there!

I remain your bumbling n disobedient servant,

'Grumpy' Gibson

FUSILLADE FAE FARMER

Dear Mr Gibson (or may I call you an ambulance? It would be a pleasure, believe me),

No, on absolutely no account may you refer to me as 'Tommy'. Do you really imagine that I went to the trouble of going to Buckingham Palace to be knighted by the Queen, only for peasant-class Leith commoners to impudently call me by a bastardisation of my Christian name? It won't wash, sir, and from what I hear through the grapevine, neither will you! As to your incomprehensible missive concerning deep fat fryers, child cruelty, irresponsible fathers, a long-ago closed down pub in Albert Street and chips, I find myself lost for words. Which is fortunate, because I am certainly not going to waste any more of them, replying to the likes of you. Except to say this – if I, Mr Petrie or Ms Dempster receive any more of your unwanted, unsolicited, unstamped, ridiculous green ink communications, you'll be getting a quick fit up the arse, courtesy of my highly-polished cherry-red size 10 Dr Martens.

Yours unfaithfully,

Sir Thomas Farmer

WHITNEY HOUSTON

So there I wis, waitin in the Arrivals Lounge at Leith International Airport, tae greet the local Tartan Army fit-soldiers returnin fae the battlefields eh San Marino. N 'greet' wis the appropriate word, as aboot hauf eh them were still cryin their eyes oot in despair. Nae bloody wonder either! Another utterly shite effort fae Scotland, albeit one in which they managed – *jist* – tae scrape a win against the lowest ranked 'country' on Planet Earth in fitba terms. If San Marino are 211th, that must pit us somewhere aroond 210th, I reckon.

Mind ye, McLeish hinted that the fans were at least partly tae blame, as the sound eh mass booing apparently made his players 'nervous'. Maybe that wis why the 'lone Hibee tae the rescue' strategy failed tae pay aff, as McNutcracker fluffed the sorty heider fae six yards oot he wid pit away nae bother at Easter Road wi his eyes shut. Anyway, never mind his nerves, mine were shot tae pieces long afore that, as on a couple eh occasions the hame team might even have actually scored – which at that stage wid have brought them level at 1-1.

It can surely be nae coincidence that 'San Marino' is an anagram eh 'Iran moans', which were heard across the nation back in '78 when the Persians hud the Scots on the cairpit at the World Cup. Aye, another result which lives on in infamy – along wi the six goal humpin by Holland, the fuck-up against the Faroes n gettin pumped by Peru. So now McLeish can stand tall alongside the likes eh Bertie Vogts (although even I wid tower above that Kraut short-erse) in presidin ower pathetic performances, although he hasn't (yet) hud tae face the boo-boys tae quite the extent a previous incumbent did.

Efter a tame capitulation at Wembley back in the day when the visitors used tae account fur two-thirds eh the crowd, the hapless gaffer claimed that he didn't hear the fans chantin his name throughoot. Which didnae say much fur his hearin, as aroond 70,000 Scots let rip wi 'IF YE HATE BOBBY BROWN CLAP YER HANDS'. Goat his come-uppance later on right enough, when he ended up married tae Whitney Houston. But what wisnae in doot then – n certainly isnae the noo – is that watchin the national team is jist a complete n utter loady Colin Nish! Ye can stick thae international breaks up yer erse – bring back the Hibees!

GOD MOVES IN MYSTERIOUS WAYS

There wis another aspect eh the so-cawed 'international break' which I wis mighty keen on avoidin – I heard through the grapevine that Slasher Smith hud threatened tae break every bone in ma body, in a country eh ma ain choosin. Big eh him, tae gie me a choice in the matter, wis it no? In fact, I'd been toyin wi the idea eh fleein tae another country anyway – one as far away fae him as it wis humanly possible tae git. But – like the fabled Mountie – it wis said that Slasher ayewis goat his man. Then the next totally unexpected n contrary thing the rumour-mill threw up wis this – aw wis forgiven apparently, cos Slasher hud undergone some sort eh religious awakenin n hud found God! Well, I wisnae buyin *that* yin, no jist yet anyway. Sounded mair like a devilish scheme dreamt up by that big demonic daftie, tae lull me intae a false sense eh security.

However, I wis careless enough tae wander intae The Cenny wi'oot checkin that the coast wis clear n next thing I kent, there he wis – right in front eh me! Ma first instinct wis tae effect the 'joiner's escape' – aye, make a bolt fur the door. Problem wis, he wis standin right in front eh it. Resigned tae ma fate, I wis aboot tae start babblin apologies fur ma recent rash words, when I clocked the unnaturally beatific expression on his coupon n whit appeared tae be a halo hoverin ower his heid. Surely jist a trick eh the light...?

"Peace be upon ye, Gibby," he intoned, throwin his airms open wide like the statue eh the Big Man atop yon hillside above Rio de Janeiro. "I wish ye nae ill-will. Have ye heard aboot ma conversion?"

"Whit – have ye taken up playin rugby, Slasher?"

"No *that* sort eh conversion, ye radge! I'm full eh the Holy Spirit!"

Aha, so *that's* it – he's full eh spirits awright! Whisky n voddy, jist fur starters. But I hud tae admit he seemed a different gadgie n on the plus side, he hudnae plucked ma eyes oot – yet. Instead, he indicated a handy table n politely invited me tae take a seat.

"Let me tell ye aboot it. I wis on ma way hame fae The Hebrides..."

"I dinnae ken ye'd been tae the Western Isles," I interrupted, in genuine surprise.

Never imagined that Slasher wis exactly the rural type, partly cos the public lavvies were so few n far between.

"I'm talkin aboot the pub in Market Street, no the bloody chain eh islands, ye auld goat!" he retorted, revertin tae type fur a moment.

But then he seemed tae relax n the calm expression wis restored tae his countenance, as he carried on.

"Of course I wis well-pished as per usual, n wis beginnin tae think I'd taken a wrong turnin in life. So I wis ploddin along wi ma heid doon, when aw eh a sudden I felt as if I wis bein sucked intae a long, never-endin tunnel. Aw wis dark n I wis devoid eh hope, eh ever findin ma righteous path. Then, jist at the blackest point, I wis suddenly engulfed by a great white light, which seemed tae be travellin taewards me at a supernatural speed. Hallelujah, I wis blind, but now I see!"

Christ, this wisnae bad stuff fae auld Slasher! I wis fair poised on the edge eh ma seat n couldnae wait tae hear whit happened next. But I hud nae choice, cos he'd gone fur another pish.

When he came back, I lost nae time in proddin him intae continuin his tale – or wis it some sort eh *parable*? I'd never hud much time fur that pie-in-the-sky religious shite masel, but there wis nae doot that this sounded like the real deal. Ye read aboot folk in hospitals whae thought they were peggin oot n then hud similar experiences. I started tae uneasily ponder on ma ain life as an unreconstructed sinner n wonder if redemption wis still possible...

"Aye – so whit happened next, Slasher?"

He went quiet fur a moment, afore turnin tae face me. His eyes blazed in Holy Passion – which wis a bit disconcertin, cos ye'd swear it wis jist one solitary peeper giein ye the eyebaw, so tae speak.

"N then I saw him, Gibby! Indeed, I *found* Him!"

"Whae – God?"

"Aye – it wis Pat Stanton himsel!"

Several conflictin thoughts churned through ma brain at this juncture, the principal amongst them bein that the psychotic bampot hud totally flipped his lid – but again, on the plus side, he still hudnae seen fit tae inflict Grievous Bodily Herm on ma guid self. But I hud tae tread carefully here, so as no tae upset him. Humour the bastirt at aw costs...

"So where dae ye reckon ye were – Heaven?"

"Naw – I wis on Platform 21 at Waverley Station."

"Whit!?"

"Aye – I'd been that ratarsed I'd taken a wrong turnin efter cuttin across the concourse n actually walked straight intae a tunnel. Jist kept stumblin on, on automatic pilot ye ken, but I didnae really ken *where* I wis."

"But... but... how aboot bein engulfed by the great white light?"

"Well that wis the last train fae London Kings Cross hurtlin taewards me at a hunner mile an oor! If I hudnae hud the presence eh mind tae press masel right up against the waw, I'd have been kilt outright! So when it hud passed I began tae sober up a bit wi the shock n realised how precious life wis, efter aw. I carried on walkin oot the other side n that's when I saw Him."

"Pat Stanton? God??"

"One n the same. Simply waitin on the platform fur his connection, jist like a mortal human being! I tell ye, Gibby – it wis a miracle!"

Fuckin miracle ye huvnae kicked ma heid in yet, I thought, keepin well schtum.

"Whit dae ye think aboot that then?" he persisted.

Honesty *almost* goat the better eh me, n it wis on the tip eh ma tongue tae say 'pish!" but it wis tae late – he'd awready gone fur another yin.

I tottered ooty The Cenny n heided fur the chippy. If he wis dyin fur a pish, I wis dyin fur a fish (wi chips, naturally.) Mind ye, it wis gettin late, but wi a bit eh luck I thought I might jist catch the last supper.

HAME SUITE HAME

I woke up wi a terrible sense eh depression, despair gnawin at the very fabric eh ma soul. Wis it the onset eh a mid-life crisis? No very fuckin likely, no at ma age. Perhaps it wis mair eh an existential crisis, then? Moved as I'd been by Slasher's religious conversion, I'd singularly failed tae experience the same, much as I'd willed it tae happen. He found God / Pat Stanton in Waverley Station, while the nearest I goat wis spottin Sam Stanton in the Waverley Bar. Hardly the equivalent.

Of course, the neeborhood situation wisnae helpin ma fragile mental state either. Gaun doonhill rapidly, ye ken. Quite literally – subsidence hud set in n I wis gettin nearer the docks by the minute. N see thae fuckin neebors... Ever since they'd dropped me in it via that trashy telly show I found masel hatin them even mair than usual. N that Junky Johnston hud started accumulatin pets an aw, although hardly eh the 'exotic' variety. Ye'll never guess whit the cunt hud started collectin. Bluebottles, that's whit! Aye, I'm no kiddin, thoosands eh the buzzin bastirts! His windaes were that black wi them, ye could hardly see in at aw. N he must be feedin them rotten meat or somethin, judgin by the awfy stench comin fae his flat. There's some sorty weird foul-smellin fluid drippin through ma ceiling tae. Only savin grace is I've no actually seen him in the flesh fur ages, must be sleepin aff his latest cocktail eh smack n Special Brew.

Ma ain hoose wis fawin tae bits an aw. Couldnae afford the repairs, like. One eh thae days that dodgy auld boiler's will go tae. But enough said aboot Senga, I even hud some radge fae the Cooncil on the blower, makin me wish even mair that I'd never hud it reconnected.

"Mr Gibson! You haven't paid for your Council Tax!" he says.

"Listen, Ersehole, never mind the Cooncil Tax, I huvnae even paid fur the fuckin cairpit tacks," I snapped. "N I've nae intention eh daein so either. Aboot time ye installed that laminate floorin anyway. Then I could slide intae Leith Docks even faster than I'm gaun at present."

In fact, I'd been thinkin aboot sellin up fur a while n gettin it tight fae some jumped-up Jimmy Jobsworth hud finally made ma mind up. Of course, it wisnae really mine tae sell, but thae Embra Cooncil bastirts have nae business tryin tae run their big city extortion rackets in the PIROL (Peoples' Independent Republic eh Leith), so ye cannae say that they dinnae deserve it, havin their hooses impounded.

But whit *really* did it wis gettin another lippy letter fae that Dumpster wumman at Easter Road. I almost choked in rage at this blatant attempt at floggin me a new season ticket, when they hudnae even hud the decency tae return ma last yin. N Pear-Tree wis still wantin his pound eh flesh – or thirty-four thoosand pounds eh flesh, tae be precise! So I read through aw the rest eh the blurb, boastin aboot whit they were daein wi oor hard-earned money, but I wis glad that I did *persevere* until the end. Cos the very last line seemed tae offer me a way ooty ma current problems...

So a day later I hud aw ma meagre possessions packed intae boxes, n wis waitin impatiently fur the removals van tae arrive. I'd decided tae strike whilst the iron wis hot, make a move right away n thereby dodge numerous other creditors, n then flog the hoose once I wis safely domiciled elsewhere. At last the gadgies showed up n although they werenae tae happy aboot ma innovative deferred payment plan, they reluctantly trucked me n aw ma worldly goods up Easter Road, along Albion Road n roond tae the stadium's main entrance. We then sat there in stony silence until Dumpster pilled up in her Merc as I kent she wid – I hudnae been stalkin her fur weeks fur nowt, efter aw. I then gied the order fur the removals boys tae unload ma gear n stack it in front eh the main doors.

"What is the meaning of this?" demanded Dumpster, alightin fae the motor n lookin none tae chuffed at comin across yours truly once again.

"Haud yer wheesht, wumman, I'm movin in, lock, stock n two smokin David Farrells," I telt her straight. "Ye shouldnae have made the offer if ye didnae mean tae stick tae yer word. Now – are ye gonnae hand ower the keys, or will I have tae take them by force?"

Her face wis a frozen mask eh pure bewilderment.

"What on earth are you talking about? *What* offer?" she spluttered.

I almost felt sorry fur her fur a moment, but the feelin soon passed.

"Look, I'm no askin fur a lot," I explained reasonably, moderatin ma tone. "One eh thae Executive hozzy suites will dae fine. Once I get ma furniture sorted n ye make sure the beer-taps stay on n the gantry's well-stocked, I'll get settled in. Then I'll no get in yer road efter that."

"Before I call the police, I'll give you *one* last chance to explain yourself," she replied.

Triumphantly, I pilled oot the formulaic missive she'd jist sent me n waved it under her hooter.

"Read that!" I said, jabbin ma finger at the last line.

As she fumbled fur her glesses, I could see the removals boys were takin a great interest in the proceedings.

"Read it *aloud*," I ordered, fur the benefit eh ma audience.

She shot me a look of loathing, but somewhit surpisingly complied, once she'd found her place.

"Hibernian is your team," she began, frownin ower the small print. "Easter Road is where we belong. There's a home for you here."

"See?!" I yelled gleefully. "The last sentence is the maist relevant, I think ye'll agree. The last sentence *afore your ain signature*, aye? Whit does it say again? *'There's a home for you here.'* There it is in black n white! I rest ma case." (Well I hud tae, it wis gettin awfy heavy. Aw thae charity boatils, ken.)

"But... but... that is not what it means *literally*," she gabbled. "You really cannot possibly expect..."

Well, I'd heard enough.

"Break doon the doors, boys," I commanded. "Then get aw ma goods n chattels inside. I'll claim squatters' rights fur the time being, if I have tae!"

I sneaked a sidelong glance at the so-cawed Chief Executive, but she wis awready dialling 999...

When I regained consciousness some oors later, I clasped ma hands tae the sides eh ma throbbin heid n tried desperately tae remember whit hud jist happened. I also wondered where the fuck I wis *now*, fur it certainly didnae look much like one eh the tap luxury Executive Hospitality suites at Easter Road Stadium. Then in a flash eh clarity, I minded rollin aboot the club car-park, tryin tae wrestle the keys aff Dumpster, efter thae removals wimps refused tae break n enter on ma behalf. Then I recawed the polis pitchin up mob-handed n one eh them raisin his truncheon high above his heid, afore aimin in squarely at *ma* heid... Then everythin went black.

I wis then jolted ooty ma painful recall by the sound eh the turn-key rattlin his chain at the cell-door. *Aw naw!* Surely that didnae mean that – *yet again* – I wis banged up at... I glared at the grinnin galoot expectantly as he carefully placed a cup eh pish-weak tea n a slice eh stale breid crawlin wi maggots doon beside me.

"Leith is your team. St. Leonard's is where you belong. There's a home for you here," he said, afore retreatin swiftly n slammin the door shut behind him.

Bastirts! Hame sweet hame, ma erse!

WATCHING SLIVVY – OWER IN LIVI

I wis released fae ma second hame (St. Leonard's that is, no Easter Road Stadium, mair's the pity) in time fur the Livingston – Hibs gemme n it wisnae long afore I wis wishin they'd jist kept me behind bars. See that bloody first hauf! Maist eh it wis like watchin Scotland v San Marino, which is low praise indeed. Mallan almost scored right at the start n that wis aboot it fur the first forty-five. The pitch wis a ringer fur San Marino's n aw – possibly even worse. How can ye play guid fitba on that? Answer – ye canny. Jist git that red ash doon by the shovelful instead eh yon drastic plastic n that'll soon sort the men oot fae the boys. No that Livi – or, tae gie them their correct name, Meadowbank Thistle – hud any notion eh playin guid fitba in the first place, bunch eh dirty bastirts that they are. Efter a while it wisnae so much like watchin the national team as endurin a typical Embra derby, which is tae damn it wi even fainter praise. Didnae help matters that referee Walsh hud apparently left his cairds behind in the dressing-room. Bottlin bastirt let them get away wi murder! N I should ken, as – *allegedly* – I've goat away wi murder masel. Twice. No that it's true, mind. Fake news...

So thank Pat Stanton fur small mercies, as Paul Hanlon strode tae the rescue wi twenty minutes left, much like he'd done in that 2-0 doon tae the Hertz in the cup jist ower three years ago. WHUMPH went his shot through a mass eh bodies, intae the back eh the net. Mallan soon doubled that wi a peach eh a solo effort n then, as usual, jist when ye thought ye could relax a bit, they only go n concede a bloody penalty! I hud the jitters that badly they soon turned intae the shitters, when Livi undeservedly clawed yin back. But the Hibees held oot fur a nail-bitin time-added-on victory, which hud the bonus eh seein us jump above the jim-jams in the league table.

Aye, I wis that pleased I even said tae Moany Tony "Macaroni!" afore treatin him tae a pie wi that fillin afore we left the Arena, whereas no that long ago I'd have happily served him up as a meal tae the Livi lions. Bastirt still owed me thirty-four grand, mind! I hudnae forgotten aboot that...

The only thing tae pit a dampener on the night wis when I goat back tae Leith only tae discover that that Dumpster wumman hud gone n changed the locks on the stadium doors! Then I found the Restraining Order in ma inside pocket, prohibitin me fae gaun within three hunner yards eh her, Pear-Tree or Sir Tommy Farmer. Aye, turned oot I hud forgotten aboot *that,* plus the fact that – contrary tae her false promises in that letter – there wisnae a hame there fur me efter aw. So half-an-oor later I wis back at the Banana Flats wi the bluebottles, pink elephants, used condoms n Senga's sex-addict clients. Life, eh – whit a loadypish!

THE NEEDLE N THE DAMAGE DONE

Of course, anythin involvin Livi ayewis brings back terrible memories eh that nightmare League Cup Final against them back in 2004. Hibs successfully repeated the feat they'd managed in 1985, by beatin baith halves eh the Auld Firm en route tae Hampden, only tae make a total erse eh it when they actually goat there. Ex-Hibs Grate Ally 'Benny' Brazil then rubbed their noses in it even further, by drivin the winnin Livi team's bus back tae the West Lothian metropolis, tae a deafenin roar eh appreciation fae one man n his dug whae were linin the streets. It wis the maist spectacular triumphalist parade that part eh the world hud witnessed, since the last time the Orange Order marched through Broxburn, on a wet Wednesday efternin in November.

Ah...Benny...internationalist by name, internationalist by nature... Stop sniggerin ya bastirts, he goat an Under-21 cap against Wales in 1978, dinnae forget! Never goat another yin, right enough. Nae point – he couldnae actually wear it, whit wi that ridiculous frizzy permed mop atop his napper, which gied the impression that some practical joker hud jist plugged him intae the mains fur a laugh. Still, one eh ma aw-time favourite Hibees though, despite bein voted 'Worst Hibs Player of The Decade' by the cruel n callous readership eh 'Hibs Monthly' fanzine.

So I decided tae pay ma ain tribute tae him, n get his handsome visage tattooed on ma chest. Now, I'm nae coward as ye aw ken, havin bravely fought ma way across Europe wi the Imperial Japanese Army durin the American Civil War, but I must admit tae a wee bit eh apprehension as the tattooist goat tae work wi the needle. The horrible buzzin sound pit me in mind eh bein trapped in Junky Johnston's mingin flat wi his swarms eh bluebottles n I almost jumped through the roof when I felt it prick ma lilywhite skin. Still, it wid be worth it in the end I thought, imaginin aw the admiring looks fae dolly burdz as I strode bare-chested along Portybelly beach in the summer. But as I wis lyin there face doon on ma back, I must have actually blacked oot wi the pain. Which wis a relief in a way, cos when I came tae, the artist hud me aw wrapped up in the clingfilm n dressing n ready fur the aff.

I quickly hurried doon the road tae The Cenny n cajoled Humpty Harry intae accompanyin me intae the lavvy.

"Whit fur?" he said suspiciously.

"I've goat something tae show ye!" I replied, wi an air eh suppressed excitement.

"Ye're no on some kind eh sick George Michael trip are ye, Gibby?" he went on, even mair suspiciously.

"Naw, ya radge, I want yer opinion on a priceless piece eh artwork!"

So we splashed oor way intae the Gents, which wis bein flooded oot by Slasher letting it aw hing oot at one eh the urinals, n I proceeded tae take aff ma grandad shirt n string vest. I gied oot an involuntary yowl eh pain as I then pilled aff the dressing, afore standin there wi ma chest puffed oot proudly.

"There! Whit dae ye make eh that?"

Efter a brief sort eh shellshocked pause, I wis rather disconcerted tae see Humpty Harry writhin aboot the pishy flair in paroxysms eh uncontrollable laughter. Finally he stood back up n wiped a tear eh mirth fae the corner eh his eye.

"Eh...I take it ye've no actually seen yer so-cawed priceless piece eh artwork yersel yet, Gibby?"

A ripple eh anxiety flickered across ma stinging chest at that point.

"Well, naw. Cos I...er...hud a wee kip tae pass the time whilst the artist wis daein the biz, ken, n when I came roond, he'd awready wrapped me up. Eh...is it no a guid likeness eh Benny, then?"

"Oh aye, it's spot on, nae worries on that score. Spittin image eh him n nae mistake! Certainly couldnae be taken fur anyone else. Have a look in the mirror."

Somewhit reluctantly, I turned tae face the gless n ma eyes almost popped ooty ma heid. Efter aw, I'd clearly telt the gadgie wi the needle I was wantin a depiction eh Benny Brazil. So whit I'd actually goat wis the ootline eh the map eh Sooth America's biggest country, wi a undeniably brilliant likeness eh that daft, dim-witted, bobble-hat wearin bampot Benny, fae yon crappy auld telly soap-opera 'Crossroads', set slapbang in the middle eh it! I mean, how the *fuck*... It wis the worst artistic faux-pas I'd made since gaun fur a portrait eh Hibs' tap scorer fur 1980-81 – but instead eh Ally Macleod the *player*, I'd wound up wi Ally Macleod the fuckin walkin disaster eh a Scotland *manager*, even worse than McLeish!

"Jesus Christ!" I groaned.

"Yes, ma son?" said Slasher, turnin roond suddenly n pishin aw ower ma brogues. "Thou shalt not take the Lord's name in vain – but whit's wrong wi ye anyway?"

"I think I've goat the blues," I whimpered pathetically.

He inspected ma artwork in critical silence.

"Nae wonder. That's quite appropriate, Gibby, because ye actually remind me eh the legendary Bluesman, Robert Johnson. Dae ye ken why?"

"Naw – why?"

"Because like you he wis a sinner, whae infamously sold his soul tae the Devil, doon at the Crossroads."

I tottered aff intae the godforsaken night, ma feelings tae deep fur words. Maybe if I goat Carol Vorderman's coupon inked ower it, it widnae look so bad...

TIME WAITS FUR NAE MAN

The followin mornin, I goat the fright eh ma life when I caught sight eh ma reflection in the bathroom mirror. Fur an awfy doom-struck moment I thought that that cunt Benny fae 'Crossroads' wis actually tryin tae burst ooty ma insides, like yon alien thing explodin ooty John Hurt's chest in that scary movie aboot aliens which fuckin well alienated me fae gaun tae the pictures fur a while. Canny mind whit it wis cawed again though... But then I remembered gettin needled, in an even mair severe manner than usual. It wisnae long afore I wis gettin even *mair* needled tae, as I went doon tae the boozer tae watch the Auld Firm kick lumps ooty each-other live on the box. Nae choice, ken, ever since thae Sky TV bastirts nicked ma ain telly. But I'd somehow missed the first oor eh the match. Then I noticed that aw the pub clocks were wrong an aw! Fur the love eh Christ, can naebody get nowt right thae days? I wis that confused I tried diallin up the speakin clock – but it widnae speak tae me. Apparently it doesnae accept reverse-charge calls. Then I went tae pit a bet on a hoarse, but the race wis ower n done wi, by the time I goat tae the bookies. Needless tae say, the yin I wis gonnae back came in at 100/1. Wis I gaun *mad??*

"Have ye remembered tae pit yer clock forward, Gibby?" grimaced Girnin Gertie, when I explained ma current predicament.

"Pit it forward fur whit? 'The Antiques Road Show'?"

"Naw, ya auld bamstick! Pit it forward by an oor. 'The Times They Are A-Changin',' as Bob Dylan said."

"He also said, 'The sun's not yelly, it's chicken'," I pointed oot. "Must've been on that wacky baccy. Or maybe he meant 'huns'..."

"Whitever. It's British Summer Time, Gibby," she sighed wearily. "So ye might as well get used tae it."

Well, that really goat ma dander up.

"I operate on *Leith* Summer Time only – n I'm no changin fur naebody," I yipped. "I blame Brexit masel. N never mind aboot Britain leavin the E.U., whit aboot Leith leavin Embra? A far mair important issue, I'll tell ye that n somethin I'd vote fur in a heartbeat! Democracy, ma erse! Never wanted tae be part eh that shitty city in the first place, wi its fur coats n nae knickers. I mind the Great Betrayal eh 1920..."

"Gibby – will ye kindly shut the fuck up? I've goat a sair heid anyway."

See barmaids thae days? Nae manners.

"Ye'll get a sair face in a minute, tae go wi it," I muttered under ma breath, afore stalkin aff, wi the sudden notion eh catchin a bus tae North Berwick. Get tae fuck away fae that auld boot n aw the other bams fur a while. But of course I'd missed it by an oor.

So I stumped aff hame tae watch Zitelli, afore mindin that I didnae have one any mair. See thae thievin Sky TV bastirts... I pit the wireless on, but aw the programmes were oot by an oor n I couldnae hear it properly anyway, ower the buzzin noise eh Junky Johnston's bluebottles. I swear tae God that smackheided simpleton's bloody well breedin them! Gettin mair eh them every day! N that smell's gettin worse... So I watched the microwave fur a while, but the timer on that wis oot by an oor as well. I paced up n doon the flair fur whit seemed like an eternity, bored ooty ma tiny mind, listenin tae the neebors screamin n shaggin n fightin (aw at the same time by the sound eh it.) Then, when I couldnae stand that any mair, I went doon tae The Spey fur a nightcap. But – aye, ye've guessed it – it hud shut its doors an oor earlier.

So I went back hame *again*, depressed, demoralised, defeated by life in general. Even Gibby kens when he's beaten at last. Whit wis it that Girnin Gertie wis sayin again? Oh aye, bring yer clock forward… I stretched oot a shaky hand tae dae jist that, but as soon as I brought it forward it fell aff the mantlepiece n smashed tae bits in the hearth. So if I'd been oot by an oor aw day, noo I hud the spooky sense that ma time hud run oot awtaegether. Cos I certainly couldnae afford tae buy another clock. I went tae bed n drifted aff intae a timeless sleep, dreamin aboot nickin yin ooty a charity shop first thing on Monday mornin. But of course I slept in, cos there wis nae bloody alarm tae wake me up! Bastirt…

WE SHALL NOT BE MOVED

Now, as ye aw ken if ye've goat this far, I'd been subjected tae a lot eh surprises so far throughoot 2019, almost aw eh them eh the unpleasant variety. So it wis wi some fear n trepidation that I opened the envelope lyin behind the door, wonderin jist whit on earth kind eh bad news that sadistic bastirt eh a postman hud brought wi him this time. But fur once I wis astonished tae receive whit appeared tae be a *nice* surprise, in the form eh a letter fae Hibernian Fitba Club. Initially, I wis suspectin another cunningly-worded inducement tae purchase a season ticket, but instead – tae ma relief n amazement – their legal representative wis informin me that ma debt eh nearly thirty-four grand hud been written aff! She described it as a gesture eh goodwill, while stressin that Pear-Tree wis still haudin oot fur his added-on seventy-two pence, the miserable tightwad. Well, I supposed I could live wi that, as the huge Christian Nade-like weight wis lifted aff ma shuders, regardin the main sum. Thank Christ fur that. Then, as I read on, it goat even better! Tae ma even greater amazement, a decision hud been taken, allowin me tae move intae one eh the Executive Suites efter aw, as Dumpster's original missive hud been ruled as 'legally binding' by the highest court in the land. I danced a jig eh joy aroond ma livin-room, occasionally coppin an eyeful eh whitever foul-smellin liquid wis still drippin through the ceilin fae the flat above. No that I could care less aboot that noo! It wis guidbye n guid riddance once n fur aw tae the bluebottles, bampots n oddly-coloured pachyderms gaun bump in the night. Easter Road Stadium – here I come – again!

So I goat on the blower tae the removals firm right away, but tae say there wis a chilly silence at the other end wid have been somethin eh an understatement. Pit it this way, when I removed the receiver fae the side eh ma heid, a large icicle hud formed on ma left lug.

"Mr Gibson," said the gadgie on the other end finally, in a voice so cauld I hud tae thaw it oot afore I could make oot whit he wis sayin, "this Company has already moved all your household items to Easter Road Stadium once, whereupon what can only be described as a major stramash then ensued. Not only were we compelled by Police Scotland to move everything back to Cables Wynd House again, but we are still awaiting payment for that job. So if you think we are going to go through all that *again*, then *you* can think again."

"Naw, ye dinnae understand, that wis aw jist a wee misunderstandin, I really *am* gaun this time!" I yelped. "Nae doot aboot it at aw."

Naturally, I wis still inwardly baulkin at the thought eh forkin ower the cash, but I supposed that noo I wis effectively thirty-four grand tae the guid, I could spare that much.

"Look, I'll pay youse up front this time, nae probs," I offered, in a mad gesture eh generosity.

There wis another lengthy frosty silence fae the other end.

"How about the money you *already* owe us, Mr Gibson? Will that be forthcoming as well, if I do agree to take this on – again?"

"Oh aye, consider it done."

"You've already done us once."

"Naw, naw, I havenae, honest, that wis aw the polis's fault! I wis concussed fur Christ's sake, there wis nae intention on ma part tae defraud youse. I'm guid fur it, I promise!"

Another icy silence fae Jumpin' Jack Frost doon the line. Wisnae shy aboot rackin up ma phone-bill wi his sulky nae-speakin act, I'll tell ye that.

"Well, against my better judgement, I will *reluctantly* agree to move you again – as long as two thousand pounds sterling *in hard cash* is lodged with our Head Office by early this afternoon. You will then be reimbursed an appropriate amount, *if* everything goes smoothly and there are no unforeseen problems."

"Like whit?"

"Like inducing my employees to indulge in breaking and entering and thus breaking the law, getting them involved in a mass altercation with police officers and subjecting them to the unseemly spectacle of a senile old coot fighting with the Chief Executive of Hibernian Football Club in the car park over a bunch of keys."

"OK, whitever ye say," I agreed, against *ma* better judgement nae doot, but I wis jist that keen tae get movin at last.

So a couple eh oors later, I wis feelin on tap eh the world, ma, jist like James Cagney in that movie 'Shite Heat'. Painful as it hud been, I'd handed ower the two grand in person plus the keys tae ma ain hoose, enablin the removal boys tae get ma gear shifted, whilst I went fur a well-deserved wee libation. By the time I came ooty The Marksman, ma stuff wid be back at the stadium – n on this occasion it wid actually be *inside* one eh the posh suites. I could hardly wait.

But as I wis recountin ma tale eh guid fortune tae Torn-Faced Tommy, a cloud descended on his careworn coupon almost immediately. See, that's the problem wi thae pessimists, they're ayewis tryin tae bring ye doon tae their level. Sure enough, he proceeded tae chuck a dirty great spanner in the works eh ma guid mood machinery right away.

"Sounds a bit tae guid tae be true, Gibby," says he doubtfully, slurpin back the Mick Jagger.

"Well, it's true awright. I've goat it in writin this time!" I replied triumphantly.

"N ye're daein awright ooty it n aw," I added pointedly, as I'd bein buyin the gloomy-faced galoot pints eh that yelly pish aw efternin. In fact, I'd been on a right auld spendin spree ever since the enormous burden eh Pear-Tree's debt hud melted magically away like snaw in the sunshine on Leith.

"Geeza deek at that letter ye goat, will ye?" said Tommy, sighin in a world-weary manner that even Moany Tony himsel wid have been proud eh.

So I handed it ower n watched his face faw even further, till it wis practically scrapin aff the flair.

"Uh-huh," he said eventually, foldin it carefully n passin it back tae me. "Did any eh the wordin in it no make ye a wee bit, er, *suspicious?*"

I didnae like the way this wis gaun at aw.

"Whit dae ye mean, like?"

"Well, dae ye really think a lawyer wid address ye as 'Dear Grumpy Guts' tae start wi?"

"I thought that *wis* a bit odd," I admitted. "But I took it as a term eh endearment. I've been cawed worse, efter aw."

"Aye, so ye have. A *lot* worse. OK then, there's also the fact that it's supposedly fae Hibernian Fitba Club."

"So?"

"Spelt H I G H B E R N I A N ?"

"Must've been a slip eh the moose on the keyboard," I replied impatiently. "It's goat the club crest embossed on it tae, hus it no? Proper heided notepaper, like!"

"True – but remind me whit's depicted on yon club badge again?"

"A harp, a castle n a ship, of course!" I yelled. "Ye ken that as well as I dae! Whit exactly are ye drivin at?"

"Well, take a closer look at yer letter again."

I unfolded it n quickly scanned the logo, set at the top. Right enough, at first casual glance it *looked* like the bona-fide Hibs crest – except instead eh a harp, castle n ship it hud a guitar, pub n fishin trawler. N despite the fact that the guitar wis a Gibson, I suddenly hud an awfy feelin that the trawler wisnae the only fishy thing aboot it...

"The clincher though hus tae be the signature eh the so-cawed 'legal representative' at the bottom eh the page," went on Tommy, as glumly as could be.

My eyes travelled doon the sheet until I located it.

"Aye – so whit's wrong wi that? A lassie by the name eh April Fuller?"

Tommy jist continued tae gaze at me, wi the saddest expression seen on a human face since Craig Levein's in front eh the 'NATURAL ORDER?' banner at Easter Road.

"Gibby – whit date is it the day?"

I hud tae think fur a moment. Cos yesterday hud been that 'Spring forward, Fall back' shite wi the clocks. Oh aye, the start eh a new month n aw that.

"It's April 1st," I said, havin finally worked it oot.

"Aye. Precisely..."

I gawped at the signature again. April Fuller...April Full...April

Fool...*aw naw!*

The penny dropped at last. N no jist the penny – I'd gied thae removal radges two fuckin grand! N I'd been spendin like a drunken lord aw day! N I'd been buyin that torn-faced tosser pints eh pish aw efternin! N noo aw ma gear wis stacked ootside Easter Road Stadium again. N I wis still due Pear-Tree thirty-four grand...

IT'S GETTIN STICKY UP THE VICKY

The jungle dreams in Leith were beatin loud n clear – n it wid be a foolish man (or wumman) whae chose tae ignore the ominous sound. Aye, the message wis oot – Gibby's on the warpath, ye'd better keep hunkered doon in the trenches! See when I found oot whae sent me that bogus letter... I even considered giein the postie a kickin, efter aw it wis him whae pit it through ma letter-box. Ye could argue that that doesnae make him culpable, but I ayewis thought he hud a sort eh furtive jambo look aboot him. Workin fur the *Royal* Mail in the first place, the name itsel speaks volumes. An organisation riddled wi erse-lickin monarchists, yams, huns n wash-hand basins, fae tap tae bottom.

However, I gied him a bye, n went on tae jot doon a list eh possible suspects. Of course, the logical thing tae dae wis itemise aw ma enemies, but I wis unlikely tae live long enough tae complete *that* particular task. Wid have been the equivalent eh writin oot the entire Encyclopaedia Brittanica fae start tae finish. But once I'd weeded oot the illiterate numpties whae were virtual strangers tae the Kween's Englush, it became a lot mair manageable. Efter much heid-scratchin, I'd settled on the maist likely culprit – Roddy the Squaddie. Ever since I'd lamped him on the neb he'd kept his distance, but he wis still ayewis sneakin aboot in the backgroond, pickin up on everythin that wis gaun on. In fact, tae ma great irritation, it seemed that I'd actually done him a favour, as he wis gaun aboot sportin a huge bandage on his coupon, tellin folk he'd hud his nose shot aff while fightin in the Yemen civil war. Mair plaudits fur Rod the dashin 'war hero', fae his gullible camp followers in cloud cuckoo land. But I'd decided he was gaun doon fur this yin, big time. So whit hard evidence did I have, ye ask? Well, fuck aw really, but so whit? I'd play him at his own gemme – it's whit the Armed Forces dae best efter aw, so he'd be sure tae appreciate the irony. Aye – shoot first, ask questions later...

A stroke eh luck then befell me, when I heard through the grapevine that Slasher Smith hud it in fur this eejit an aw, apparently fur the crime eh takin the Lord's name in vain. He'd been in the same queue in the chippy when he overheard The Fraud say 'oh, God' oot loud, in whit Smithy interpreted as a blasphemous manner. In fact, oor Rod hud jist been offered an alternative tae his usual haddock – which wis aff the menu – n hud actually responded wi "oh, *cod*', but there wis nae point in tryin tae convince auld Slashy-Poos eh that. I'd also endeavoured tae git masel intae the weak-bladdered whacko's guid books, by pittin oot the word that I tae hud stood in the presence eh the Light eh God. Which wis *nearly* true, as I'd clocked Pat Stanton leanin against the waw ootside the Hibs Club efter a function, when the security beacon above his heid suddenly blazed on.

"Ye're one eh the Lord's flock noo, Gibby," said Smithy, smilin beatifically, as I sidled up tae him in The Cenny.

I wis mighty tempted tae tell the bampot tae jist get tae flock, but held ma tongue. It wid be highly advantageous fur me tae somehow induce him intae cairryin oot ma dirty work fur me, which I wis fairly confident I could achieve, by simply poisonin his mind even further aboot the satanic proclivities eh Roddy the Squaddie. Once a psycho, ayewis a psycho, I reasoned, as Smithy could now use the excuse eh wagin holy war or administerin the wrath eh God tae the Unbelievers, when the insatiable thirst fur violence overcame him.

Sure enough, afore long n wi the help eh a few stiff swallics eh Communion wine, I hud him champin at the bit tae dae some serious damage tae oor common adversary. The resident spies hud reported that the bold Roderick wis currently spinnin his stories eh derring-do tae an enthralled audience in The Victoria up the road, as maist eh the pub clientele at the Fit eh The Walk were gettin wise tae him. Efter a while Slasher disappeared tae caw on a joiner mate, afore reappearin wi two sturdy planks eh wid nailed taegether in the shape eh a crucifix. I began tae wonder if I'd perhaps gone a wee bitty tae far in seekin vengeance…

Then, no long efter he'd left the pub again, on a mysterious errand tae 'dae the Lord's righteous work' there came the sound eh terrible ear-piercin screamin fae further up The Walk. Maist folk affected no tae notice, but efter a while curiosity goat the better eh us n a wee trickle eh bodies exited through the doors. Crossin the road in anticipation eh gettin a better view, we heided south fur a couple eh blocks n then looked back across tae ootside the pub opposite. A heavenly sight met oor eyes, causin yours truly at least tae mutter, 'Praise be tae the Lord' reverentially under ma breath. Fur there, apparently nailed tae the waw above the door via the crucifix wis the stricken form eh oor Roddy, airms outstretched like Eric Idle at the end eh 'Life eh Brian'.

"Ayewis look on the bright side eh life!" I yelled encouragingly, at the Jesus-impersonatin jackass, afore hastily scurryin aff back tae base, jist in case Slasher wis on a major *jihad* against aw other sinners in the vicinity.

Happily fur the Squaddie however, we found oot later that Slasher hud relented at the last moment n only attached him tae the crossed planks by means eh superglue, whereas the auld pre-religious Slasher wid almost certainly have opted fur the mair traditional nailin doon method. Still, the main objective hud been achieved, in that the victim wid be unlikely tae darken oor doorsteps so much in future, spoutin his tales eh tosh. He'd lost whitever credibility or dignity he thought he possessed n wid ayewis be a laughin-stock. Fur years tae come, people wid talk aboot the night that military maverick Rod the Fraud wis finally n deservedly awarded the Victoria Cross by Slasher Smith.

NIL N VOID

It wis jist as well that Rod the Fraud's misfortune hud pit a smile on ma face, cos that wis promptly wiped aff it again, efter viewin yon Hibs – Kilmarnock gemme. In fact, ma coupon strongly resembled Steve Clarke's fearsomely frownin façade, long afore the final whistle. Here we go again, Scotland v Kazakhstan / San Marino, a trad Embra derby, take yer pick. End-tae-end tedium throughoot. Ayewis says it aw, when yer main talkin point efterwards is yer goalie's performance, in oor case the one-man Israeli Defence Force that is Rocky Marciano. But if that sounds like he wis repeatedly pullin aff save efter vital save fae the rampagin Killie forwards, it gies them way tae much credit. He *did* make one superb stop, efter Hanlon made an erse eh it at the back, sendin Jones away bearin doon on goal, surely tae score at last. But he didnae, as ever since the Six Day War of 1967, ye're unlikely tae find an Israeli shitin it aff Jordan. However, naebody else wis capable eh scorin either. Wis this really the same two teams whae contested an eight-goal thriller at the same venue, no so long ago? Apparently so. Baith mair or less cancelled each-other oot in the first hauf n although there were a couple eh decent chances apiece, nowt came eh them.

"They've goat some bloody nerve, takin ma guid money tae watch that pish," I complained tae Moany Tony the day efter.

"It's youse that's goat some bloody nerve, complainin aboot it at aw," he retorted.

"Eh?! Whit dae ye mean by that?"

"Cos they never took yer money in the first place. Ye were spotted watchin it 'as live' on Alba in The Spey, at ten o'clock!"

Bastirt! Grassed up by some Nosey Brandon Barker, as per usual.

"Well, aye, I wis watchin it *again* on the telly, efter I goat back fae Easter Road."

"Oh, ye were at Easter Road awright – ye were seen in Middleton's, The Mash Tun, The Office, The Four-in-Hand, The Iona n The Persevere, aw between 7.45 n 9.30!"

Bastirt again! Whole eh Leith is over-run wi spies n snoopers, I tell ye! I've a guid mind tae move tae Gorgie.

Still, it wisnae aw doom n gloom, no by any means. Ye ken me, I like tae end on an optimistic note. A tap six spot wis noo guaranteed, we were right up the Hertz's erses in the table n Sidebottom hud jist scooped 'Manager eh the Month' award. Although, personally, ma ain accolade in that department wid have tae go tae the manager eh The Victoria, whae hud tae eventually cut Roddy the Squaddie doon, n pack him aff tae the Royal Infirmary, still sufferin fae the effects eh inadvertently sniffin so much glue.

MOANY'S IN THE MONEY

Woke up this morning (there's a song in there somewhere) n ye'll be astonished tae hear I wisnae in the best eh moods. No like me, I ken. But that soon altered, when I goat a phone-call fae Moany Tony. Tae be honest, I wis still regrettin havin the bloody thing at aw n tended tae jump like a startled deer every time it rang. Cos it wis seldom tidings eh comfort n joy bein relayed fae the other end, nae matter whae wis callin. Usually demands fur money, court summonses, cheeky polis askin nippy questions, ye ken the script I'm sure. I even hud two miss-calls – one fae Miss Senga McGlumphar n one fae Miss Fifi Phanni-Phlapz, but as they'd only be efter dough an aw I chose tae ignore them. So I wisnae exactly overjoyed tae hear the Moanin One's voice, fur obvious reasons. See whit that bastirt hud pit me through... But I soon changed ma tune, when he piped up in surprisingly chipper tones.

"Gibby! Aw yer worries are ower!"

"Are they really?" I replied, wi a distinct lack eh enthusiasm.

"Gibby, we've been mates fur donkey's years, ma auld pal, have we no?"

"Have we?"

"Aw, dinnae be like that. Look, ye ken I've been feelin awfy guilty aboot losin yer loot, so that's partly whit I'm phonin aboot. I should have said – aw yer *money* worries are ower!"

Ma enthusiasm jumped up a notch at that statement, I must admit.

"Oh aye? In whit way exactly?"

"I'm finally in a position tae pay ye back! N no only that, there'll be a wee bit extra in it fur ye n aw, tae make up fur aw the pain n sufferin I caused. Maybe even the same amount ower again!"

Well, he definitely hud ma attention noo!

"How come?"

He took a deep breath – or he wis maybe jist sighin as usual, it wis hard tae tell the difference – n continued in an unexpectedly dramatic fashion.

"Cos I've only gone n won the Lottery!"

I almost dropped the receiver.

"Ye've whit?"

"Aye, won the Lottery!"

Ma brief sense eh relief n freedom fae crushin financial worries that hud hot-wired through ma body wis suddenly replaced by a familiar sinkin feelin.

"Dinnae tell me – ye've scored a tenner?"

"Naw, naw, honest tae God, cross ma Hib n hope tae die, I'm talkin aboot the big yin!"

"Billy Connolly?"

"Naw! Gibby – I hope ye're sittin doon – cos I've jist landed *five hundred thousand pounds!*"

At that moment, I felt that droppin the receiver wis appropriate efter aw.

Sittin in The Cenny a short time later, there wis a general air eh supressed excitement n anticipation as the usual worthies awaited the imminent arrival eh oor very own hauf-millionaire. I wis consolin masel wi the fact that Moany never told porkies eh *that* magnitude, he simply didnae have the imagination. N he certainly wisnae one fur jokes, the moanin-faced auld get. So, sceptical as I'd been at the ootset, I hud tae accept that it wis almost certainly true. Finally he breezed in, no quite lookin like a million dollars, mair like eighteen shillings n sixpence in auld money. But there wis a definite jaunty spring in step, despite his sartorial elegance bein akin tae that eh a meths-drinkin tramp wi nae fashion sense bein gied a free pass in a charity clothin shop. I wis mildly disappointed tae see that he wisnae humfin a bulging briefcase full eh greenbacks, cos the world eh cheques n electronic transfers werenae really his bag, as he didnae trust banks. Which wis a two-way street, cos they certainly didnae trust him either. Mainly cos he used tae rob the fuckers fur a livin, back in the day.

"Tony ma man, whit can I get ye?"

He looked well-chuffed, as well he might. Poor bastirt hud never enjoyed such a warm welcome in his puff! Everyone wis shakin his hand, clappin him on the back n toastin his guid health.

So the oors rolled by n the drinks went doon n delighted as I wis fur ma dear auld mucker, I couldnae help noticin that he hudnae exactly started splurgin the hauf-mil in oor direction. In fact, the tight cunt hudnae bought a roond aw day! So I wis aboot tae press him on the delicate topic eh whether he'd actually goat his paws on it yet n also tae find oot when the fuck he intended tae weigh me in, tae the tune eh thirty-four grand, twice ower. But afore I could pose the questions, Humpty Harry came in through the door n pilled up a seat.

"I jist heard aboot yer guid fortune, Tony – well played, that man! How much wis it again – I heard five hundred thou, but then I thought, naw, surely no?"

Tony nodded his heid vigorously.

"Aye, Harry, spot on – five hundred thousand pounds it is! No a penny mair, no a penny less. N no jist that, but –wait fur it – I'm talkin aboot five hundred thousand *Nigerian* pounds n aw!"

I swear tae Christ, ma jaw hit the flair wi such a loud 'THUNK' the glesses jumped aff the tables up the road in The Spey. He jist leaned back in his seat, lookin awfy smug. Efter a while, he became aware eh a sea eh faces gawpin back at him, wi quizzical expressions well tae the fore.

"They're worth mair than Scottish or English pounds," he clarified. "Somethin tae dae wi the Exchange Rate n Overseas Tarrifs, ken."

Will ye listen tae Mr High Finance, here, eh! Sir Fred fuckin Goodwin wi a lobotomy. I mean, whit the *fuck…?*

There wis a deathly silence fur a few moments.

"Tony," I said finally, tryin desperately tae keep ma composure. "When ye said ye'd won the Lottery, we took it tae mean ye'd won the *National* Lottery. So whit's aw this fuckin shite aboot Nigerian pounds?"

"Well, that's jist it, ye see," he goes on, smirkin like the cat that goat the cream n swallyed Tweety-Pie at the same time. "I won the National Lottery awright – but no the *British* yin, I won the bloody Nigerian yin instead!"

Another awfy silence ensued, afore Humpty Harry cleared his throat noisily, prior tae speakin up.

"So, er...how exactly have the Nigerian authorities paid oot? Did they dae a bank transfer or did they send ye a cheque?"

"They're sendin the cheque right noo!" crowed Moany happily, takin a huge gulp ooty a triple-measure rare thirty year auld Glenmorangie that I'd jist wasted the best part eh twenty quid on. "I goat the confirmation this morn. Be wi me in twenty-four oors, the boy there says. Aw they hud tae dae wis wait fur the cheque I sent them tae clear at their end first."

"Whit cheque?"

"Well, ye see, I hud tae send them a grand up front, tae cover administration costs n internal taxes n aw that sort eh pish. I did think it wis a bit steep. But hey-ho, when they pay oot, I'm still £499,000 better aff!"

Whae'll jump ower the table n strangle him first, I wondered – Tommy, Harry or masel?

Completely oblivious tae oor open-moothed reactions, the silly cunt prattled on.

"N it gets better than that, tae! See, I must awready be famous ower there as a result eh winnin the big prize, n ma name well-kent, fur I'm aboot tae make *another* financial killin, directly fae the same country!"

He beamed at us expectantly, until I wis forced tae croak oot a demand fur further explanation.

"Cos the big movers n shakers there have sat up n taken notice. I jist goat an amazin offer through the post, fae a member eh the Nigerian Royal Family!"

I didnae think it wis possible fur ma jaw tae drop even mair, but I swear it did.

"Get this," he says, "Crown Prince Odinga Obama Badabing Badaboom himself sent me a letter n he's prepared tae deposit tens eh thousands intae ma bank account afore the week is oot!"

It wis Humpty Harry whae hud the courage tae step up tae the plate this time. Mind ye, he loves tae revel in other gadgies' misfortune n misery, it hus tae be said.

"Lemme hazard a wild guess here, Tony – did the, er, so-cawed Crown Prince ask fur yer bank details first, afore offerin tae transfer the dosh fae a secret account which he cannae access in his ain country fur complex legal reasons?"

Moany jist gawped at Harry in bemused amazement.

"That's bang on there, Harry! How on earth did ye ken that? Dae ye ken the Crown Prince yersel, likes, or whit?"

Finally, I could stand it nae longer.

"Of couse he fuckin disnae, ya moanin-faced muppet, fur the simple reason that CROWN PRINCE ODINGA OBAMA BADABING BADABOOM DOESNAE FUCKIN EXIST! It's aw a scam, ye great dozy dippit eejit, as is the so-cawed Nigerian National Lottery, fur fuck's sake! Ye've been hud, ya bam!"

There wis an awkward, drawn-oot pause, afore Moany slowly goat tae his feet n pit his empty gless doon (aye, the rare Glenmorangie, the dear stuff!). He then turned tae face me n announced wi great dignity, "The trouble wi you Gibby, is that ye have nae faith in yer felly man. Ye're a cynical, bitter auld bastirt n that's a fact. However, due tae ma joy at ma great windfall, I'm gonnae forgive ye fur yer harsh words spoken in anger – n I'll still see youse OK when ma cheque comes through."

He then swanned oot the door like a Leith version eh Bill Gates, a modest moneyed man on a mission, aff tae answer the call eh destiny.

There wis another Godawfy protracted silence – Christ, the efternin hud been full eh them n nae mistake.

"Imagine bein duped by a bogus letter like that, whit a daft gullible bastirt," I observed, drainin the dregs ooty ma single 25ml measure eh Whyte n Mackay (aye, the cheap stuff!). "Ye widnae catch me fawin fur a trick like that."

Ma compatriots aw nodded sagely, but fur some reason nae-one wid meet ma eye...

I HAVE A DREAM

I wis standin at the border checkpoint, gettin ever mair antsy as thae Customs officials continued tae drag their heels, takin forever tae go aboot their business. Finally it wis ma turn n the gadgie wi the mirrored shades n peaked cap proceeded tae scrutinise ma Leith passport wi great suspicion. Seemed reluctant tae let me through, the cheeky bastirt, but he hud nae choice. N as far as whit I wis cairryin on me wis concerned, I'd checked the regulations carefully tae make sure I wis clear in that department tae.

"Anything to declare?" says this jumped-up Jimmy Jobsworth.

"Aye – Hibs are gonnae win 2-1," I telt him. "I hud a premonition."

"Is that a fact? Well, I've got a premonition that you spell trouble with a capital 'T', possibly with the letters 'YL' before it, if I let you through. But I don't suppose I've got any legal reasons for stopping you. So I'll ask you once again – barring any smart remarks, do you have anything *else* to declare?"

"Only these flares n a single coconut," I stated truthfully.

"You're not shy, I'll give you that," he sighed, reluctantly raisin the barrier at last.

So, wi a defiant flick eh the vickies in his direction, I crossed fae the Peoples' Independent Republic eh Leith intae the city eh Embra. Aye, Tiny Castle, here I come! They rake in their buckets fur something tae drink / In front eh their bus shelter, coloured in pink / In their Gorgie slums...

Mind ye, as per usual, I wis soon wishin I hudnae bothered. Fur Hibs looked like they were gonnae get absolutely pumped! I could hardly bear tae watch. When Haring scored, it took an immense amount eh willpower no tae go haring oot eh the Roseburn Stand, directly in the direction eh the Roseburn Bar, afore scorin a one-way ticket on the tram, straight back tae the border wi the PIROL. But, jist as I wis tryin tae take a wee surreptitious drink ooty ma coconut (I'd replaced the milk wi McEwan's Export earlier), that Barryl Organ went n equalised wi a brilliant strike fae his right boot.

"Ya beauty!" I yelled oot tae the right boot sittin next tae me (Girnin Gertie), as I jumped up n doon, causin the spontaneous combustion eh ma green flare, which wis cunningly concealed in the pocket eh ma green flares (purchased fae Cowan Tailoring in Lothian Road, circa 1974.) Unfortunately that somehow ended up on the park as I frantically tried tae kick it clear, as did ma coconut. But I wis soon gaun nuts again, as the Hertz almost immediately reasserted their dominance n it wis a grateful Gibby whae goat tae hauf-time wi his team still on level terms.

Still, I hud faith in the gods above, especially efter ma premonition, in which Slasher Smith appeared tae me in a dream, swathed in long trailin robes eh green n white n telt me it wid be 2-1 tae Hibs. Annoyingly, he must have pished the bed whilst he wis at it, cos I woke up wringin wet. But noo I wis jist wringin ma hands in anxiety, until whae else but the best player in green by a country mile stuck away another peach in the tap corner. They were aw dancing tae Barryl Organ's tune awright n they should have wrapped it up wi a third courtesy eh McNutsack. Seemed like he thought he wis back playin fur Scotland against San Marino, wi a replica eh the miss fae that gemme, which made fur a nail-bitin finish. I wis that nervous it wisnae even ma ain nails I wis bitin, it wis those eh the boy sittin next tae Girnin Gertie. N it wisnae even his fingernails either, I'm talkin aboot *real* nails, ooty a bargain bag he'd jist bought at Wilkes on Stevenson Road, at a very reasonable price. But he wis quite unreasonable aboot me munchin ma way through them n I hud tae pay compensation tae keep the peace, but I didnae really care. No wi Hibs hingin on fur a famous victory.

Back at the border checkpoint, I wisnae in the mood tae pit up wi any mair pish fae pernickety pen-pushers – but much like the case eh Americans crossin intae Mexico, they dinnae really bother their fur-coated nae-knickered Embra erses when ye're heidin the other way. But I gleefully stuck the vickies up at the Customs clowns again, jist tae symbolise the two Hibs goals n then danced on doon the Walk tae the green green gress eh hame.

RIVALRY WI RESPECT

Aye, that wis the zingy new soundbite-type phrase, apparently dreamt up by club officials on baith sides pre-derby, only tae be greeted by cynicism n doonright disdain by the fans. Tae which I can only add – rivalry wi respect, ma erse! Whitaloadypish. Ten reasons why ye shouldnae respect the Hertz, straight aff the tap eh ma heid – Craig Levein, Wallace Mercer in general, hostile takeover bids in particular, the Oli Shaw goal that never wis, Natural Order nonsense, big team / wee team in Embra fantasies, scarf-twirlin, horrible colours, livin in a big Pink Bus Shelter n Craig Levein again.

"But it has a certain buzz about it!" claimed the fitba establishment lackeys.

Aye, well, so does Junky Johnston's bluebottle menagerie, but I'm no exactly gaun ooty ma way tae show that any respect either!

However, as a man whae hus been kent tae have a few catchy wee phrases eh his ain – not aw eh them a loady pish, he says modestly – I thought I'd gie it a try-oot in a non-fitba context. Ma first chance came when I saw Senga n Fifi havin a handbag-wieldin catfight in Duke Street, ower the financial charms eh a rich American tourist they'd waylaid. He'd gaun doon that way hopin tae see the Royal Yacht, but the closest he goat tae royalty wis bein takin fur a ride in The Duke's Heid.

"Rivalry wi respect, ladies!" I admonished, in an avuncular fashion.

Whereupon they instantly pit their temporary rivalry aside n turned on yours truly instead! Battered the shite ooty me wi thae hauf-ton handbags – whit dae they keep in there, brick condoms? I'd mair prominent lumps on ma heid than John Merrick, by the time I goat tae The Cenny.

Once inside, I soon became embroiled in a heated debate between two gadgies, whae were arguin ower the jukebox selection. One wanted tae pit on an Otis Redding soul classic n the other wis optin fur Aretha Franklin's interpretation eh the same song.

"Rivalry wi 'R-E-S-P-E-C-T', boys?" I enquired.

"Whit fuckin business is it eh yours, grandpaw?" retorted one aggressively.

"I've changed ma mind anyway," said the other. "I think I'll pit on Nick Lowe instead. Then we can baith sing along."

He shoved his pound coin intae the slot n brought his pint tumbler doon on ma heid at the same time.

"I love the sound eh breaking gless," they then chorused in harmony, as I staggered aff tae the cludgie in search eh towels.

So I wisnae in the best eh moods as I made ma way hame later, havin stopped aff tae shoplift six boatils eh Real Ale ooty Scotmid. Suddenly I saw a familiar figure across the road on Constitution Street. He wis giein me the sort eh dirty look that ye can only get fae a gadgie whae's been superglued tae the outside eh a pub n strongly suspects that *you* might have hud a hand in it. Aye, that khaki-camouflaged cunt Roddy the Squaddie! Well, I'd hud enough eh folks' lip fur one night n needless tae say, I'd hud enough eh a certain trite little phrase n its ramifications tae...

As he continued tae gie me the evil eye, I swiftly crossed ower, opened ma bag n pilled oot one-sixth eh the contents. I then proceeded tae dae tae him whit the soul music aficionado hud jist done tae me in The Cenny. The Fraud rolled aboot in the gutter squealin like a stuck pig, efter I brought the boatil doon on his napper.

"Whit the fuck wis that aboot?!" he howled, forgettin his clipped military tones fur once.

"Disrespect – wi Deuchars," I explained, hurryin aff hame wi the rest eh ma ill-gotten gains. Pity tae waste yin on that bam I suppose, but in consolation I still hud five left.

OF COPS N COCONUTS

So there I wis, back at that bloody border barrier again, between the PIROL n the city eh Embra. Same bloody Jimmy Jobsworth on duty of course.

"Anything to declare, sir?"

"I have nuthin tae declare, but ma genius," I telt him. "Oscar Wilde said that."

"We're the kids in America, whoa-oh," says this cheeky bastirt in reply. "Kim Wilde said *that.* So what is the purpose of your visit to the city of Edinburgh today, sir?"

"Mind yer ain bloody business!"

Thing wis, I hud a dark suspicion that *his* business hud been tae drop me in it wi the authorities, efter ma last visit. I hudnae been cairryin contraband as such, but nae doot the cameras hud picked up on that as well as him, n noo aw the hysteria bein generated by the media aboot events at Tiny Castle wisnae helpin matters. I hud a feelin that ma *real* purpose in visitin Embra – a summons tae St. Leonard's fur a wee chat – must be connected wi that somehow.

"Do you know why you're here, Mr Gibson?" says this Uniform, playin guid cop, bad cop or jist plain crap cop, I hudnae hud time tae work oot which wis which yet.

"Because ma legs carried me in through the front door n then intae this claustrophobic wee room, I wid imagine. Whae the hell designed the place – an architect specialisin in accommodation fur circus midgets? Christ, ma bloody fridge is bigger!"

"Be that as it may, Gibby," says the other yin – he must be the 'guid' cop, cawin me by ma nickname, ken – "I'm wanting a wee word with you – and that wee word happens to be 'flare'. What do you have to say about that?"

I dropped ma eyes n scrutinised the area under the desk carefully.

"Aye, I can see the flair, I'm no fuckin blind. Looks awfy spick n span, I must say. Do gie ma compliments tae yer cleaner, along wi a box eh Milk Tray chocolates n a big bunch eh flooirs."

But the other Plod wisnae gaun tae be distracted by ma crafty verbal tactics, designed tae delay n confuse.

"We're not talking about the *floor*, Mr Gibson," snaps Bad Cop. "We're talking about the *flare*, the pyrotechnic on the pitch at Tynecastle Park, during Saturday's derby encounter between cheating Leith-based scumbags of dubious Irish heritage and those fine upstanding Presbyterian representatives of this city's august Establishment and direct descendants of McCrae's Battalion, the glorious Heart of Midlothian. Any idea who might have conveyed that onto the playing surface, eh?"

"Eddie Turnbull, I would assume," says I, thinkin that it wis morally OK tae gress up a deid guy, cos they could hardly go n gie him the third degree noo, could they?

There wis a brief puzzled silence, afore Guid Cop spoke up again.

"Are you trying to tell us that a former legendary Hibernian player and manager was responsible?"

"Aye, it's obvious, isn't it? Says so in the song efter aw."

I could see the dafties were still scoobied, so I proceeded tae treat them tae a wee musical snippet eh 'Hibernian (Gie us a Goal)'.

"Hibs, Hibs, Hibs, Hibs, that's the team wi *FLARE* / Eddie Turnbull, the man whae pit it there..."

Their coupons were still registerin dual expressions eh incomprehension. Aye, they sure as fuck dinnae dish oot brain-cells along wi the truncheons at Tulliallan Polis Trainin College, I'll tell ye that!

"OK, we'll come back to that one in a bit," says Bad Cop hesitantly, beginnin tae lose his earlier air eh steely assurance. "But what about the coconut?"

"Youse tell me – whit aboot the coconut?"

"Did you throw it onto the pitch?"

"Well of course I did! But I chucked it in the direction eh the touchline, didn't I?"

"Did you? What difference does that make – throwing a coconut towards the touchline?"

"I wis only tryin tae be helpful."

"In what way?"

"Because someone wis aboot tae take a shy."

"Are you taking the piss, Mr Gibson?"

"Only if ye're giein it away free this time. Seem tae remember ye charged me fur it last time around. *Over*charged, in fact."

"Eh?"

"You forced me tae pit ma hard-earned cash in that drinks machine in the corridor, efter offerin me a cup eh tea. Well, it wis maybe *meant* tae be tea, but it tasted mair like pish tae me. Two quid fur that! Ye should find oot whae's responsible n charge them wi Daylight Robbery, no tae mention causin Grievous Bodily Herm, instead eh persecutin law-abidin citizens like masel."

They exchanged brief glances.

"This was just an informal chat, Mr Gibson – for now. Is that clear? You have not been charged with any offences – *yet.* Aye, you're a slippery customer alright."

"No hauf as slippery as yer fuckin stairs," I muttered. "So I'm free tae go?"

"Free as a bird – *for now.*"

And this bird youse cannot ch-a-a-a-a-a-nge... I quickly flew the coop, afore they ch-a-a-a-a-a-nged their minds.

NEVER MIND THE POLYPS

Next mornin, I wis that convulsed wi rage ower whit I read in the sports pages, I swear I almost choked on ma bowl eh cornflakes n Smirnoff. Aye, that Dumpster wumman, wastin ma hard-earned season-ticket money again! Says she's gonnae spend £100,000 on daein up the CCTV system – jist think whit ye could dae wi that amount spent on chip fryers instead. Aye, make some bloody chips! Ye may think I've goat a bit eh a (Hi)bee in ma bunnet aboot the subject, but fur Chrissakes, Leeann baby, there's hungry Hibbies starvin oot here in the stands.

I dinnae haud wi aw this 'Big Brother is watchin ye' shite in any case, as if George Orwell hud visualised the omnipotent figure eh Rod Pear-Tree as the Great Dictator when he wrote '1984'. N Dumpster says the clarity eh the new set-up will be such that ye can 'read a tattoo on someone's arm.' Well I've goat news fur her, if she points the lens in ma direction when I've goat ma tap aff gettin a suntan on Leith, she'll bloody well see Benny fae 'Crossroads' lookin right back at her! Whae-ever said the camera never lies wis clearly lyin an aw – I've been dubbed up tons eh times by photographic 'evidence' which wis highly suspect. Thank God cameras hud yet tae be invented, when ma two previous spouses accidentally fell doon the stairs.

I soon hud mair tae worry aboot than intrusive cameras spyin on ma every move at Easter Road tae, when a situation wi another kind eh intrusive camera-work presented itsel. I'd been cawed in tae see the doaktir efter some routine tests n tae say the gadgie looked grim aboot the gills wid have been a major understatement.

"Mr Gibson, I'm afraid to say that we've found some blood in your stools."

I shifted uncomfortably on hearin that, as ye can well imagine. Cos how could he ken that the stools I'd choaried ooty The Cenny were heavily stained wi the stuff, mainly as a result eh it gushin ooty Rod the Fraud's hooter ontae the fabric?

"It's probably tomaty sauce," I lied unconvincingly. "Makes an awfy mess eh the furniture."

He regarded me in a scoobied fashion fur several moments.

"I'm not referring to *those* kind of stools, Mr Gibson," he finally said, wi an air eh impatience. "I mean the other kind."

"Whit – toadstools?"

"No. No, no, no. Not stools that grow under trees, not stools that you sit on, stools that result from bowel movements!"

Aha! I wis wi him now. But I suddenly wished that I wisnae...

He then went on tae try n reassure me – failin miserably in the process. It wis like listenin tae Dr Harold Shipman tellin me that the injection he wis aboot tae gie me wid dae me the world eh guid. An *internal camera* wis gonnae be unceremoniously shoved up my jacksie, courtesy eh the hospital, he explained, tae check oot the scene in mair detail. N despite his airy description eh an instrument so microscopic in size that I wid hardly feel a thing, I remained somewhit unconvinced.

So, a frighteningly short time later, I found masel up The Western, awaitin ma fate. I nervously tugged up ma pyjama bottoms, as if tae subliminally protect ma posterior fae whit wis aboot tae ensue. I then goat some shock when a go-go artiste shaped like an emaciated pipe-cleaner wi rickets n mair tattoos than that bampot Beckham shuffled up ontae the tiny Confederate Flag-bedecked stage, tae the strains eh 'Sweet Hame Alabama'. Wi a flash eh realisation I instantly saw ma schoolboy error. Aye, I wis in The Western awright – The Western *Bar* that is, no the bloody Western *General*!

Three dances later (tits only, mind – nowt below the belt) I reluctantly left, n hailed a taxi tae the Crewe Road Sooth medical facility. Once there, they rushed me straight through intae the operating theatre wi indecent haste n then some gadgie in a white coat started giein me a spiel, which sounded suspiciously like some sort eh sales-pitch. He wis dronin on n on aboot NHS cut-backs n whit-not, n how they were so short eh money they sometimes hud tae improvise wi whitever equipment they could lay their hands on. Tae be honest, I wis hardly payin attention tae the radge. Hud other things on ma mind, ken.

"So, Mr Gibson, I assume your own doctor explained the procedure and the method by which we seek to clarify your, er, internal condition and so on?"

"Aye, aye," I muttered. "Tiny wee camera up ma bahookey n aw that. Jist get on wi it, will ye? I dinnae ken why ye're wastin yer breath tellin me aw that other shite. I'm no interested!"

He coughed awkwardly.

"Ah, but you see, you *should* be interested, Mr Gibson, because it directly concerns you. Your own practitioner may well have given you the impression that a camera of miniscule dimensions would be the preferred option, but unfortunately the last one got broken and we can't afford a replacement. They cost a fortune! So we've been forced to adapt an earlier model, to do the same job..."

Lyin there face doon on the slab, I uneasily tried tae glance back ower ma shuder, jist in time tae see two giant orderlies each built like Mike Tyson suddenly move forward tae secure ma airms. Then the surgeon yanked doon ma pyjama troosers n reached fur an auld-fashioned *Box Brownie* – wi tripod attached. Holy Mother eh Christ...

"Just try to relax, Mr Gibson. But I must warn you, this may hurt just a *little* bit..."

DON'T BE VAGUE, ASK FUR CRAIG

In the continuin aftermath eh derby day dystopia (media focus on flares, nutty milk receptacles, racist abuse n stand closures conveniently obscurin the small fact that Hibs actually *won*), oor Craigie wis bravely standin his ground. Bravely, as it might have gaun up in flames at any moment, thanks tae another mis-thrown pyrotechnic. Appropriately, he then proceeded tae shoot doon in flames the rumour that he wis heidin fur exile in Iberian parts, sayin, "I don't even like Spain." Christ Awmighty, whae in their right mind doesnae like Spain? Sun, senoritas, sangria, cheap bevvy in general, Barcelona, Real Madrid, aff tae make a gallant bid...

In his usual contrary mood (n few folk dae contrariness quite so well as Craig), he rubbished claims that many Hertz fans wanted rid eh him, citin the historical evidence thus:- "The fact is that we played Partick Thistle in the cup, we were 1-0 up and the fans were singing 'There's Only One Craig Levein'." He omitted tae mention that they included the 'thank fuck' refrain at the beginnin n end. But apart fae the obvious mair relevant fact that – even if true – that wis *then* n this wis *noo* – it widnae be the first time that Craig's lugs hud failed him. A couple eh seasons back he embarrassingly claimed that the fans were cheerin him tae the rafters as he emerged fae the tunnel, which occurred as 70,000 rugby fans at Murrayfield hud unleashed a huge roar tae celebrate a try, at *exactly the same time.* But nae-one thought tae tell him that sound travels on the breeze... Hears whit he wants tae hear though, sees whit he wants tae see. Which doesnae include watchin his team playin ‘Route One’ fitba apparently, despite the majority eh fans moanin aboot that very tactic bein used, tae the exclusion eh any alternative.

“I had to laugh when that came up on Saturday,” he said, referrin tae an impudent journalist’s question on that topic efter the derby.

Craig – *laugh?* Someone’s havin a laugh awright, but it’s unlikely tae be him. Then he moderated his initial denial somewhit, by concedin that, “*sometimes* we do play the long ball.” Whit did he mean by ‘sometimes’ I wonder? Only between 3 n 4.45 p.m. on a Setirday efternin?

Then mind that notorious time managin the national team? He sent oot a side comprisin a goalkeeper, six defenders, four midfielders...n *nae* forwards! Efter predictably losin tae the Czech Republic, he then hud the gall tae defiantly respond tae the critics by sayin that he’d been right aw along, as, “it *nearly* worked.” Try tellin that tae thoosands eh Czech fans (n Scots) whae paid guid money tae watch such shite! Well, thank the Lord he’s no at the helm there any mair – although McLeish is showin promise in bein equally pish – n let’s no forget he’s only back in the hot-seat at Tiny Castle cos naebody else wanted tae dae it. First, he goat shot eh the wee hobbit, Cathro, efter bullyin him intae submission by sendin him threatenin notes throughoot matches, then pretended he didn’t *really* want the gig himsel, when Annie Budge hud exhausted aw other possibilities. Big names were floated n the same big names sank wi’oot trace. Never fear jambos, it’s Craig tae the rescue again! Thinkin, as long as I beat thae Hibees noo n then, they’ll forgive me anythin.

Oops, canny even ‘manage’ that any mair, it seems...

EMBASSY REGAL

Noo, as ye aw ken, havin that bloody telephone in workin order again wis daein ma heid in, mair often than not. Ower the course eh one mornin, I hud an Eskimo salesman on, tryin tae flog me an igloo (only partially melted), some joker askin me tae invest in his ice-lolly business n a rep fae Walls', invitin me tae take part in a survey aboot their products. Turned oot they were aw cold callers, but they goat me a bit hoat under the collar n nae mistake. However, even I've goat tae reluctantly admit that it occasionally hus its uses.

I'd been fancyin a wee break tae hook up wi the London Hibs Supporters Club anyway, n as I watched the main news, the lead story gied me inspiration tae maybe have a hell eh a lot mair than jist a short vacation. Why no get the fuck ooty here n move tae The Smoke mair or less permanently? The opportunity wis there noo, efter aw. So I goat on the blower immediately. As soon as the gadgie at the other end picked up, I pitched it tae him straight away.

"I'd like a room," I started aff, afore thinkin, dinnae sell yersel short, Gibby, why no go fur the whole shebang?

"A room?" replied the boy, soundin a bit scoobied.

"Naw, sorry. When I said a room, whit I actually meant wis a full suite," I explained, jist tae clarify matters.

But Daftie doon the line still wisnae gettin ma drift! There wis a silence eh the pregnant variety, afore he spoke again.

"There must be some mistake, sir. This is not a hotel."

"I ken it's no!" I yelped impatiently. "Whit wid I want wi a bloody hotel, fur Chrissakes?"

"I'm sorry, sir, but I'm a trifle confused here. You are aware that you are through to the offices of an international diplomatic mission?"

"Aye, aye! But cut oot the fancy terminology, pal, eh? Is that or is that no the Ecuadorian Embassy?"

"Yes, sir – it is."

"Well then, at the risk eh repeatin masel, I want a room, at the very least. N dinnae tell us ye've no goat yin spare, cos I've jist seen that Assange boy get cairted aff by the polis on the national news! Ken him, that released aw thae secret documents on Prickileaks or somethin, although that does sound mair like a medical condition pertainin tae Slasher Smith. But that's neither here nor there. I'm here, ye're there, ye've goat a room gaun spare, n I'm gaun spare if I dinnae get ooty here! Dae I make masel clear?"

There wis an extremely long pause this time, afore the boy finally deigned tae reply, albeit in a hesitant sort eh manner.

"No, sir, you most emphatically do *not* make yourself clear. But if you are seeking to gain some sort of advantage from Mr Julian Assange's current difficulties, bear in mind that he was granted political asylum here. He did not just blatantly attempt to blag free accommodation in central London, as you appear to be doing."

Christ, this boy wisnae hauf hard work! I'd have tae change tack a bit, tae achieve the desired result.

"Aye, same situ here, gadgie, political asylum is whit I'm claimin!"

"Really, sir? And may I enquire just whom exactly you are seeking political asylum from?"

"Embra!"

"I beg your pardon?"

"The *City eh Embra*, in *Skoatland*," I telt him. "Their fascist dictatorship is persecutin the Leith minority. The PIROL hus goat its back tae the wall n canny haud oot much longer!"

"The *what*, sir?"

"The People's Independent Republic eh Leith!"

"Yes, sir, I see. Well, I'm just scrolling through our alphabetical list here of countries, nation states and overseas territories recognised by the Government of Ecuador. Unfortunately, neither the city of *Embra* as you call it, or that bearing the acronym of PIROL is on it. In any case, do you have any personal connection with Ecuador?"

"Aye – Ulisees de la Cruz!"

"I'm sorry, sir, the line is breaking up a bit – did I understand you to say that you are 'useless on the booze'?"

"Naw, naw! Well, aye, I *am,* but that's no the point! I used tae watch two eh yer felly countrymen on a regular basis. Played fur the Hibees, ye ken. Ye're no listenin tae me properly..."

I began tae sense I wis losin the argument here. But I wis startin tae forget whit the actual argument wis... Ah well, might as well try one last throw eh the dice.

"Look," I said imploringly, "ye'll have heard eh the Hibs, have ye no?"

"I would assume that everyone here has indeed heard of them, sir, if you are referring to the popular slang term for Hibernian Football Club. Almost certainly, every man, woman and child in the entire continent of South America is familiar with that name, as they taught Brazil how to play football – allegedly. Anyway, before I terminate this fascinating call, is there anything else you'd like to add?"

"Jist two words, pal, startin wi initials same as the Embra postcode – Eduardo Hurtado!"

"In response, I have just two words for *you*, sir, starting with initials same as Foreign Office..."

But I'd quickly banged the receiver doon, tae deny him the satisfaction. Bastirt!

MURDER, POLIS

Well, unfortunately, it wisnae long afore I wis on the receivin end eh even *mair* cold callers. N even mair unfortunately, these yins came in person, no via the phone, n were cauld tae the point eh bein doonright frosty. Aye, ye've guessed it – the polis!

"Gibby, we've come aboot yer neighbour," says the first yin, wi'oot any eh the usual preamble.

"Thank Christ fur that! Jist take him away in handcuffs n make sure he doesnae come back!"

"*He,* ye say, Gibby, *he*? Whit makes ye think we were referrin tae a male?"

See thae bloody bizzies n their stupit bloody mind-gemmes! Spend tae much time watchin repeats eh 'Taggart', n that's the truth!

"He, she, it, I couldnae care less whae it is! They're aw a load eh bloody pests anyway. Be guid tae see the back eh them," I stated succinctly. Then, clockin the grave expressions on their coupons, I couldnae resist addin, "whit – hus there been a *mur-durr?*" in the tones eh yon deid actor boy, that Mick McManus, ken.

"Maybe there hus, Gibby, maybe there hus. N if there hus, it hus long been suspected that ye've goat a bit eh form in that department. Goat a police record, have ye no?"

"I bought 'Roxanne' when it came oot," I admitted. "But that wis jist a wee birthday prezzy fur Senga McGlumphar, as she's in the same line eh work as the burd in the song. I wis never a huge fan masel."

"Same auld Gibby." sighed the other cop. "Ayewis prevaricatin away n tryin tae change the subject. *A police record?* Christ, ye've goat mair like the equivalent eh their entire fuckin album back catalogue, fae 'Outlandos D'Amour' on! Noo – when wis the last time ye saw Mr Johnston?"

Aw shite!

"I've no seen him fur ages," I said, truthfully fur once. "But if it's *mur-durr* ye're talkin aboot, well, I can probably help ye oot there."

Suddenly they were aw ears.

"Ye can?"

"Aye – I've seen the deid bodies wi ma ain eyes!"

Christ, I hud their attention noo awright!

"*Deid bodies*, ye say? Like, mair than one?"

"Oh aye!"

Yet despite ma helpful 'eager-tae-please' attitude, I dinnae like the way they were lookin at me at aw, as if I wis Leith's answer tae Denis Nilsen or somethin. Then I remembered that documentary aboot the infamous serial killer, where the first investigatin officer described how he'd asked him if he wis talkin aboot *one* deid body – or maybe *two* – whereupon Nilsen, calm as ye like, turns tae him n says politely, "It's actually *fifteen* or *sixteen*, I kind of lost count after a while." N that wis the kind eh look Leith's finest were noo bestowin upon yours truly, whae'd never so much as hermed a fly! Christ Awmighty!

So efter they'd read me ma rights, righted ma wrongs, asked me if I wanted a lawyer present, aw the usual shite, they seemed quite surprised that I wis happy tae gie them chapter n verse. Cos fur once, I hud nuthin tae hide!

"How many bodies are we talkin aboot, Gibby – one, or maybe two?" the first yin says quietly, openin his notebook in an ominous fashion.

Christ, he must've seen the same documentary aboot dear auld Denis!

"A few," I said. "I canny be sure."

They exchanged meaningful glances.

"Now, ye said that ye actually saw the deid bodies wi yer ain eyes? Did ye have anything tae dae wi their murder?"

"Aye n naw."

"Well, which is it?"

"Aye, tae yer *first* question, ye dozy cunt, I *saw* them awright, but I hud nowt tae dae wi it!"

"Remindin ye right now that swearin at a police officer is a criminal offence in itself, I must ask you – *where* did ye see the bodies?"

"In Junky, er, I mean in *Mr* Johnston's flat."

They were aw agog noo, on the edge eh their seats.

"Jist tae be clear, Gibby, ye saw mair than one deid body in the flat belongin tae the almost certainly late Johnny 'Junky' Johnston?"

"Aye, I swear on ma wives' lives. Baith eh them."

"Mmm, that might no be the maist ringin endorsement eh the truth that I've ever heard. Can ye explain the circumstances by which ye saw them?"

"I saw them through the windae, simple as that."

They baith looked a bit disappointed aboot that revelation. First Cop pursed his lips thoughtfully.

"So ye werenae actually *inside* the flat, in person?"

"Naw, like I'm tellin ye,I saw the deid bodies, or *corpses* if ye prefer, through the gless. The minute I saw them, I thought tae masel – there's been foul play here. N of course there wis a foul smell n aw, Christ, the place hus been mingin fur weeks, worse than a Gorgie slum!"

"Yes, Gibby, the smell is whit alerted us in the first place. Did ye no think tae report that weeks ago then, when ye first became aware eh it?"

"Naw – I jist thought it wis masel. I hudnae hud a bath fur six months."

Cop Two cleared his throat impatiently.

"Look, can we get back tae thae corpses..."

"Aye – their legs were stickin up in the air tae! Like that rigor mortis-lock hud set in, ye ken?"

"Really?" he said, scribblin away furiously.

"But I must say, I think ye're makin a lot eh fuss aboot fuck aw," I went on. "In any case, I'd have thought that this wis mair a job fur the SSPCA, rather than the polis."

"Come on, Gibby, I appreciate ye didnae exactly see eye tae eye wi Johnston, but there's nae need tae make bad-taste jokes n speak ill eh the deid."

"Whit? He's no actually deid, is he?"

They exchanged mair highly meaningful looks.

"Ye seem genuinely surprised at that possibility, Gibby. How come? N whit wis that crack aboot the SSPCA again?"

"It wis nae joke! I thought they'd be the obvious yins tae be daein the investigation, seein as it involves cruelty tae animals. Animals, that are noo – no tae pit tae fine a point on it – deid! As ye ken fine anyway!"

Noo there wis merely a stunned silence. Tweedle-Dum n Tweedle-Dumber were starin at me in dumbstruck amazement. Finally numero uno regained his power eh speech.

"Gibby – whit the fuck are ye haverin aboot?"

"Bluebottles of course, whit else?"

"Bluebottles?"

"Aye, fuckin heaps eh deid bluebottles, by the hunners! Aw ower the fuckin place! I tell ye, that junky ersehole's been ill-treatin them or starvin them, I dinnae ken which, but the result is the same, they're aw brown breid!

They baith goat slowly tae their feet, shut their notebooks n started floatin taewards the front door like sleepwalkin spacemen.

"Glad tae have been eh assistance!" I shouted sarcastically at their retreatin backs. "N whit were ye sayin aboot that smackheided numpty – is he really deid n aw?"

"We believe so, Gibby. The remains found in his flat have yet tae be forensically examined in detail, but we're pretty sure it's him."

Killed by his ain bluebottles, eh, whae wid have thought it? But, as the Big Game hunters ayewis warn, *these beasts can turn at any time.* Jist goes tae show, ye cannae be tae careful, dealin wi exotic pets. Of course, by the time I'd remembered I should've telt them aboot that other radge keepin the pink elephant in an unnaturally small space, they'd shot the craw.

TAE THINK I FOUGHT THE WAR FUR THE LIKES EH YOUSE

I dinnae ken aboot youse lot, but I wis startin tae get a bit narked aboot aw the extra gaps in the season. First, we hud that unnecessary winter-break nonsense, then we hud the even mair unnecessary international yin (cos the chances eh Scotland ever daein anythin are zero), then we get *another* yin, tae accommodate the cup semis! As a Hibbie, aw I can say is – whae gies a toss aboot the Scottish Cup? We've won it often enough, thank ye very much, n have nae interest in riskin injuries tae players wi the tap six run-in tae the League jist up ahead. It's a Mickey Moose competition that Disney matter, unless ye're some sort eh Goofy gadgie fae the planet Pluto whae wants tae waste yer Setirday lunchtime watchin Hertz v Inversnecky Cameroonian Thistle kick lumps ooty each-other.

Different story durin the war though, noo that wis a *real* break! Never mind a three-week shutdoon in case eh a couple eh snawflakes, there wis a *seven* year hiatus – aye, mind the bloody gap, awright! I dinnae ken if I've mentioned the war afore – probably not – but youse youngsters dinnae ken the hauf eh it. N I *am* talkin aboot the Second World War, no one eh thae daft wee skirmishes since then, maist eh which barely lasted six oors, never mind six years. Aye, it wis me against Hitler, much tae ma auld man's disgust. Admittedly, I did try tae register as a Conscientious Objector, but ma commandin officer wis havin nane eh it. Usually ye have tae dae it on religious groonds, kid on ye were a Jehovah's Witness or a Quaker or somethin, but I jist gied him it straight.

"Ma conscience objects tae me gettin shot at," I explained.

"Does your conscience object tae the idea eh warfare in general and the possible maiming and killing of innocent civilians?" he asked.

"Aw naw, I couldnae gie a fuck aboot that," I said. "Nor have I goat any problem aboot shootin other folk masel. Germans, Jews, Gypsies, Tramps n Thieves, Scotch, Irish, Russians – ye name it, I'll kill it! I jist object tae them tryin tae kill *me!*"

So I wis quickly posted tae Falkirk, tae stave aff a possible German invasion through Larbert. I wis jist in time tae be on the receivin end eh the first salvo eh the Scottish War Cup – five shots aimed wi deadly accuracy – intae the Hibs net! Aye, pumped 5-0 by the Bairns! So winnin the second-leg 4-0 at Easter Road wis aboot as much use as Stauffenberg's plot tae kill Hitler.

The followin year the war-time League wis set up n although Hibs did fuck aw in that either, they *did* lift the *big* trophy eh the day. The Scottish Cup's far superior replacement, The Summer Cup, wis carried aff in triumph, efter a thrillin showdoon wi Rangers. Naturally, as Hibs were 2-0 doon, I left wi a despairin cry eh 'worst gemme I've seen in ma life!' afore findin oot later they'd gaun on tae win 3-2. Pity they couldnae win by that score in a *Scottish* Cup final, I'll tell ye that! But the year efter that they met the huns in the final again n lost – on the toss eh a coin! A 0-0 draw resulted in the Rangers' captain daein the biz wi his dodgy penny, which hud the King's heid on baith sides. Whit a bloody liberty. Never mind fightin the Jerries, Leith should've declared war on Glesgie immediately efter that yin!

Talk aboot exactin revenge though, which occurred on September 27th, 1941. As I wis walkin doon the Albion Road, I met a total stranger, n he said tae me, are ye gaun tae see, the famous Glesgie Rangers? So aff I went tae Easter Road, tae see the famous Glesgie

Rangers – but the team eh the hun, goat fucked 8-1, by the famous Embra Hibees. Hibs scored four in each hauf n have a wild guess how the huns goat their solitary goal? Aye, via a bloody penalty! Some things never change.

Of course, I wisnae tae experience the rest eh Hibs' early 1940s campaign, as in an unwelcome development I wis posted fae Falkirk tae France. Quite literally – the Army jist sealed me in a crate n sent me First Class Air Mail tae Paris. Efter that, I wis involved in some eh the bloodiest theatres eh the war – youse youngsters have never seen the like. I thought it wid be safer stayin in the theatres rather than bein oot on the streets, ken, but ye could hardly settle doon n enjoy 'My Fair Lady' in French, cos eh the German Occupation bastirts eatin popcorn loudly throughoot. Ended up rollin aboot the aisles punchin fuck ooty Fritz n his friends on many an occasion, I can tell ye.

I wid have been at the D-Day Landings n aw, but unfortunately I wrote doon the wrong date in ma diary n wound up on some deserted bloody beach in northern France on ma ain! Nae sign eh Germans, sun-loungers, towels or even ice-cream vendors!

I wis there fur the Liberation though, n whit an experience that wis. Thoosands eh civilians linin the streets wavin flags n cheerin, whilst yours truly wis busy liberatin the contents eh their wine cellars, afore hijackin a lorry n fleein ower the border intae Spain. Later on I wis tried as a war criminal n passed wi flyin colours. Churchill himsel presented me wi a medal – naw, no auld Winston, I'm talkin aboot the dug aff the adverts on the telly. Aye, some eh us lost oor minds due tae the horrors we'd witnessed n some eh us hud nae minds tae lose in the first place.

Still, by the time I goat back tae Blighty, the war-time League wis in its last season n aff I went tae Killie tae see how the Hibs hud been gettin on in ma absence. Tae be honest, I wis far fae impressed. Get this – makin his debut up front, they hud a *sixteen year-auld laddie!* Looked like he couldnae have knocked snaw aff a dyke. I ken they were short eh players due tae the conflict, but this wis plain ridiculous.

"Well, we'll never clap eyes on *him* ever again, once they bring the boys back hame," I remarked tae the boy next tae me. "Whit's his name anyway?"

Noddin in agreement, he opened his programme n scrutinised the team-sheet.

"Lawrie Reilly," he said.

N as usual, I wis proved correct in that assessment!

I'D RATHER BE A NAZI THAN A JOCK

I wis then brought back abruptly tae the godawful present day (a guid war wid almost be welcome) wi news eh McLeish finally bein sacked as Scotland gaffer. Whit took thae bunglin bastirts in the blazers so long? Should've been handed his jotters directly efter the Kazakh catastrophe, n if no then, certainly efter pittin us through aw that extra sufferin against San Marino. His record wis absolutely abysmal, eh the twelve gemmes under him, only *one* could've been considered a reasonable result, the 3-2 victory ower Israel. N even that wis far tae close fur comfort n relied on a stand-oot performance on the night fae Forrest tae seal the deal. Utter pish!

So he hud tae go, but of course he should never have been appointed in the first place, definitely a case eh the wrong man at the wrong time. Ye can thank Pear-Tree in part fur that, in his position as underling tae the equally clueless Blazers' Chief Executive, Ian Maxwell. Oor Rod is tae easily distracted by tryin tae recoup the cash he says I owe him, tae dae the job properly n that's a fact! Naturally, despite the inexplicable time delay in emptyin Eck once the official announcement wis made, there wis nae hint whitsoever if they hud anyone else lined up or under consideration. Probably still tryin tae contact Willie Ormond, Ally McLeod n Jock Stein tae see if they fancied another crack at it.

I did briefly consider selflessly savin the nation by takin on the gig masel, but efter ma calamitous attempt at securin the Easter Road hoat-seat, I somehow dooted Pear-Tree wid be amenable tae that either. Certainly couldnae dae worse than some eh the other duffers they've hud. Vogts, Levein, Gordon Short-Erse 'Leigh Griffiths isnae tall enough' Strachan... Jawohl, mein herr, it is surely aboot time fur me tae reclaim ma Teutonic birthright, embrace ze Fatherland again n save masel the embarrassment eh bein Scottish. Aye, I'm gonnae dae an Erich Schaedlar in reverse. Awtaegether noo – Deutschland, Deutschland, Uber Taxis...

GLOBAL WARNING

At last, the first eh the post-split fixtures wis upon us, wi a visit fae Sellik. The weathermen were promisin sunshine on Leith n biChrist, they werenae kiddin! I wis that owercome wi heat I collapsed in

Albion Road ootside the Albion Bar – which hud mysteriously disappeared aff the face eh the Earth by the time I came roond. I looked up intae the unsympathetic face eh this glaikit-lookin polisman (mind ye, aren't they aw?) whae didnae appear tae happy.

"Ye canny kip there, grandpaw," he says sternly.

"I'm no kippin! I'm daein ma bit fur the 'Extinction – Hibernian' movement," I telt him. "This is a protest aboot climate change. Which, in case ye hudnae noticed, is changin a bit tae bloody fast fur comfort! I'm fair meltin here, worse than yon Polar ice-caps! So whit are ye gonnae dae aboot the greenhoose gases, eh? Nae social conscience, youse polis, that's the problem. Aye, we're the environmental Hibees, baby, we've goat class."

"I'll dae ma bit fur the environment, by leavin ma carbon footprint firmly embossed on yer erse, if ye dinnae move *now*," he says, giein me a threatenin preliminary prod wi the size 10s.

So ten minutes later I wis inside the stadium, but it felt mair like I *wis* sittin inside a giant greenhoose! I wis bloody beelin! But the heat wis on that mob fae the west tae, right fae the start, wi the Hibees absolutely cookin. Barryl Organ went close, Omeonga went closer, n I felt like stickin ma heid in the oven later on, when Oli the Wally passed up another great chance. But the undisputed Man eh the Match fur Hibs wis the big felly between the posts, he's magic you know, it's gotta be Marciano. Pilled aff a string eh fine saves, especially right at the end, when a veritable rash eh Sellik corners hud me in a right auld sweat. In fact, by that time I'd perspired that much throughoot that ma Bovril hud become fatally diluted, ma chips wid nae doot have been a soggy mess in ma lap *if they'd been available* n I'd lost aboot hauf ma body weight intae the bargain. Aye, it wis almost genuinely Extinction – Hibernian fur yours truly, fried tae death in the midday sun, aw that – jist tae watch a nil – nil draw!

See the things that team pit me through... A lesser man might have complained, but ye ken me, it's jist no in ma nature. I never even goat a shot on one eh thae sniffer dugs, that Dumpster hud said wid be daein the roonds, tae prevent drugs, flares or smoke bombs gettin intae the groond. Which wis maybe jist as well in retrospect, cos I wis cairryin aw three. Aye, ye'll have mair tae worry aboot than that, Leeann ma love, when global warming causes the whole stadium tae go up in a big puff eh smoke! It's comin, mark ma words, Mark McNulty, even. Mind where ye read it first – the end is nigh!

CONTRACT KILLER

In the wake eh the Sellik gemme, the welcome news came through that baith Knight eh the Hibernian Realm, Sir David Gray n Darren McGregor hud signed four-year contracts. Well, bully for *them*, I thought, but whit aboot yours truly? As usual wi Hibs, there's one law fur the players n another fur the fans. It's no right. Efter aw, I'd been giein everythin tae the Hibernian cause fur a lot longer than that pair. I thought aboot gettin on the blower tae Pear-Tree, but nae doot he'd jist refuse tae take the call or start bitchin aboot his mythical thirty-four grand again. Dumpster? Nae bloody way, she'd been refusin tae take ma calls an aw, even when I tricked the operator intae connectin me, by usin a range eh cunningly-crafted aliases, based on the names eh Hibs' players. Only the other week I got through claimin tae be Mr Omeonga Malonga-Agyepongo,

Snoddy Stanton, Tortolano O'Rourke, Riordan O'Connor n Kenny Brazil, but she tippled it wis me every time. Christ kens how, cos I used different voices fur every one, no tae mention speakin in different languages. Anyway, that only left George Craig, Heid eh Fitba Operations. Must've been instrumental in agreein terms wi Sir David n Daz ye'd have thought, so I phoned Easter Road again n telt them tae pit me through tae Dode pronto.

"Who shall I say is calling, sir?"

"My name is Ma Kalambay Zltelli, n I'm no a sir, I'm a wumman," I said. "A *French* woman in fact, ken, one eh thae Madam Mozelles."

"I'm sorry, madam, your deep voice had me confused there. As did your extremely peculiar accent. May I ask what it is in connection with?"

"I'm a famous player in the French Burds' League, tap scorer fur the Hunchbacks eh Notre-Dame two seasons on the trot n I'd like tae join Hibernian Ladies as soon as possible."

"Hold the line, madam, and I'll try to connect you."

N that wis it, easy as pie! Straight through tae the Dodester himsel! Of course, I'd have tae confess I'd jist used a clever ruse tae get through tae him in the first place, n then hit him wi ma demands.

"That's not you *again* is it, Gibby?" he sighed.

Well, *that* threw me a bit, n nae mistake!

"Eh...naw...well, aye, but, naw, but...aye... How did ye ken it wis me?"

"Gibby, you have been plaguing Hibernian Football Club with a series of ridiculous phone-calls incessantly for weeks, under a raft of increasingly implausible pseudonyms. You are well aware that you are banned by law from trying to contact either the Chairman or the Chief Executive of this club anyway and now the telephone operators and reception staff are sick to the back teeth of you as well, which is the only reason I am speaking to you now. So what is it this time – not more nonsense about chips, by any chance?"

"Naw, Dode, nae worries, nae chips – on ma shuder or anywhere else – n especially no in the Famous Five Stand feedin-trough," I said quickly, afore he could hang up. "It's a disgrace fur sure, but I'm no here tae talk aboot chips. Thing is, I wis jist wonderin if there's any chance eh giein me a four-year contract, same as ye've done fur Davie Boy n the Dazmeister? I ken they were integral tae the Scottish Cup win, no that I can mind anythin aboot it, but bear in mind I wis there when they won it the first two times, so I wis integral tae thae triumphs by virtue eh cheerin the boys ontae victory! N I've been gaun ever since – apart fae the times I wis layin doon ma life fur ma country in two World Wars. So whit dae ye say tae that, Georgie Porgie? Fair's fair, efter aw. I dinnae even want aw the money up front, ye can pay me fur ma on-goin support in instalments. Have we goat a deal?"

There wis the kind eh irritatingly lengthy silence at the other end that seems tae be a mair or less permanent feature eh ma personal telecommunications. I wis jist rememberin that I forgot tae ask fur his views on climate change but there wis nae need, cos when he finally did speak his voice wis that cauld it wis obvious that the temperature in EH7 5QG hud awready dropped alarmingly.

"Oh, we've goat a deal alright," he said flatly.

"Glad tae hear it!"

"Let me finish, Gibby. The deal is this – you promise to *never* make another phone-call to this club for as long as you may live, and I'll not phone the police and instantly have you arrested for making malicious calls with underlying threats of extortion. Not just yet, anyway. So – deal or no deal?"

But the bastirt hung up, afore I hud the chance tae tell him tae stick it right up his chorus n verse!

So it wisnae long afore I wis relatin the tragic tale eh bein ruthlessly cast aside n done ower by Hibs – again! – tae a largely unsympathetic audience in The Cenny. Then, that great bearer eh bad tidings, Humpty Harry himsel, pit in his tuppenceworth, wi whit appeared tae be unseemly glee.

"Of course, it must've been a disappointment tae ye," he said. "But look on the bright side, at least ye've still goat a contract deal eh sorts."

"How dae ye mean?"

"Oh, have ye no heard yet?" says the sadistic shitebag wi a smirk. "Slasher Smith's only gaun n pit a contract oot on ye!"

"Whit?!"

It took a while fur the penny tae drop. N then it took even longer fur the second penny tae drop. So by the time I'd taken on-board the humpty yin's tuppenceworth eh terror, I wis pure shitin ma breeks.

"Whit...whit...whit have I done tae upset Slasher?" I stammered, visions eh Rod the Fraud n his Victoria Cross still aw tae fresh in ma mind.

"Says ye've been takin the pish."

I wis jist aboot tae refute this suggestion, when an awfy realisation dawned on me. Ye see, I *hud* been takin the pish – quite literally. Slasher's bladder problem meant that the urinal trough in The Cenny wis usually full tae the point eh owerflowin, so I'd been siphoning it aff when naebody wis lookin, mainly jist tae help wi health n hygiene, ken.

"I dinnae ken whit he's in a strop aboot that fur," I puzzled oot loud, once I'd explained the situ. "It's no like he's goat any mair use fur it, surely?"

"Aye – but someone telt him that *you* did. Telt some boy it wis fur the roses. Come aff it, Gibby – ye really expect us tae believe ye're fertilisin yer flooirs courtesy eh Slasher's slashes? Ye've no even goat a windae-box, fur Chrissakes!"

I jist goat slowly tae ma feet n tottered oot the door in a haze. I suspected that any further explanations wid only dae mair herm than guid. Cos in truth, it *wis* fur The Roses – The Bunch eh Roses, that is! I'd been sellin it by the bucket-load tae the bar-staff by the back-door n passin it aff as Tennents Lager. N so far, naebody hud noticed any difference! But strictly speakin, I suppose I wis therefore guilty eh takin the pish, by, er, takin the pish. Right enough, jist a metaphor fur ma miserable life fae beginnin tae end – a pure loadypish, when aw wis said n done.

CRAZY IN LOVE

I wis doon The Shore fur a wee daunder, checkin oot the rumour that a Great White shark hud become disoriented at sea n wis noo stuck in the Water eh Leith, ootside the Malt n Hops. Of course, there wis nae sign eh any such thing, so either some radge hud been talkin pish or they'd jist caught a glimpse eh Slasher Smith ooty the corner eh their eye. It wisnae hard tae confuse the Great White wi the Great Shite – aw cauld deid eyes, razor-sharp gnashers n a taste fur human flesh. I wis hopin Smithy wis gonnae find God / Pat Stanton again a bit sharpish n cancel the contract, but best tae be on the safe side. So I wis intent on avoidin the usual haunts, until this stunnin-lookin American lassie came shimmerin ooty The Malmaison n asked me fur directions tae The Marksman.

"I'll take ye there masel," I said gallantly. "Er...are youse meetin anyone there at aw – say, a local wi occasional religious mania n weak bladder fur example?"

Couldnae be tae careful, ken. She threw back her lovely heid n laughed uproariously.

"Gee, I just *lurve* the *Skattish* sense of humour, even though I don't understand it," she replied, with a Texan twang. "No, I'm just on my own. Fancied a break from all the showbiz pressure and read about this quaint little tavern in 'The Good Pub Guide'."

Must be the special edition yin, written by the owners eh The Marksman, which doesnae have any other pubs listed in it, I thought somewhit cynically. But fur once, I hud the guid sense tae keep ma opinions tae masel.

So fifteen minutes later we were in the Duke Street dive n I chivalrously allowed her tae get the drinks in, just tae gie her a gen-u-ine Skattish experience, ken. But she'd looked awfy familiar fae the start n her remark aboot showbiz hud me wrackin ma Roy Baines fur some clue as tae her identity. She wis clearly *somebody* – but whae??

Luckily, she wis knockin back the pints eh Export at such a rate that she soon hud tae go tae whit thae Americans demurely refer tae as 'the rest-room' tae 'powder her nose'. (Although nose-powderin eh the other sort hud been known tae take place in The Gents n aw). It wis at that moment, as I stood starin blankly at auld music videos on the telly screen, that it suddenly hit me like a bolt fae the green. Fur there she wis, on Zitelli, frontin an aw-girl group, singin 'I'm A Survivor'. Aye, it wis only her that used tae be in Dysentery's Child n wis noo a global superstar efter gaun solo! Whit wis her name again though...something tae dae wi trampolines flickered through ma mind fur some reason...

"Alright, Gibby, can I get you another one?"

I almost jumped ooty ma skin, as she suddenly reappeared at ma elby. I couldnae help starin.

"I... I... I've jist realised whae youse are!" I gasped.

A glorious blush spread ower the broon skin on her gorgeous coupon.

"I was hoping to remain unrecognised today, but I suppose it was only a matter of time," she said shyly. "So who do you think I am?"

Then I remembered the name! Thank Christ fur that, jist as well I wis thinkin aboot whit kind eh movements ye make on a trampoline!

"Ye're Bouncy, aren't ye?" I croaked. "N dinnae deny it, doll, cos I've jist seen ye shakin yer funky booty on the box there!"

"It's *Beyoncé* actually, but close enough," she admitted. "Look, Gibby, I feel a bit self-conscious now that you and probably half the bar know who I am. Goddam that freaking television! Do you fancy moving on somewhere else? How about The Central?"

Holy Moly!

"Lead the way, doll! I'm right behind ye, bringin up the rear!"

(I felt obliged tae bring up her rear an aw, two globes eh gorgeousness encased in tight, *tight* denim. Phwoarr! A bit on the big side fur some tastes, ken, but no fur this connoisseur eh curvaceousness!)

So we swaggered intae The Cenny n tae be honest I couldnae have gied a flyin duck if Slasher *hud* been in the place, crucifyin some poor bastirt tae the waw. In fact, I wid have positively welcomed the sight! Cos, hard as it is tae believe, it's no every day I stroll intae a Leith boozer wi the likes eh Bouncy Knowles on ma airm! Jist wait till thae bevvied-up bitter bastirts spillin their lager ower The Racing Post get an eyeful eh Gibby n his gal! I'd be the envy eh aw the single laddies, aw the single laddies...

Aw very well, but the annoyin thing wis that *nane* eh ma usual circle eh pathetic pals n parasites appeared tae be on the premises. Even Girnin Gertie must've been on a day aff, cos her stand-in didnae even bat an eye when I strode up tae the bar n yelled, "Pint eh Export fur me n whit aboot youse, BOUNCY? Same again?"

I mean, it's hardly a common name is it, but still got no reaction.

“I think I’ll go for the half-pint and nip offer,” she replied, scrutinisin the sign on the waw.

“OK, make that a hauf eh McEwan’s Ecky n a Whyte n Mackay fur MISS KNOWLES!!” I practically screamed, castin furtive glances around at the other punters. But naebody wis payin any attention.

So we settled doon on two stools at the bar, where *someone* wis bound tae clock us sooner or later. Ma drinkin companion explained that she’d jist felt the need tae unwind efter heidlinin a HUGE concert in London, n hud simply hopped on a plane tae lap up the Skattish culture fur a few days, afore returnin tae The Smoke.

“Tell me though, Bouncy, are ye related tae the late Cyril Knowles, whae played fur Spurs in the 1970s?”

“Er...I don’t think so,” she replied, a bit uncertainly.

“Cos he wis kind eh musical tae, as well as bein a barry fitba player,” I went on, warmin tae ma theme. “Did vocals on that song ‘Nice One Cyril’, ken – nice one Cyril / nice one, son / nice one Cyril / let’s have another one. It wis credited tae The Cockerel Chorus, ken, cos eh the big cock on the Tottenham badge, likes, but it wis really jist the team singin it. Goat intae the charts tae! No a patch on ‘Hibernian (Gie us a Goal)’ though. Ye ever thought aboot daein a cover version eh that? The Hibs song that is, no the Spurs yin!”

“Um...I’m not actually familiar with either,” she admitted, lookin somewhit scoobied. “Maybe a bit before my time.”

“Are ye familiar then wi the late kids’ entertainer n telly star Roy Castle, or wis he afore yer time tae? Cos I wis thinkin how funny it wid have been if ye’d married his laddie, instead eh yon rapper felly.”

"No, I don't know of him either. But how do you mean?"

"Cos then ye'd be a Bouncy Castle."

"Mmm. Yes – no doubt that would be *extremely* funny – *if* my name was Bouncy. But it's not – it's *Beyoncé!*"

Oh, how we laughed. Or at least I did. She sort eh scowled in a bad-tempered but still pretty way. So we were gettin on that well I wis beginnin tae idly wonder aboot tryin tae tap her up fur thirty-four grand, when this pished jambo staggered past.

"See that fuckin team eh yours on Sunday, couldnae have scored in a brothel," he slavered.

Bouncy arched a perfectly plucked questionin eyebrow in ma direction.

"Hibs," I clarified. "Drew 0-0 wi Sellik."

"Ah. I thought it must have been. So, Gibby, do tell – is Joe Tortolano still advertising sun-beds?"

"Whit?!"

"There's no need to look so surprised! I thought Joe was a very sexy man, back in his heyday. Quite a pin-up figure with the rock chicks of Hollywood, I can tell you, as well as the rest of Destiny's Child."

When I'd finally stopped chokin on ma pint, I became aware eh two worthies approachin, commonly kent as Rory the Choarie n Tea-Leaf Keith. The latter's claim that he wis so-cawed as a result eh his fortune-tellin skills via readin tea-leaves at the bottom eh yer cup wis generally tae be taken wi an extremely large pinch eh salt.

"Scorpio?" he inquired, jerkin a greasy thumb in ma companion's direction.

"I dinnae ken whit her star-sign is," I said shortly.

"Naw, ya radge – does she no work at Scorpio Leisure wi Senga n Fifi?"

"Naw, she maist certainly fuckin doesnae. Fur Chrissake, dae ye no recognise her, ya bam?"

He proceeded tae study her critically, lookin her up n doon like he wis checkin oot a slab eh meat in the butcher's windae.

"Right enough, it's no her efter aw. No a bad-lookin doll, though!" he added cheerfully, whilst I manfully resisted the temptation tae ram ma pint tumbler intae his glaikit pus. Meanwhile, Rory the Choarie wis movin in fur the kill.

"Are ye interested in a brand new DVD player – cash on the nail n nae questions asked?"

"No thank you," said Bouncy politely, takin a big belt eh the Whyte n Mackay.

"How aboot dresses?"

"I'm sorry?"

"Nae need tae be, hen. They're no exactly *hoat*, ken, but a wee bit on the warm side, I must admit."

Then, afore I could grab him by the scrawny throat n throttle him on the spot, he'd moved ontae paint.

"Paint?" enquired Bouncy faintly, as if she'd jist been inhalin that very substance's fumes fur a bit tae long.

"Aye, stacks eh it. I've goat aboot 450 tins – *giant* yins – eh bright yelly stuff, ken it aw kind eh fell aff the back eh a lorry wi'oot spillin, if ye get ma drift. I can have it delivered, if ye want!"

Finally I cracked.

"Look, ya choaryin bastirt, she doesnae want DVDs, dresses, paint or anythin else ye're puntin, right? So afore ye sling yer hook, take another look. Dae – ye – no – ken- whae – she – is?"

His eyes grew wide n his jaw dropped. At last, I thought, at long bloody last. Then a fearful expression crept ower his face n he raised his stick-thin airm as if tae ward aff an imminent blaw.

"Fur the love eh Christ, she's yin eh thae undercover bizzies is she no?" he gasped.

At the utterance eh that phrase, Tea-Leaf Keith slithered aff his stool n oot the door at remarkable speed, closely followed by his partner-in-crime.

"The Undercover Bizzies?" queried Bouncy. "Are they a band?"

"Somethin like that. Sort eh like The Police," I added, in sudden inspiration.

Well, it wis a relief tae get rid eh that pair eh Highland Dancers – *but where the fuck wis everybody else?* Right enough, Moany Tony hud been lyin low in embarrassment ever since his Nigerian nightmare, Humpty Harry wid be revellin in some other poor bastirt's misery in The Bam O' Shanter, Slasher wid be havin a slash or slashin someone else, Roddy wis in the infirmary, Junky Johnston (or whit wis left eh him) wis in the mortuary... It wis quite spoilin ma efternin oot wi one eh the maist famous burdz on the planet, that naebody wis there tae witness it. Then aw eh a sudden, Torn-faced Tommy shuffled in the door wi a face on him like a wet Wednesday in Wilkies.

"Tommy!" I yelped, wi mair enthusiasm than I'd ever greeted him afore.

"Whitever it is, the answer's naw," he muttered suspiciously, clearly pit oot by ma demeanour.

"Dinnae worry, I'm no efter yer dough," I said reassuringly. "I jist want ye tae answer a simple question."

"Which is?"

I birled Bouncy roond on her stool so fast she spilled maist eh her Export intae her crotch, but at least she wis facin him heid on.

"Dae ye ken whae this is?"

He stared at her fur a few seconds.

"Naw."

"She is a singer," I continued, as ma sense eh rage n frustration bubbled up tae a dangerous level. "A *very famous* singer."

"I still dinnae ken."

"Ye bloody must dae!" I yelled. "Fur Chrissakes, man, think hard!"

He proceeded tae gawp at her afresh, but wi a bit mair concentration this time.

"Oh aye," he finally said. "Now I've goat it."

Well, it wis hardly the awestruck reaction I'd hoped fur, but that's that torn-faced tosspot fur ye.

"It's her fae that Country n Western band that play doon The Dockers Club, is it no?"

"Whit?!"

"Aye," he went on, wi greater conviction. "That's her awright. Krystle Shan-de-Lier, the crossover Dutch – Leith Dolly Parton eh The Dockers. Looks a bit different in the daylight, right enough. Tidy piece eh crumpet, though."

By this point, it seemed that Bouncy had jist aboot hud enough eh The Cenny n I couldnae say that I blamed her. Efter aw, I'd cowped Export ower her, subjected her tae the attentions eh two notorious criminal scumbags n wis noo showin her aff like some prize exhibit in the zoo. She blootered back the rest eh the whisky n informed me curtly she wis heidin back tae her hotel pronto, n catchin a flight back tae London the followin day. Then she wis oot the door, afore I'd even broached the matter eh a wee five-figure loan.

I gargled back the remainder eh ma drink, feelins tae deep fur words. Then, swingin roond, ma anguished gaze fell upon the motley collection eh jakeys, flakeys, junkies, cheeky monkeys, hooks, crooks n comic singers n of course that fuckin eejit Tommy.

"Ye bunch eh blind bastirts!" I howled. "That so-cawed *tidy piece eh crumpet* wis nane other than Bouncy Knowles! Understand whit I'm sayin? Only the international megastar, Bouncy Knowles!"

A prolonged awkward silence followed ma wee ootburst. I poured another pint doon ma throat in a oner, jist as an irritatin cough sounded behind me, the sort that someone gies when they want tae attract yer attention. I turned roond angrily, tae see an incredibly dirty auld vagrant sittin by the door. His coat wis black wi dirt n tied wi string n his boots were fawin tae pieces. He regarded me intently through a pair eh sharp eyes set deep in his filthy grime-encrusted battered coupon.

"I've jist been listenin tae whit ye've been sayin, pal," he said. "N I think youse hud better watch yer fuckin step. Noo – dae ye ken whae *I* am?"

"Naw," I replied coldly.

"I'm Jay-Z."

It wis the first time in ages I'd actually lamped someone even aulder than masel.

* In the interests of accuracy, it must be pointed out that after we, the publishers, sought to clarify the veracity of the above, a spokesperson for Ms Knowles issued the following statement:- *'Beyoncé categorically denies ever drinking pints of McEwan's Export and / or nips of Whyte & Mackay whisky in The Marksman or The Central, in Leith, Edinburgh, Bonnie Skatland. Furthermore, nor has she ever met or socialised with anyone by the name of 'Gibby', 'Gibson', or 'Grumpy'. She does admit to once fancying Joe Tortolano though.'*

When we put this to Mr Gibson, his first reaction was, predictably, "The lassie's talkin pish." However, when we further presented Mr Gibson with irrefutable evidence that Ms Knowles was in fact attending a barbecue at Snoop Dogg's mansion in San Antonio,

Texas, at exactly the same time as he claimed to have been in her company, his story changed somewhat. He went on to claim that if it wasn't actually her then it was almost certainly her stunt double, but failing that perhaps he merely dreamt it, or, possibly, it never actually happened at all. In fairness, we must add that we were unable to ascertain the exact whereabouts of Jay-Z (a.k.a. Mr Beyoncé) at that particular time, so it *might* have been him who got punched in the pus by Gibby in The Central. However, being a self-styled 'bad-ass dude from the 'hood', he would be unlikely to admit to it.

GO ASK ALICE WHEN SHE'S TEN FOOT TALL

So, derby day wis upon us once more, n as tradition long dictated I was havin a pre-match pint in The Bam O'Shanter wi Lady Gaga. Noo, if ye believe that, ye'll believe anythin, cos that wis in fact a blatant lie. But I wis jist sayin that tae make a point, which is that whilst I wis lyin *there*, I maist emphatically *wisnae,* wi regard tae boozin wi Bouncy. Thae Braidwood Books bastirts are jist tae damned suspicious, questionin the veracity eh hauf the things I come oot wi, n then tryin tae prove that I'm talkin pish. Christ kens why. I tell ye this, if publishers in the past were so pernickety aboot the truth, some eh the maist well-kent factual books eh aw time wid never have seen the light eh day!

Take Alice n her dubious 'Adventures in Wonderland' fur example. The lassie claimed tae have fawin doon a rabbit-hole, gaun tae a Mad Hatter's Tea Party, met loads eh animals whae could talk, taken advice fae a hookah-smokin caterpillar, seen a Cheshire Cat whae kept disappearin (except fur its grin) n played croquet wi the Queen eh Hearts (naw, no Justin Fashanu or Annie Budge) n naebody accused *her* eh makin up stories. Does any eh that sound as plausible as yours truly knockin em back wi Knowles? Naw, it does not. So I hope that Mr Braidwood bloody Books sittin in his ivory tower in Carluke takes on board whit I've said. N jist tae reiterate – I *wisnae* drinkin wi Lady Gaga at aw. I wis actually havin a pint wi Lord Gaga himsel.

"How dae ye let her go oot dressed like that?" I asked him. "See yon ootfit made ooty meat – surely every dug in toon wis on her tail?"

But he jist gied me the big Poker Face n said nowt. Well fuck him, I wis aff tae continue ma Bad Romance wi the Hibees.

First eh aw, there wis a minute's applause fur oor former goalie, Andy McNeil, fur some reason n then we goat doon tae business on the hottest day at Easter Road since April 21st, 2019. Aye – baked alive fur the second week in a row! If thae clueless catering staff hud jist thought tae bring along bags eh frozen McCain's oven chips (which they didnae, needless tae say) they'd have cooked themsels in nae time at aw!

Anyway, jist like New Year's Day 1973, the Hertz were soon seven doon. In yelly cairds that is, the dirty nigglin bastirts that they are. But it wis a typical derby stalemate n nae surprise when the trooped aff level at 0-0 efter the first hauf. I hud a feelin I'd seen this yin afore. Several times...

In the queue fur a scran at the break (certainly wisnae fur chips either, I can tell ye that), I wis so sunburned that I initially got mistaken fur Stephane Omeonga. Then, by the time I goat tae the coonter, the lassie servin thought I wis Marvin Bartley. Or, should I say the lassie *no* servin – she refused tae gie me a pie on the groonds that it might adversely affect ma performance if I came on as a sub! Whit a bloody nerve! A measly single pie is hardly gonnae make any difference tae a superb physical specimen like masel wi a slimline figure tae be envied. I pilled up ma top defiantly tae show her ma six-pack n half-a-dozen cans eh Export instantly fell oot ontae the deck. She fainted deid away on the spot – but I think that wis maybe doon tae ma Benny fae 'Crossroads' chest tattoo.

However, it goat better fae a Hibs point eh view in the second period – at least until McNut-Roast skelped a pish-poor penalty the wrang side eh the upright. Christ, how hard can it be, man?! Mind ye, I blame the groondsman tae, he should've thought tae widen the gap between the posts afore kick-aff. But then, the newly-crowned Hammer eh the Hertz, Barryl Organ, stepped up n did the biz, although it ws actually credited tae Yogi Berra as an o.g. "Oh gee," wis his reaction n aw, if ye were skilled in the art eh lip-readin. On the other hand, he might have been sayin something startin wi the latter afore 'g' instead. But rather than pressin hame the advantage, Hibs sat back tae much n let that lot regain the initiative. There wis a sense eh inevitability aboot it when that huge great galumphing galoot Ikpea-Soup equalised wi six minutes tae go. Makes Christian Nade look positively anorexic, so he does. "Disappointin tae say the least," as Alex Miller wid nae doot have said, n fur once I'd have hud tae agree wi him.

Hertz fans covered themsels in ignominy as usual, by disruptin the minute's applause at the start, throwin a flare ontae the park n wreckin seats in whit I insist should still be cawed the Karen Dunbar End. Match-day safety officer Alan Marshall hud a curious take on it, as he wis quoted in the papers efterwards as sayin, "I would say the Hearts fans were pretty well-behaved. There were around 28 seats broken but no major destruction." Which is a bit like the mayor eh Hiroshima, Japan, remarkin on August 6th, 1945 that it wis a wee bit warm fur the time eh year. "I would say the American pilots were pretty well-behaved. There were around 60,000 people killed but no major destruction."

It only goat worse tae, when I returned tae The Bam O'Shanter efterwards. Belligerent barman Erse-Faced Eddie took great delight in informin me that Lord Gaga hud been splashin the cash non-stop right up until 2 p.m., buyin drinks fur aw n sundry, by which time his wallet wis as shredded as his other hauf's claes. Like the Hibs, sometimes ye jist canny win.

* In the interests of accuracy, it must be pointed out by we, the publishers, that contrary to what Mr Gibson appears to believe, 'Alice's Adventures in Wonderland' has never been presented as a 'factual' book. Leaving aside Gibson's outrageous slurs against Braidwood Books, we also remain somewhat sceptical about the genuine existence of Lord Gaga.

RAISING KANE

"May-Day, May-Day! N if ye think that's a distress call ye're hearin, ye're bloody right it is. Cos although it actually *wis* May Day, I wis in some state eh distress awright. Fell aff the tap eh Arthur's Seat, ken – *or wis I pushed?*"

Humpty Harry regarded me critically.

"Were ye pished, did ye ask? A rhetorical question I assume, cos it wid hardly be the first time, wid it?"

"Naw – *pushed,* ya deef daftie!" I reiterated.

I wis relatin this tale eh woe tae him as we sat there in The Cenny – me wi some difficulty as I wis bandaged up like yin eh thae Egyptian mummies efter ma wee 'accident'. *But wis it an accident at aw??*

"Whit were ye daein up Arthur's Seat anyway?" queried Humpty.

"Christ, man, it's a long-standin Embra tradition datin back hunners eh years," I said. "Gaun up there at the crack eh dawn on the first day eh May. I even asked the Hibs goalie tae come along."

"Ye whit? Which yin? N whit fur?"

Get a loady auld Humpty Dumpty there! Question efter question efter question. He's ayewis been a questionable character, right enough.

"Well, Marciano of course! Whae else?"

"But why him?"

"Cos the tradition is tae go up there n wash yer face wi the Jew."

There wis a pregnant silence, durin which he looked as if he wis aboot tae have triplets.

"Naw, ye silly auld goat, the tradition is tae go up there n wash yer face *in the dew*!" he finally replied.

Noo it wis ma turn tae look as if I wis aboot tae gie birth.

"Ye're talkin pish as usual," I scoffed. "Anyway, he didnae want tae come, as he prefers takin the Rocky Road, rather than the Radical Road.

So I hud tae climb up there masel, cos thae Cooncil bastirts havenae installed an escalator yet. Christ, it wis like scalin the auld main terracing at Easter Road back in the day! A thick mist came doon as we approached the tap, n I lost sight eh the team eh Sherpas whae were luggin the cairry-oot."

"Thought ye said ye were on yer ain," objected that nitpickin numpty, guzzlin back the Mick Jagger.

"I *wis* on ma ain, servants dinnae coont," I ploughed on irritably. "But luckily I still hud one oxygen cylinder left, plus a distress flare that I forgot tae chuck on the park at Tiny Castle. The summit wis almost within reach, when, aw eh a sudden, it happened!"

"Whit?"

"Whit dae ye mean 'whit?' – dae ye no read the papers or watch the News? Fur the first time in thoosands eh years the volcano erupted, that's whit happened! The pyroclastic flow totally wiped oot the whole eh Dumbiedykes!"

"Paul Kano erupted, ye say? Wis he there in place eh Rocky, like?"

See that corn-beef catastrophe sittin opposite me? I swear I'd pay tae get his lugs syringed masel. Maybe get his brain syringed at the same time, fur aw the guid it wid dae.

"I felt the burnin lava surgin aw aroond me, as I hung on there fur dear life," I went on, ignorin his last question. "Then, jist when I thought the worst eh it wis ower, I felt a sinister presence in the misty gloom, reachin oot fur me. That's aw I can mind, afore the ambulance gadgies nursed me back tae consciousness at the foot eh the Crags."

Humpty contemplated this chain eh events thoughtfully.

“So... are ye sayin that ye were pushed oot intae thin air by...”

“Aye, aye – I reckon it wis him awright,” I butted in excitedly. “Bigfoot, the Yeti, The Abominable Snowman, whitever ye want tae caw him!”

“Oh,” responded Humpty glumly, “I thought ye were gonnae say it wis Slasher Smith.”

I shot bolt upright in ma seat, as if someone hud suddenly dunked ma taes in a basin full eh molten lava.

“Slasher...”

See, up tae that point, I’d somehow managed tae pit that radge tae the back eh ma mind. Drinkin wi Bouncy Knowles n Lord Gaga can fatally distract a man, efter aw. So wis it possible that either him or one eh his henchmen hud follyed me up that bloody mountain, wi a view tae daein the dirty deed? A bit like Professor Moriarty tryin tae shove Sherlock Holmes tae his doom doon that waterfall! The mair I thought aboot it, the mair likely it seemed n havin an Abominable Snowman on ma trail instead seemed like a far mair attractive proposition. There wis nae doot I wis gonnae have tae reimburse Smithy fur takin the pish, afore the contract wis fulfilled, one way or another.

N ma troubles werenae ower in other departments either, once his Humptiness started bumpin his gums aboot ma experience, aw ower Leith. Next thing I kent, I wis gettin huckled ooty The Four-in-Hand by the owner n telt in nae uncertain terms no tae come back! Appeared he wis less than happy tae hear I’d been gaun around sayin that Paul Kane hud spontaneously combusted up Arthur’s Seat, or words tae that effect...

WHIT'S IN A NAME?

Tae be honest (n despite thae publisher bastirts' allegations, I'm never anythin less than that), I've never hud much luck wi pubs owned by former Hibees. When Lawrie Reilly hud The Bowlers' Rest, I wis kind enough tae point oot tae him that people might therefore assume it wis run by a famous ex-bowler rather than an ex-fitballer. Could be losin oot on potential custom, ken? But efter I suggested a change eh name fur his ain guid, he immediately suggested a change eh location fur yours truly, also fur ma ain guid.

Ye ken me though, I'm no one tae take offence. So I went up tae The Footballers' Arms, n pointed oot tae Willie Ormond that as thae appendages fitballers have danglin doon fae their shuders were largely superfluous tae their gemme, he'd be better aff cawin it The Footballers' Legs. In response, he suggested I used ma ain legs tae pit as much distance between masel n his hostelry as wis humanly possible.

Next stop wis whit used tae be Mac's Bar, until a famous ex-player n manager took it ower n renamed it E.T.'s.

"Folk will think ye're aimin tae attract aw thae sad sci-fi bampots n movie buffs," I complained.

"Really? Well, I'm sensin an unwelcome *alien* presence in ma pub right noo," growled Ned. "It's about time *you* phoned home – preferably fae the phone-box at the tap eh Easter Road. N dinnae bother comin back."

Charmin, eh?

So I did go up tae the tap eh Easter Road, but only tae catch a bus along tae the end eh London Road.

"Jock's Lodge is a shite name fur a boozer run by an ex-Hibee," I telt Jimmy O'Rourke. "Fur a start, the second word implies an affinity wi sash-wearin flute-playin wash-hand basins, n whae's Jock fur Chrissake? In that context, it could be the ex-hun manager Wallace, whae used tae enjoy runnin up n doon the sand dunes at Gullane."

Wordlessly, the proprietor handed me a timetable fur the 124 bus.

"Whit's this fur?"

"Ye can catch that service right outside the door, which'll take ye directly tae Gullane," he said. "When ye get there, folly the sand dunes until ye find yersel facin the open sea..."

"Aye – n then whit?"

"N then jist keep walkin."

Well, I can take a subtle hint as well as the next man. I retraced ma steps tae the bus-stop, but rather than heidin fur the seaside, I jumped an LRT 44 doon Willowbrae Road.

"The Right Wing is a shite name fur a pub next tae a workin-class area," I telt Gordon Smith. "Ye're jist gonnae attract a Tory clientele wi a handle like that n alienate the fine upstandin Labour Party populace eh Mountcastle n Northfield. Why no caw it The Left Wing instead?"

"Cos Willie Ormond usually played in that position," he replied.

"I've jist spoken tae Willie Ormond n he's goat his airms n legs aw mixed up," I informed him, jist as two big bruisers ominously stepped ooty the shadows n started flexin their knuckles.

"Aye? Well these gentlemen will be happy tae mix yer airms n legs up n aw, tae such an extent that ye'll no be able tae tell yer erse fae yer elbow. Kindly leave these premises *now* – n dinnae come back."

So a dizzyingly whistle-stop tour eh Embra then ensued, durin which I castigated Cropley n Marinello fur havin unimaginative pub names like Cropley's n Marinello's (Cropley hud Cropley's n Marinello hud Marinello's, by the way, cos it widnae have made much sense eh Cropley hud Marinello's n Marinello hud Cropley's, wid it,) n then I ticked aff Schaedlar fur 'Shades' n telt George Stewart aff fur runnin a pub in Hertz territory. Then at last I wound up in Cairns Bar, where none other than mine host Pat Stanton wis pourin me a pint. This wis mair like it! Ye'd get nae complaints fae me wi God lookin doon upon me beatifically... Still, I felt obliged tae use up *one* mair complaint anyway, n an opportunity presented itsel as I bade farewell tae Pat n carried ontae Abbeyhill. Stoppin aff in the first howff there, I decided tae get them telt n aw.

"Giein this place's location, I wis wonderin why it's cawed The Station Bar?"

"Well, Gibby," said the bar-keep, "whit form eh transport dae ye generally associate wi stations?"

"Eh...trains?" I suggested.

"Precisely."

"But I still dinnae get the connection..."

"Oh, but ye will – any moment now."

Aw a sudden I goat a fuckin connection awright, as wi a terrible WHOOOSH n horns soundin deafeningly, I wis promptly flattened by an incomin Inter-City 125.

THE FOE, DEFOE, FLO, N A SAIR TOE

"Gaun tae Ibrox?" enquired Torn-Faced Tommy, as the final encoonter eh the season against the Innis & Gunns came upon us.

"I wid love tae," I lied. "But the auld war wound is playin up somethin terrible again."

"Oh aye?" he said disbelievingly. "Which yin?"

"The yin fae the *Second* World War. Thing is, when ye've laid doon yer life fur Queen n country as often as I have, it's hard tae remember sometimes. Efter aw, I've goat wounds fae World Wars One, Two n Three n fae wars yet tae be fought."

"I mean, which *wound*?" he persisted. "No which conflict ye allegedly sustained it in."

I grabbed a haud eh ma leg dramatically n simultaneously winced, in Oscar-winnin style.

"The shrapnel in ma left pin is giein me gyp."

"Funny that – seein as it wis apparently lodged in yer *right* pin, the last time ye tried tae get ooty gaun tae a gemme."

"Well, it's moved since then," I snapped. "Same as the bullets lodged aw ower ma body. The doaktir says that if the yin near ma spinal cord shifts by one *millimetre* I could be paranoid fur life!"

"Don't ye mean 'paralysed'?"

"Naw, I bloody dinnae! N if ye ask me any mair stupit nosey questions ye'll be runnin the risk eh bein paralysed fur life yersel!"

So that wis *him* telt.

But judgin by the telly footage beamed live fae Eye-Brocks, it looked like the Hibs team were paralysed an aw! Couldnae get ooty their ain hauf tae save theirsels. Mind ye, they only hud one man up front – McNut-Allergy – as Camembert hud been dropped like a hoat tattie, n no afore bloody time either. So Sidebottom opted tae stick an extra body in midfield instead, but that didnae really prove tae be any advantage. Gauld looked lively fae the start but soon faded, seemingly aboot as match-fit overall as yours truly – aye, n his internal organs werenae full eh bits eh shiftin metal which could kill him at any moment either!

Then, when the gaffer replaces dyin Ryan wi Swiss piss, ye ken ye're in trouble. He did however have one terrific chance tae level things up, but blew it. At this stage fairly late on, Hibs were still only trailin by one goal n so were never really ooty it, despite an almost total lack eh punch up front. But they struggled tae contain the maist ancient man on the park, Daniel Defoe's aulder brother, whae pit the Currant Buns one up jist afore the interval, n never really looked like turnin the tables. Young Tommy Agyepong looked the yin maist likely tae dae the biz when he came on, but it wis soon peterin oot intae a typical end eh season affair.

Although Hibs still hud somethin concrete tae play fur (a possible third-place finish n Euro spot), the media hud kept stressin afore the gemme that fur the hame team it wis very much 'a dead rubber'. An apt reference fur the day as it turned oot, cos I proceeded tae step on a deid rubber on the landing outside ma front door as I made ma way hame, nae doot dropped by one eh Senga's clients. Aye, there wis mair spunk in there than in Hibs' attack, sad tae say, as I stumbled in n heided fur the fridge.

When I awoke in the armchair later on, ma war wounds were playin up again n tae ma horror I could feel the shrapnel hud shifted even mair! I swear tae Christ a big lump eh metal wis workin its way oot via ma left foot! I hirpled through tae the bathroom in mortal agony n gingerly removed ma sock – but it wis only a ring-pull fae the tap eh an Export can which hud somehow goat stuck there. Whew! A relief eh sorts tae be sure, but – as Senga's customers often remarked – a 'Gentleman's Relief' never lasts that long. My life wis still hingin by a thread, nae doot aboot it.

EUROPE IS A LOADY PISH: THE EVIDENCE

The maist disappointin aspect eh the last two results wis that Killie n the Sheep hud now surged well ahead eh Hibs in the table, so there wid be nae European berth fur us next season. Well, disappointin fur *some*, maybe, but no fur *moi*, as they say in France. Cos I've been tae Europe n it's pish, I tell ye! Totally n utterly Michael Fish. They canny speak the Kween's Englush, they've goat funny food n if their trains run on time, that's eh little consolation. Cos when I goat unexpectedly hit by that 125 in The Station Bar yonks ago, it wisnae the first time it hud happened. Back in the late ‘60s when I wis followin Hibs in the Fairs Cup, I goat struck by a locomotive in Leipzig efter watchin ma team win 1-0. I wis jist admirin the Teutonic efficiency eh ze Master Race, mein herr, but unfortunately I chose tae admire it fae right in front eh the 9.50 Express tae Dresden. Goat the tae eh ma winklepicker stuck in the railtrack, ken, when I wis tryin tae take a short-cut. As a result eh years eh mental conditionin caused by bein fucked aboot by British Rail, the notion eh a train runnin on schedule never entered ma heid, n I thought I hud plenty eh time tae cross. Should've kent better eh course, where the Jerries were concerned. Efter aw, they hud plenty eh practice a couple eh decades afore that, ensuring a brisk n punctual service tae that charmin wee Polish village they renamed Auschwitz. Moany Tony declared that he couldnae believe that anyone could have the misfortune tae be hit by a train on two separate occasions, likenin the odds tae that eh bein struck by lightnin. Dinnae ken whit he wis on aboot there though, cos I've been struck by lightnin loads eh times n it certainly husnae done me any herm so far.

But watchin Hibs in Europe wid continue tae be an accursed business. They goat through tae the next roond, so it wis aff tae Germany *again* – the capitalist West this time though, no the Communist East – but I promptly ended up hospitalised, rather than capitalised. Aye, wi awfy poetic irony I wis laid low by a dodgy hamburger in Hamburg – ye couldnae make it up. I also goat mistaken fur one eh The Beatles, whae were still big news in the port city efter their early ‘60s residences there. Canny mind which one though – Mick Jagger maybe. But that wis probably cos ma lips swelled up tae a monstrous size efter contractin food poisonin. Oh aye, n Hibs lost 1-0 n aw, so it wis a poisoned chalice awright, in mair ways than one.

Therefore it couldnae get any worse, could it? Oh aye, it could. Cos at the start eh the new decade a similar fate befell me efter travellin tae see Hibs in Malmo, where I came doon wi some terrible disease efter eatin a dodgy Swede. The brothel owner hud claimed she wis clean as a whistle tae. By the time God in his infinite wisdom hud secured a Hibs victory (aye, Stanton notched the winner), I wis hooked up tae a drip in Stockholm Royal Infirmary. (I dinnae ken whae the drip wis, but he looked awfy like one eh thae grinnin gadgies ooty Abba.)

However, wi'oot doot the worst experience came two years later, when Hibs were in the European Cup-Winners Cup. They'd qualified through the tried n tested method eh gettin gubbed 6-1 by Sellik in the Scottish Cup Final, but as the weedjie mob went intae the European Cup as usual by winnin the league, Hibs claimed the second Euro-slot. Fur starters, I couldnae recognise *any* eh the players in green on the night – which wisnae surprisin, as I wis in Lisbon n Sporting were unsportingly sporting the sacred colour instead. N whit were Hibs wearin? Purple, that's whit, bloody Deep Purple! Aye, it wis a Black Night awright, so far from home... So efter watchin them lose 2-1, I goat well pished on the cheap vino n as a result I couldnae find ma feet, let alone ma hotel. But it wis a nice warm night, so efter blunderin aboot fur ages gettin angrier n angrier n swearin colourfully in Portuguese, I wis resigned tae kippin in the open air. I spied a nice wee patch eh greenery, which fur some reason wis situated behind a high barbed-wire fence, but that posed nae problem tae a superb athletic specimen like yours truly. Well, apart fae the small problem eh rippin ma erse tae shreds on the way ower, but I wis tae shattered tae care. I bedded doon n slept soundly aw night long until bein awoken the next mornin by an awmighty bloodcurdlin roar.

As ma eyes flickered open, I wis strugglin tae remember where I wis, but once I rolled ower I wis instantly gripped by a sense eh unholy terror. I wis pinchin masel tae make sure it wisnae a dream, cos I appeared tae be surrounded by the Lisbon Lions. Naw, no the Sellik European Cup-winnin side eh 1967, I'm talkin aboot the *real* thing! See, I'd only climbed intae the Big Cats' enclosure in the city zoo the night afore by mistake n noo thae big hungry-lookin bastirts were eyein up Gibby as potential breakfast! It didnae hauf gie me food fur thought, tae gie them thought eh food, as I backed intae a corner murmurin "nice kitty, nice kitty," somewhit unconvincingly.

"... n if thae keepers hudnae arrived on the scene wi the tranquiliser guns *at that very moment*, it certainly widnae have been cool fur cats," I telt Humpty Harry later on. "I'd never have made it back tae watch us tankin Sporting 6-1 in the second leg at Easter Road. Cos I widnae have hud a second leg left masel. In fact, I widnae even have hud ma *first* leg, once thae big furry fuckers hud got tae work wi their gnashers."

"Lisbon Lions, eh?" he mused thoughtfully.

"Aye, ye'd better believe it!"

"Lisbon lyin, mair like," the cheeky bastirt concluded, giein us his well-worn cynical look. "Ye dinnae hauf talk some pish, Gibby."

I wis that black affronted I stormed aff on the spot, so he missed oot on hearin aboot how I goat arrested by the secret police at FC Besa v Hibs in the next roond, afore heroically owerthrowin the Communist dictatorship fae inside ma prison cell n then bein declared a national hero eh the Albanian people, right up there alongside Norman Wisdom. Ah well, his loss...

JOYLESS KILMARNOCK BLUES

Robbery! Doonright daylight robbery! Worse than Brinks Mat, Hatton Gairden n Moany Tony's machinations wi ma thirty-four grand combined! Aye, I'm talkin aboot the theft eh three points at Killie, thanks tae that one-man soap-opera Dallas – again! He gied them a penalty which at first the radio pundits assumed he'd cawed correctly, as he wis only five yards away – but naw, when they reviewed it, aw agreed there wis nowt in it. As I wis fulminatin fulsomely on the subject in The Cenny, thae nitpickin ne'er-dae-wells started questionin ma commitment tae the Hibernian cause – again!

"Whit were ye daein listenin tae the radio commentary, if ye were actually at the gemme?" they demanded tae ken.

See thae suspicious nosey bastirts in that bloody boozer...

"The sun wis in ma eyes at the time," I snapped. "That's why I pit the radio on."

"But the only radio ye've goat is the one that goes wi that expensive choaried hi-fi system that sits in yer livin-room," objected Humpty Harry. "Are ye tryin tae tell us ye lugged that – amplifier, speakers, turntable, the lot – aw the way tae Rugby Park n back?"

"Well, I didnae lug it there *masel*, did I – I employed some casual labour tae dae it fur me. N I dae emphasise the word *'casual'*, ken?"

"But how did ye get it intae the stadium?"

I tell ye this, I felt like I wis aboot tae go Radio Gaga at any minute. I banged ma pint gless doon ominously, goat tae ma feet n drew masel up tae ma full height. Which wis far fae impressive tae be honest, so I climbed on a stool, drew masel up tae ma full height fur the second time an issued a warnin.

"I'm tellin youse aw one mair time n one mair time *only* – n if anyone says differently we'll take this ootside pronto – Rugby Park wis ma destination on Setirday efternin, cross ma Hib n hope tae die, Stanton strike me doon if I should lie."

Job done! No a peep ooty anyone at aw. Then, aw eh a sudden, I *did* hear a faint peep, fae behind the bar. I leapt ower the coonter in a blind rage, fists ready tae fly.

"Which smart-erse made that fuckin irritatin noise? Show yersel right noo!"

"Calm doon, Gibby, it's only the toaster," muttered Girnin Gertie.

I glowered aroond the sea eh silent faces, satisfied I'd made ma point. See, I wisnae *totally* tellin porkies – cos on the Setirday I'd sneaked intae Goldenacre tae watch George Heriot's FPs take on Watsonians, so I wis definitely at *a* Rugby Park.

But at the one doon in Ayrshire, efter faffin aboot like heidless chickens fur the first ten minutes or so, the Hibees clawed their way intae the gemme. Like yours truly in The Cenny they were makin a decent fist eh it when that dimwit Dallas stuck his oar in jist efter the hauf-oor mark n Brophy duly converted the spot-kick. So it wis ayewis gonnae be an uphill struggle efter that, bearin in mind that we didnae really have anythin tae play fur. The Dons hud dumped the Hertz the night afore, so there wis nae way the latter could pip us fur fifth spot in the table noo, thanks tae oor much superior goal difference. Killie on the other hand still hud the incentive eh finishin ahead eh the Sheep n the lure eh Europe (which, as I believe I've already made clear, is a loady pish, fae France tae the Faroes n fae Luxembourg tae Lithuania n back again.)

So Hibs matched the hame team fur maist eh the second hauf, but wi'oot ever really lookin like scorin, which can be somethin eh a disadvantage if ye're actually tryin tae win the gemme. Sidebottom realised this n threw on three subs at the same time, which almost paid aff when young Tam Agyepong went close wi a twenty-five yard screamer. But that wis in the last minute n Killie hung on fur the narry victory.

"Aye, ye must have goat back fae Kilmarnock in record time, Gibby," said Torn-Faced Tommy. "Did ye fly?"

I bridled instantly.

"Whit dae ye mean by that?"

"Aw, nuthin really. It wis jist that when I spotted ye at the Fit eh the Walk at 6 p.m. on Setirday, I couldnae help but be impressed by the speed eh yer return."

Bastirts! See Leith, full eh nosey pryin spyin busybodies, wi nowt better tae dae wi themsels than stalkin innocent hard-workin God-fearin folk, n notin their every move!

"Naw, I didnae fuckin fly. Although I might be flyin in the direction eh your fuckin throat in a minute. I left at hauf-time n went straight tae the station."

"Oh aye? Still, amazin ye goat back so quickly, what wi havin tae change trains in Glesgie, no tae mention makin yer way fae Central tae Queen Street n then waitin on a connection tae get back through here."

"I DIDNAE CATCH A FUCKIN TRAIN!" I yelled. "They were aw full up so I goat a taxi, right? Cost a small fortune, but it wis worth it. The boy goat on the motorway n floored it aw the way back tae Embra at a hunner mile an oor! Noo, does any other lippy bastirt want tae cast doot on the fact that I wis at the gemme in person? Dae ye want tae see ma taxi receipt, will that convince youse aw?"

I wis aware I wis takin a bit eh a chance wi that yin, but reckoned they widnae have the bottle tae keep pressin the point. N right enough, they aw jist sat there, shakin their heids dumbly. But I wisnae finished yet. I dramatically whipped oot a big wad eh notes n waved them in front eh Humpty's ugly kisser.

"There's two hunner quid here. N I'll happily gie it aw tae *anyone* whae can conclusively prove that I wisnae at Killie v Hibs. Dae we have any takers?"

No a peep ooty a soul – no even fae the toaster this time. (Which wis jist as well, cos I wis quite prepared tae lamp that cheeky bastirt intae the middle eh next week n aw, inanimate object or no.)

"I rest ma case," I announced wi great dignity, stuffin the notes back in ma pocket n preparin tae take ma leave.

"Eh...afore ye go, Gibby..." piped up Humpty, hesistantly.

"Aye, whit?"

"When ye pilled oot that wad eh cash, ye dropped yer match programme on the flair. Here – ye'd better have it back. Funny though, I couldnae help noticing the mis-print on the cover..."

"Whit mis-print?"

"Well, rather than sayin 'Kilmarnock v Hibernian', it says 'George Heriot's v Watsonians', but nae doot ye've goat a perfectly rational explanation fur that."

Bastirts!

A DAY IN THE LIFE

When I heard the terrible news two days later – n I'm no talkin aboot Jim McIntyre bein emptied by Dundee fur the crime eh actually winnin a gemme – I jist hud tae confide in someone.

"Another auld flame gaun oot then," I sighed pathetically, takin a deep philosophical gulp ooty ma gless.

"Well, I've been tellin ye tae get that dodgy boiler fixed fur yonks," retorted Torn-Faced Tommy tetchily. "Christ, if memory serves right it wis in that hoose when ye moved in. Nae wonder the flame's gaun oot. Of course, the fact that ye never pay the gas bills doesnae help matters."

"I'm no referrin tae a dodgy auld boiler," I snapped irritably, although in the back eh mind wis the uncomfortable thought that maybe I *wis* talkin aboot a dodgy auld boiler efter aw. A human yin though, rather than a faulty gas appliance. But every time I used tae see her up there on the silver screen, I used tae visualise masel playin opposite, in the Rock Hudson role, ken. Of course, I soon changed ma tune when the truth came oot aboot *him*, but still...

"Ye're lookin awfy thoughtful n far away, Gibby," remarked Humpty Harry. "Although no quite as far away as Kilmarnock, it hus tae be said."

"Look, will youse comedic bastirts jist show some respect n stop talkin pish fur once? I've jist heard that one eh ma ex-burdz hus passed on."

"Passed on whit? A contagious disease?"

"Naw, ya radge! She's deid!"

"Fell doon the stairs 'accidentally', did she?"

"Naw she bloody didnae! Fur yer information, she passed away surrounded by her loved ones – apart fae me – in Hollywood."

"So she snuffed it in that doss-hoose at the tap eh yon road, on the junction wi the Pleasance?"

"No Holyrood in Embra, ya bams, Holly*wood* in Kaliforny, USA! I met her when she wis a young strollin player on tour n I wis workin at the Gaiety Theatre..."

A collective groan went up fae the company at that pronouncement.

"So ye're sayin that *another* eh yer formerly famous actress burdz hus copped it? Which yin wis it this time?"

"It wis Doris."

"Doris Speed, whae used tae play Annie Walker in 'Coronation Street'?"

"Naw, ye fuckin parochial eejit, I'm referrin tae Doris *Day*!"

There wis a stunned silence at that revelation, jist as I'd anticipated. Finally, a voice piped up fae the assembled throng.

"Awfy sorry tae hear aboot yer tragic loss, Gibby. I dinnae want tae intrude on yer bottomless pit eh grief at a time like this, but wid it possibly help even in a small way, if we aw jist stood ye drinks aw efternin, jist tae deaden the emotional pain?"

At last! *Noo* we were gettin somewhere!

"Dae ye ken this," I said in mock thoughtfulness, effortlessly slidin intae an actin performance eh such consummate skill that it wid have knocked the socks aff Rock Hudson, even afore he went aw poofy, "I think it really might."

"Oh aye? Well, ye can *get tae fuck*, Gibby, cos ye tried the same sympathy scam when June Whitfield turned up her taes, we're no fallin fur that again! So ye pulled Doris Day did ye? Ye couldnae have pulled *Robin* Day, even if ye'd goat a haud eh his bow-tie wi a handful eh superglue."

I goat tae ma feet slowly n proceeded tae stroll laconically taewards the door, jist like Howard Keel in 'Calamity Jane'. Inside though, I wis pure ragin. Selfish, suspicious bunch eh penny-pinchin bastirts, I thought it might have been guid fur at least a hauf-decent swally. I decided there n then tae get tae fuck awright, as advised, aye, get tae fuck ooty Leith once n fur aw n move tae North Korea *permanently.*

Jist then, a certain bulldog-faced barmaid came roond the bar wi a bucket eh soapy water which she unceremoniously cowped aw ower me, prior tae pickin up a mop n furiously sweepin me physically taewards the exit.

"Whit the hell are ye daein, Gertie?" asked Tommy.

"I'm gonna wash that man right outta ma lair..."

EXTREMELY WICKED, SHOCKINGLY EVIL N VILE

Well, it wis time fur another wee break fae Leith – until I could make ma long-planned irreversible move tae doontoon Pyongyang. But at least I'd get some respite fae aw thae nosey bastirts fur a while – *or wid I?* Cos ma fledgling TV career wis aboot tae be rebooted, although no quite in the way I'd anticipated. It seemed that I'd made the classic mistake eh gettin ma Jeremys mixed up – which wis hardly surprisin, given the plethora eh the bastirts in Tellyland. Ye've goat Clarkson, Paxman, Vine (nice, but dim), Beadle (no nice, but deid) n it wis the Chelsea-supportin host eh 'Dickheads' that I *thought* I'd signed up fur. No fur the aforementioned teatime quiz-show, but fur his Channel 5 mornin number, mainly cos I've goat a wee thing fur that cute Scottish lassie on it, wi the daft name. Ken her, that's named efter a weather condition, 'Whirlwind' or 'Hurricane' or somethin similar... Anyway, that turned oot tae be immaterial, cos when I goat tae the TV studio in deepest, darkest Englandshire somewhere, ma error became aw tae apparent. Aye, I'd only gaun n signed up fur the fuckin Jeremy Vile Show!

However, ye've goat tae get up awfy early in the mornin tae catch Gibby cauld. 'Ayewis be prepared', that's ayewis been the Gibson family motto – sometimes wi 'tae run away at tap speed' tacked ontae the end eh it. So I wis wise tae Vile n his tricks n decided tae jist go along wi it. Lie-detector tests n aw that shite – bring it on!

Then, when I saw aw thae bastirts fae The Cenny in the audience grinnin like a pack eh mentally retarded jackasses, I wis even mair convinced that I'd been set up. But I kent whit tae expect. Sordid accusations relatin tae ma two dear departed wives, the problem eh slippery stairs in the Banana Flats, I kent the script awright, afore Vile even opened his mooth.

In fact, it appeared that the host hud awready opened his great flappin gob, but bein temporarily distracted by the sight eh Humpty Harry sittin there in his three-piece aff-the-peg Matalan suit, I hudnae been payin attention. I became aware eh Vile glarin at me expectantly.

"Whae are youse lookin at, Bawbag?"

"I'm lookin at *you*, Gibson!" snapped Vile, gaun intae his 'let's bully the hapless doontrodden workin-classes' routine right away. "And I'll repeat the question, as you appeared to be more interested in gawping at the audience – are you prepared to take a lie-detector test or not?"

Christ, that wis quick! Nae beatin aboot the bush fur oor Jerome, eh?

"Course I am – I've goat nowt tae hide efter aw!" I declared defiantly.

A ripple eh excitement ran aroond the studio, as some gadgie came on n proceeded tae wire me up tae this contraption, which looked like some sort eh medieval torture apparatus the Embra polis utilised at St. Leonard's. But I'd sailed through many a question n answer session there wi nae problems, so I wis hardly gonnae be fazed by this version. I hud aw possible replies carefully filed away in ma heid, ready fur use at the drop eh a hat. *Naw, I didnae push her / Naw, I wisnae even there at the time / Aye, that new-fangled polish the*

Cooncil cleaners were usin in the Banana Flats that terrible day hud an unusually high slippery content... Wi a start, I realised that Vile wis glarin at me again, clearly keen tae get gaun.

"Are you ready, Gibson?"

"Ready tae rumble, Radge-works! Hit me wi yer first question."

"OK. Did you or did you not attend the Kilmarnock v Hibernian game on Saturday, 11th May, in person?"

Whit?! Christ, I ken I said I kent the script, but this wisnae it! Fur fuck's sake...

"Well?" barked Vile, in gleeful expectation. "Would you like to answer the question?"

"Er...aye...uh-huh, yesss...on that day I wis at, er, a rugby park..."

Vile slammed his palm skywards, like a stormtrooper giein a Nazi salute.

"Stop right there! You say you were at *a* rugby park, not just that you were at *Rugby Park.* Which is the home of Kilmarnock Football Club," he added, fur the benefit eh the Sassenach audience, "not to mention the crappest plastic playing surface this side of the Tony Macaroni Arena. Anyway, serious allegations have been made about this guest's purported support of Hibernian Football Club and his questionable attendance at numerous matches. *Were you at that particular match or not, Gibson?"*

"Er, aye...I wis at a match fur sure..."

I swear tae Christ I could feel that bloody lie-detector machine jumpin aboot aw ower the shop, as Vile turned tae the next page eh his notes.

"The year 1919 – does that mean anything to you, Gibson?"

Sweet jumpin Jesus! Whae telt the cunt aboot...

"Er...it wis the year I wis finally demobbed fae the First World War, ken. I'd jist goat back fae battlin the Zulus at Little Big Horn..."

"Never mind all that. It was also the *last* time you paid for a Hibernian F.C. season-ticket! The *last* time, ladies and gentlemen!" he repeated dramatically, playin tae the gallery big style.

A great hissing noise eh disgust n disapproval arose fae the studio audience, whae were aw glarin at me in a similar manner tae Vile. He then spun roond n pointed an accusatory finger at yours truly.

"And don't try to deny it! We have written testimony from Mr Roderick Pear-Tree, Supreme Dictator of Hibernian Football Club, to the effect that you have systematically defrauded them – the team you claim to love and support wholeheartedly – for years! *Decades,* even! So what have you got to say about *that?*"

"Er...um...it wisnae me, likes...a big boy did it n ran away..."

The host repeated his Nazi 'Heil Hitler' act tae signal fur silence.

"Of course, we also have evidence showing your undoubted attendance at certain matches played at Easter Road Stadium..."

A brief sense eh relief flooded through me on hearin that – perhaps the sadistic bastirt wis gonnae cut me a bit eh slack, efter aw? Fat chance, as it turned oot.

"But on *one* occasion we have verified, you also *exposed* yourself to the Chief Executive of Hibernian Football Club in the stadium toilets and permanently damaged the club blowtorch, which was being utilised to remove your frozen penis from the urinal! That's right, ladies and gentlemen, you heard correctly – his *FROZEN PENIS!!"*

Well, that did it. As the supercilious cunt practically *screamed* the last two fateful words, it proved tae much fur the unwashed, tracksuited, homemade tattooed, benefit-cheatin bayin mob eh psychopaths n sad cases in the cheap seats. They proceeded tae pelt me wi rotten fruit, afore invadin the stage n bootin ma erse fae one end eh the television studio tae the other. The last thing I saw afore losin consciousness wis Vile eagerly handin oot the chibs, knuckledusters n basebaw bats tae enable them tae finish me aff completely.

Still, ye canny fault the telly gadgies fur their efter-show care taewards their guests – once I goat discharged fae the hospital they gied me a one-way bus ticket hame. Or at least that's whit they *said*, but they neglected tae tell me it wis only valid in England, so I hud tae hoof it hame fae Berwick, gettin fucked aboot by the border-guards at Gretna Green on the way, prior tae bein attacked by a flock eh rabid sheep jist north eh Dumfries.

But once back in Leith, ma main concern wis noo the second roond eh awfy humiliation that wis bound tae folly, once the show wis actually aired. Every mornin fur a week I hid behind the sofa n peeked oot at the TV screen in fearful anticipation, but mercifully I failed tae materialise on it. Then one day I goat a phone-caw ooty the blue. The gadgie identified himsel as a researcher on The Jeremy Vile Show n informed me that unfortunately he hud some very bad news. Ma hert sunk tae ma boots. Fur the love eh Christ, whit noo?

"Whit sort eh bad news?" I groaned weakly.

"Well, Mr Gibson, I'm afraid that due to tragic circumstances out-with our control, we are unable to now publicly screen the episode of the show featuring yourself. We realise that this must come as a great disappointment to you, and you will of course be financially compensated."

Ma heid wis spinnin that fast I hud tae grab a haud eh it wi baith hands tae make it stop. I could scarcely believe ma lugs.

"But...but...why can ye no screen it?" I heard masel askin.

"Another guest who was on the same show as yourself regrettably topped himself two days later, so out of respect for the sad daftie's family, we feel it would be inappropriate to show it. You see, he was devastated after failing a lie-detector test, having been confident beforehand of passing it. When we checked the machine later, we discovered that in fact it had been malfunctioning since going haywire after being attached to your body. So it turned out that he was telling the truth after all. Shit happens, eh? Is there anything you would like to say in response?"

"YA FUCKIN BEAUTY!"

Jeremy Vine Show, here I come...

SHEEP DIP

Afore aw that though, wis the small matter eh Aiberdeen at Easter Road. Last gemme eh the season, ken. I sat there in Wilkies, stoically boozin, recklessly spendin The Jeremy Vile Show compo cash which I hudnae actually goat ma hands on yet.

"I suppose I'd better make the effort," I declared wi a distinct lack eh enthusiasm, knottin the auld green n white muffler aroond ma neck.

"Make an effort tae whit? Concoct another cock n bull story aboot how ye went tae the match, whereas in reality ye were either in some other boozer or hidin under yer bed instead?" piped up this pestilential pip-squeak.

"Naw, I'm gaun tae the bloody gemme awright!" I snapped, seek tae ma back teeth eh aw thae Doubtin Thomases. "Hospitality an aw!"

Of course I wis lyin aboot that, jist tae make them aw jealous. The only way I'd be experiencin hospitality wis if n when Slasher pit me in the hospital, which wisnae that far aff the mark at aw.

But I wound up in the peasants' viewin gallery as usual, wi nae chips (as usual.) Christ, I actually *wid* fork oot fur a hozzy package if I thought there wis any chance eh gettin chips that way. Aye, n I bet Pear-Tree's no short eh them up in that Directors' Box either, where they're rumoured tae grow on trees. Eats chips fur breakfast, that bastirt, or so they say.

Still, fur a match wi absolutely nowt at stake as far as Hibs were concerned, it wisnae lookin tae bad. I hud tae dae a double-take when I thought I spied Anthony Stokes on the park wi his back tae me, but it wis only Fraser Murray sportin a similar haircut. He hud the best chance eh the gemme later on – which he fluffed – but he did set up McNutcracker sweet, tae put the Hibees one up in the first hauf. I wis that happy I'd briefly forgotten aboot chips, but then a chip intae the box by McLennan brought me crashin back doon tae earth. There hud looked bugger aw danger, but Cosgrove goat on the end eh it n stuck it past Rocky. 1-1 at the break, which left me in a decidedly vinegary mood, n the only chips I hud were on ma shuders.

Aye, Hibs hud done it again – failed tae capitalise when they were in the ascendancy n scorned guid chances. Jist past the oor mark their defence opened up inexplicably n Sheep sub Stevie May (whae's been pish ever since he left Perth) prodded it on tae Wilson, whae made it 2-1. Hibs should still have equalised – but needless tae say they didnae – n the Mutton Men's merriment wis short-lived really, as they still failed tae clinch third spot in the table, thanks tae Killie dumpin the huns by the same scoreline.

So Hibs couldnae win any eh their tap six fixtures n hud also succeeded in losin three on the trot. Pish, whichever way ye look at it! We're in Terry Butcher territory, I'll tell ye that fur nowt. Youse ken it n I ken it – Sidebottom must go! Time tae bring back Fenlon (or maybe Jocky Scott...)

ODDS N SODS

The Hibees' season might have been ower n done wi, but that wisnae the case wi the nightmare neebors, whae still hud a Scottish Cup Final tae negotiate. Aw the focus wis on Sellik n their 'Treble Treble', until Craig Levein blithely stated that the Hertz were gaun fur a 'Single Single'. Laugh? I nearly started. Aye, he's a right comedian is oor Craig, up there in 'the natural order', somewhere between Bernard Manning n Jimmy Tarbuck. In other words – tae paraphrase Billy Connolly – 'aboot as funny as a burning orphanage'.

It wis nae laughin matter fur his team n their skerf-twirlin followers as expected, although they did take the lead n Sellik were far fae convincin at that stage. But Eduardo looked *odds on* tae score (see, that's *real* comedy fur ye right there, Craig), n once he hud done so, there wis only gonnae be one winner. But aw the talk eh 'Treble Treble' (David Bowie once hud a hit wi a song eh the same name), n 'Single Single' widnae wash wi yours truly, whae's ayewis been mair eh a man fur a double double.

Then, jist as Girnin Gertie grimly sloshed the aforementioned quadruple Whyte n Mackay intae ma gless, I felt a tap on ma shuder. Which wis a bit eh a surprise, cos last time I looked it wis still attached tae the sink in the lavvy. However it turned oot tae be an animate object rather than an inanimate yin, mair's the pity, in the fearsome form eh Slasher Smith. N he wis fuckin well animated awright, tae say the least.

"I've been lookin fur ye, Gibby," he announced, wi a terrifyin shark-like smile spreadin across his crater-ridden coupon.

Ma knees turned tae water on the spot. So either Gertie hud added it tae the whisky wi'oot me noticin or I wis scared shiteless, take yer pick.

"Heard ye goat yer compo fae The Jeremy Vile Show," he went on conversationally. "Seem tae recall that I'm also due some compo – fae *you* – fur takin the pish. *Quite literally* takin it, I might add."

Bastirts! See that bunch eh loose-lipped babblin bampots that I choose tae drink wi, goat tae tell every other bastirt yer business – even when that bastirt happens tae be auld Psycho Smithy here. Fur that's the only way he could have found oot aboot ma guid fortune, as I'd been proudly flashin ma cheque aroond the other highspots eh Leith earlier on the same day. There wis one *slight* problem however...

Efter ma initial call fae the show, I goat a folly-up tae say that I'd been awarded a four-figure sum, which naturally hud me jumpin fur joy – briefly. When the envelope did come through, I felt obliged tae stab that bastirt eh a postie – again – cos efter openin it I saw I'd goat a four-figure sum awright, namely £34.00! It wisnae only that poxy show's presenter whae wis vile, noo ma temper wis an aw! I wis jist aboot tae rip it intae a thousand tiny little pieces, when a brilliant idea suddenly flashed through ma awready brilliant brain. How much did Pear-Tree claim I owed him again? Thirty-four big yins wis it no? I looked at the cheque again. Aye, surely a crafty piece eh forgery wi the trusty black biro could dae the biz, by changin the decimal point tae a comma n addin a cheeky wee zero tae the end...?

So that wis the version eh the said article I'd been airily wavin aboot in the faces eh worthies fae the Bar Brig tae the Bam O'Shanter earlier, n naebody noticed it hud been cunningly altered! Granted, maist eh them were blind as bats as well as blind drunk, so in hindsight perhaps that wisnae overly reassurin. I wis awready gettin cauld feet n havin second thoughts aboot actually tryin tae cash the thing in the bloody bank, when Slasher hud made his presence felt.

"Thirty-four grand, wis it no?" went on the latter, still smilin ferociously.

"Er...aye, that wis the amount awright."

"I'll tell ye whit I'll dae," he said thoughtfully, whilst helpin himsel tae ma double double the cheeky bastirt, "if ye agree tae sign the cheque ower tae me, we'll say nae mair aboot ye pauchlin ma pish."

"Uh-huh. N if I dinnae agree?"

"Then I'll remove yer eyebaws wi this cocktail stick, prior tae rammin them up yer erse."

"Ye drive a hard bargain, Smithy," I observed calmly. "Done!"

"Done?"

Aye, ye've been done awright, ya big mad daftie.

"Ma word is ma bond," I said wi great dignity, "n if ye jist bear wi me a minute, I'll sort it oot fur ye right here."

"I'm gaun fur a pish," he replied, which wis hardly the maist unexpected thing I'd ever heard issuin forth fae his mooth. "Dinnae move fae that spot till I come back."

The suspicious bastirt then applied superglue tae the soles eh ma shoes as a precaution, whilst he disappeared in the direction eh the cludgie. As soon as his back wis turned I whipped oot the cheque, scraped some bird-shit aff ma bunnet, n used it tae blot oot 'Grumpy Gibson' in the 'Pay' column. I then inserted 'Slasher Smith' in its place wi ma biro.

"There ye go, Slashmeister, ma dear auld china," I said sycophantically, on his return. "It's aw yours!"

He glanced at it quickly, afore shovin it intae his inside pocket.

"OK, Gibby, nae hard feelings, I hope. Aw is forgiven. I'm a man eh God efter aw."

Aye, n I'm a man eh Fraud...

"Ye're welcome, Slasher. Jist dinnae go spendin it aw at once!" I joked merrily, provin I wis right up there wi Craig Levein in the Comedy Gold stakes.

Unfortunately though, I foresaw that when he eventually attempted tae cash it in Santander next door, he wis odds on tae end up the same way as Craig's comedians hud done at Hampden earlier on. Aye, well fucked...

PARTY CENTRAL

So it wis a ruminative Gibby heidin taewards The Cenny in the dyin days eh May (the month, as well as those eh that disaster eh a Prime Minister wi a face like a bad-tempered prayin mantis tryin tae pass a particularly sharp gall-stone.) She ended up greetin her eyes oot n tae tell the truth I wis on the verge eh joinin her. The fitba season wis ower n the empty days stretched oot afore me, each yin emptier than the yin afore it – Christ, life wisnae hauf a loady pish when ye chose tae think aboot it. Then things took a turn fur the worse, as the bloody pub door appeared tae be jammed. I pushed n pushed tae nae avail. Bastirts! I then noticed that the bloody place seemed tae be in total darkness, despite it bein a Friday night. Surely tae Christ it hudnae been shut doon wi'oot anyone botherin tae tell us? Widnae pit it past them, right enough. Then, I heard a faint yet distinct sound eh voices fae within. I began tae suspect that the bloody doors hud been jammed on purpose, jist tae keep yours truly oot! "If it at first ye don't suck seed, try, try n try again," I muttered under ma breath, repeatin the proud motto eh the Gibson clan (or one eh them anyway.) Try tae barricade the boozer against *me* wid they? Right then, I'll show them...

I took a huge run up fae the kerb-side, preparin tae pit aw the weight eh ma left shuder tae the woodwork, but, jist as I goat there, the door suddenly swung open unannounced n I went racin heidlong intae a pitch-black space, skitin uncontrollably across the flair afore crashin intae the puggy machine. I mean, whit the f...??

Then aw the lights instantly blazed on, as I lay there dazedly wi pound coins fawin on ma heid. I blinked intae a sea eh familiar-lookin grinnin faces.

"Surprise, surprise! Hibbie birthday tae ye Gibby, ye miserable auld goat!" they aw chorused in unison, raisin their brimmin glesses in ma direction. Tae say I wis deeply touched wid have been nae exaggeration. But that wis mainly because Senga hud her hand inside ma jaikit, tryin tae choarie ma wallet.

"Aye – many Hibbie returns tae ye, auld-timer! Lang may yer lum reek!"

I hud a sudden strong inclination tae get reekin masel. Fur as far as I kent, it wisnae ma bloody birthday at aw, although it *might* have been. See, ma dear auld maw, God rest her soul, once telt me that I wis a very special bairn as she dandled me on her knee. As I wis wrapped in a plaid shawl, ye might even say that I wis tartan special. No least, cos by an astonishin stroke eh fate, ma birthday actually fell on the same day as that on which I wis born! Aye, there's no many can claim that distinction. Only problem wis that the dementia-ridden auld bat forgot tae mention which bloody date it actually fell on – n I've been in the dark aboot it ever since! Even worse, as a result eh that circumstance, I wis born wi nae star-sign either! Ye can imagine the embarrassment when folk used tae read oot their horoscopes fae the newspapers in front eh me, aw thae show-aff Aries n Geminis n Virgo bastirts n whit have ye.

"Whit sign are *you*, Gibby?" they'd smirk.

I'd jist grit ma teeth n tell them it wis nane eh their bloody business. But Christ, it hurt inside, I'll tell ye. Poor Gibby, left oot in the cauld again...

"Whit are ye lookin so depressed aboot?" demanded Girnin Gertie, her voice joltin me rudely back intae the present.

"Well, I dinnae think it's ma birthday at aw!" I explained, shakily gettin tae ma feet. "Whae says it wis in the first place?"

"Yer pal Tony there. He organised the whole shindig."

Moany bloody Tony, I might have kent it! Been absolutely conspicuous in his absence, ever since that ludicrous Lottery louse-up. I could vaguely pick him oot in the crowd, sittin at a table wi this big black felly, whae wis dressed in this purple ermine robe n drippin wi gold trinkets, a big crown atop his heid.

"Whae the hell's Tony's new pal?"

"Oh, that's the prince."

"The whit?"

"The prince. Or, tae gie him his full title, *Crown* Prince Odinga Obama Badabing Badaboom eh Nigeria."

Jesus H. Kherrist, I'd heard it aw noo!

Next thing, the gullible moanin bastirt wis up close n personal, tears eh emotion wellin up in his eyes.

“Gibby, I hope ye take aw this in the spirit in which it wis intended – as ye ken, I’ve never forgiven masel fur losin aw yer hard-earned dough...”

“Well, it wis actually the proceeds eh a bank robbery,” honesty compelled me tae admit.

“... never mind that. I’ve felt awfy ever since n we – yer loyal pals – aw ken that ye dinnae actually have a birthday eh yer ain. So we aw goat taegether n decided that fae noo on yer birthday will be on the anniversary eh Hibs winnin the Scottish Cup in 2016.”

“Aye? I certainly dinnae remember *that* happenin.”

“Naw? Well maybe jist as well, cos I goat the date wrong anyway. They won it on May 21st, n this is actually May 31st. But whit’s ten days between friends, eh?”

“Whit indeed?” I mumbled, still strugglin tae take in the full picture, as it were. N nae bloody wonder! Cos it wis some picture tae behold, I can tell ye. I hud tae gie the daft auld get credit, he’d done a fair job eh roundin everyone up.

“Aw yer pals past n present are here,” he went on, “n acquaintances tae numerous tae mention.”

“Eh...Slasher’s no here, is he?”

“Naw. Did ye no hear – he goat done fur passin a dud cheque!”

“Whae – Rudi Skacel?” chipped in Humpty Harry, whae wis clappin me enthusiastically on the back whilst surreptitiously tryin tae pick ma pocket.

“Or maybe that Vanacek – he’s another dud Czech,” observed Torn-Faced Tommy. “Craig Levein said so himsel. Signed him on fur the Hertz n then telt him he wis rubbish! So where did Slasher pass him? Up the Walk?"

"No a dud *Czech*, ya bams!" moaned Moany mournfully. "I says, a dud *cheque*!"

"That sounds exactly the same, whichever way ye say it."

"I could maybe use that in this book I'm writin," I mused oot loud, rememberin that thae Braidwood Books bastirts hud hinted darkly that deidline day wid fast approachin.

"I wouldnae bother, Gibby. A crap pun like that doesnae work on the printed page, only verbally."

"Aye, I suppose ye're right," I conceded reluctantly. "I'll maybe no bother then."

As the night wore on n well-wishers continued tae buy me drink n toast ma rude health, I began tae feel a warm glow taewards ma fellow man (n wumman.) Nae wonder, I'd carelessly leaned back n the candles on ma cake hud jist burned a big hole in the erse eh ma troosers. I couldnae even count the number eh candles either, but the cheeky bastirts claimed tae have stuck a hundred n fifty on it, as that wis their rough estimate eh ma age. (Which hus been a closely-guarded secret ever since I goat ma telegram fae Queen. Very decent eh Freddie, Brian, John n Roger tae send it n aw, I must say.)

"Hibbie birthday, Gibby!" sang oot this cute wee blonde piece, as I birled roond in amazement tae clock the lassie aff 'Countdoon' on the telly!

"Carol! It's yersel!"

Her lovely face instantly composed itsel intae a thunderous expression eh distaste.

"No, it's *Rachel*! So away n fuck yersel!"

Well, ye canny win them aw.

Even crotchety auld Dick-Nick wis there, up shakin ma hand, whilst lookin tae be well away wi the goalie. I found oot later that he'd sustained permanent brain damage efter I'd clattered him ower the heid wi yon dictionary n hud nae idea where he wis or whae I wis either. Maybe jist as well. Aye, at least I won *that* yin...

I wis disappointed that Carol Vorderman wisnae there of course – n neither wis Bouncy Knowles, stuck-up Texan tart that she is. But two other grand auld dames mair than made up fur it – Senga McGlumphar n the irredeemable Ms Fifi Phanni-Phlapz eh this parish. Fur years Tony n I hud been arguin ower the authenticity eh the latter's name – I held that it wis clearly a made-up yin, whilst that daft bastirt thought it sounded awfy exotic n wis definitely fur real. Noticin her handbag hud been left open, I spied whit appeared tae be her passport near the tap n nudged the Moany yin urgently in the ribs. There wid never be a better chance tae find oot. As she wis aff makin a move on Dick-Nick (or his wallet tae be precise), I quickly reached oot n palmed it.

"Right! A hundred quid says that Fifi Phanni-Phlapz isnae her real name! Whit dae ye say?"

"Well ma hundred quid says it is!" he declared confidently.

"I'm tellin ye, Tony, I bet it's somethin totally lame like Fiona Smith or whitever. That handle she's goat is jist a sort eh stage-name, I'm sure eh it. Noo, I dinnae want tae take yer money (I did, obviously), so are ye *sure* you want tae take the bet?"

"Aye, I'm in. Quick, take a look then!"

I flicked swiftly tae the back page n instantly let oot a long involuntary groan.

"Well?" said Moany eagerly. "Whae's right?"

"Neither eh us," I admitted. "Here – see fur yersel."

I stuck the incriminatin evidence in front eh his pus n watched as his eyebaws promptly leapt ooty their sockets on two springs.

"Her real name is *Fanny* Phanni-Phlapz?!" he sort eh croaked.

"Apparently so."

I reeled aroond the bar fae one end tae the other, gleefully lappin up aw the plaudits as well as the endless drinks that came wi them. Whit a night! I must start havin birthdays mair often, I thought, as I went aff tae get a nice big slice eh ma cake, but it turned oot Rory the Choarie hud awready choaried it. Even that wisnae gaun tae pit a dampener on proceedings though, as Tea-Leaf Keith promptly went oot, broke intae a cake-shop n came back wi an even better replacement.

Then, jist when I wis thinkin the evening couldnae get any better, I felt a tap on ma shuder. Noo last time such a thing occurred, Slasher wis on the other end eh it, n I must admit tae experiencin a wee shiver eh deja-vu. But when I turned roond, it wis only Rod Pear-Tree himsel – wi that Dumpster wumman!

"Gibby, we've decided to write off your debt once and for all, and issue you with a brand new season ticket," he beamed magnanimously. "We suspect that since the sad passing of Sam Martinez aged 106, you are now almost certainly Hibernian F.C.'s oldest surviving fan. You are –

and always have been – a cantankerous old pest of the highest order, but at least you're *our* cantankerous old pest of the highest order."

He then raised a gless tae the multitude eh gaggin-fur-it Gibson groupies n declared, "Hib Hib Hooray for Gibby!"

"Hib Hib Hooray!" roared back ma fan club, n even the Dumpster wumman gingerly stretched oot a clammy paw tae shake yours truly by the hand.

Of course, nae party wid be complete wi'oot a spot eh live music, n even long-time Leith n Cenny favourite Andy Chung hud tae make way n step aside fur the heidlinin act eh the evening. Ladeez n gennilmen, whae else but the legendary Dutch-Leith crossover act, Krystle Shan-de-Lier & The Dim Bulbs!

Now, as in the situation regardin Fifi, the authenticity eh the aforementioned chanteuse's name hud often been cawed intae question n aw. But in this instance, Moany Tony wis bizzarely adamant that Krystle Shan-de-Lier *wisnae* her real name.

"Why are ye so sure, where she's concerned?" I once asked him.

"Well, even her ain husband doesnae believe it," he'd replied.

"How dae ye mean?"

"Cos he once said tae me – n I'm quotin him directly here – 'if that's her real name then I'm a Dutchman'."

"But he *is* a Dutchman!" I pointed oot, wi some asperity.

"Oh aye, I forgot aboot that..."

Aye, that's Moany fur ye, no exactly at the front eh the queue when they were dishin oot the auld 'Saughton Mains'. N as fur Krystle...

"Yeah, I can see how ye mistook Bouncy Knowles fur her," I couldnae resist sayin tae Torn-Faced Tommy, as the band soared intae their big No.1 hit in Holland, the oral sex classic 'Chewed Lips From Amsterdam'.

"Ye can, aye?"

"Aw, definitely. They're jist so strikingly similar, aren't they? Bouncy's tall, black n beautiful, whereas Krystle's built like the Hunchback eh Notre-Dame, weighs aboot twenty stone, hus a cannabis leaf tattooed on her forehead n is frequently taken fur the late Jocky Wilson in a bad light."

"Aye, they *are* like two peas in a pod, aren't they?" responded the daft blind bastirt, peerin at the band vaguely through his coke-boatil specs.

I tell ye, sarcasm's wasted on some people...

Tae be honest, I wis noo startin tae feel a bit wasted masel, n wis thinkin eh cawin it a night. But jist as I wis makin ma way somewhit unsteadily through the door – disaster! The priceless artistic artefact that the singer hud originally brought wi her fae the Netherlands wis of course afforded pride eh place behind the band fur the occasion. As befitted its country eh origin, it wis rumoured tae be a genuine Van Gogh! No *Vincent* Van Gogh admittedly, no even his brother Theo, but their slightly lesser kent cousin twice-removed, Jimmy Van Gogh. But reputedly still worth millions. The Cenny hud it insured tae the hilt, naturally, but nae-one hud actually ever goat roond tae framin the thing. Which proved unfortunate, as Krystle hud jist absent-mindedly discarded the stub eh a traditional herbal 'Amsterdam cigarette' she'd been tokin on, when takin a bow tae the ecstatic audience. As I turned roond one last time afore sneakin aff intae the night, I saw tae ma horror that one corner eh the masterpiece hud caught fire, n the flames were awready spreadin rapidly. I simply couldnae bear tae look.

As I slipped oot the door n scurried aff hastily, I wisnae even at the Queen Vicky statue when I heard the band startin up again n aw thae drunken bams singin along. I hud tae strain ma lugs tae make it oot, but it soon became 'Krystle' clear whit high note they were endin the night on.

"Oh, that Krystle Shan-de-Lier, lights up the painting on the wall..."

Terrible, terrible stuff. Ye couldnae make it up, could ye?

There wis jist one final surprise left, when a bolt eh lightnin suddenly lit up the Leith skyline like a surrealistic movie-set, n Pat Stanton descended fae the clouds ridin a green n white stallion, handed me a six-pack eh McEwan's Export n then vanished in a puff eh smoke.

So whit can ye say efter that, except tae remind youse aw tae behave yersels, keep yer noses clean n yer underpants cleaner, n dinnae dae as I dae, jist dae as I say, OK, n I'll see youse aw behind the goals afore long. C'mon the Hibs!

G.G.T.T.H.

(Grumpy Gibby the Total Hibbie)

BRAIDWOOD BOOKS THANK YOU FOR YOUR ATTENDANCE AND CONTINUING SUPPORT; WE HOPE YOU HAVE ENJOYED THE SHOW

YOU HAVE BEEN WATCHING:-

Grumpy Gibson: Star of the show and senile old coot, aged somewhere between 75 and 130 (allegedly). Born Hibbie, born liar.

The late Mrs Gibson (Christian name unknown): The above's first wife. Died in mysterious circumstances.

Mumpy Minnie: The above's second wife. Died in even more mysterious circumstances.

Adolf Heinrich Goebbels von Gibson: GG's father and Nazi war criminal (deceased).

June Whitfield: Dead actress. Alleged former paramour of GG.

Humpty Harry: Associate of GG.

Moany Tony: ditto.

Torn-Faced Tommy: ditto.

Barry Parker: Hibs' former assistant coach (possibly mis-named).

Girning Gertie: Barmaid of fierce repute.

Erse-Faced Eddie: Barman of unfortunate appearance.

Rod Pear-Tree: Heid Bummer and Chief Bottle-Washer (because he's too fucking miserable to pay anybody to do it) at Hibernian Football Club.

Leeann Dumpster: Second-in-command to aforementioned HB & CBW.

Senga McGlumphar: Lady of the night. Voted 'Top Hooker in Leith' three years on the bounce.

Fifi Phanni-Phlapz: Ditto. Best pal and work colleague of above. Won 'Best Blow-Job in The Bar Brig' Award in a close-run contest back in 2016.

Irving Walsh: Edinburgh-born novelist, whose real age is sometimes as flexible as Gibby's. Life-long Hibbie, he once wrote some book about trains.

Jakey Rowling: Boy wizard literary plagiarist (allegedly).

John Humphrys: Stern-faced host of TV quiz show, 'Fastermind'.

Dick-Nick: TV quiz show host who isn't Richard Whiteley.

Joseph Tortolano: Politically incorrect soccer raconteur.

Elsie Tanner: Former 'Coronation Street' man-eater (deceased).

Roddy the Squaddie: War hero / military fantasist with mental health issues too numerous to mention.

Slasher Smith: Feared gangster with a distressing urinary tract problem.

Junky Johnston: Neighbour of GG. (Possibly deceased).

Pat Stanton: Omnipresent Deity / Secular God

April Fuller: Legal representative of HFC. (Possibly fictitious).

Tea-Leaf Keith: Fortune-teller (allegedly).

Rory the Choarie: Does what it says on the tin.

Krystle Shan-de-Lier: Top Country 'n' Western chanteuse of mixed Dutch / Leith heritage.

Bouncy Knowles: International singing megastar and one-time admirer of Joe Tortolano.

Lord Gaga: Not Lady Gaga.

Jeremy Vile: Controversial suicide-inducing trash telly 'star'.

Crown Prince Odinga Obama Badabing Badaboom: Nigerian financial entrepreneur.